Also by Karin Roffman

*From the Modernist Annex: American Women Writers
in Museums and Libraries*

The Songs
We Know Best

"controls"

1.

Here is everything for everyone.

you gets a delicious picnic lunch

leathers...sleek fit...perspiration

a yellow straw profile

(made of a strong paper-like substance),

Correspondence should be

what Kleenex is to the handkerchief-

'uminous lovelies that help to lighten that load.

A particularly interesting effect can be seen if a solid tube is inserted in the window through one of the openings.

2.

Before his coming the city was singularly devoted to the raucous,

3.

surrey to take you up into the mountains—

a marvellous idea for travelling.

buy packages of snap-in sections

of a small room the inside of which is completely covered with leaves.

...tawny, tantalizing

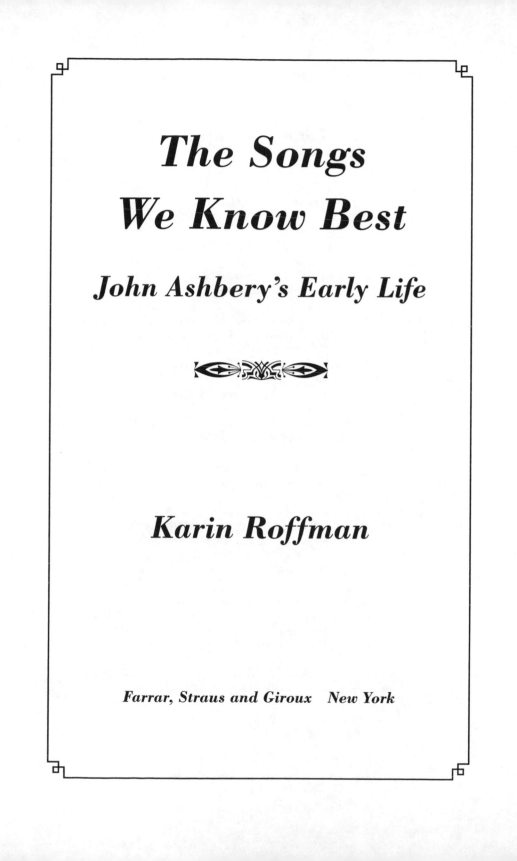

The Songs
We Know Best

John Ashbery's Early Life

Karin Roffman

Farrar, Straus and Giroux   New York

For my parents

Farrar, Straus and Giroux
18 West 18th Street, New York 10011

Copyright © 2017 by Karin Roffman
All rights reserved
Printed in the United States of America
First edition, 2017

Owing to limitations of space, all acknowledgments for permission to reprint illustrations
and previously published material can be found on pages 317–18.

Library of Congress Cataloging-in-Publication Data
Names: Roffman, Karin, author.
Title: The songs we know best : John Ashbery's early life / Karin Roffman.
Other titles: John Ashbery's early life
Description: First edition. | New York : Farrar, Straus and Giroux, 2017.
Identifiers: LCCN 2016045038 | ISBN 9780374293840 (hardback) |
    ISBN 9781429949804 (e-book)
Subjects: LCSH: Ashbery, John, 1927– | Poets, American—20th century—Biography. |
    Ashbery, John, 1927– Criticism and interpretation. | BISAC: BIOGRAPHY &
    AUTOBIOGRAPHY / Artists, Architects, Photographers. | BIOGRAPHY &
    AUTOBIOGRAPHY / Literary.
Classification: LCC PS3501.S475 Z83 2017 | DDC 811/.54 [B]—dc23
LC record available at https://lccn.loc.gov/2016045038

Designed by Jonathan D. Lippincott

Our books may be purchased in bulk for promotional, educational, or
business use. Please contact your local bookseller or the Macmillan Corporate
and Premium Sales Department at 1-800-221-7945, extension 5442, or by
e-mail at MacmillanSpecialMarkets@macmillan.com.

www.fsgbooks.com
www.twitter.com/fsgbooks • www.facebook.com/fsgbooks

1 3 5 7 9 10 8 6 4 2

Frontispiece: John Ashbery's "controls," October 20, 1982

Our knowledge isn't much it's just a small amount
But you feel it quick inside you when you're down for the count

—"The Songs We Know Best"

Of course Eurydice vanished into the shade;
She would have even if he hadn't turned around.

—"Syringa"

Contents

Preface

John Ashbery and I met at Bard College in the spring of 2005, when he visited a class I was teaching on modernist poetry and painting. Not long after, he and his partner, David Kermani, invited me to their nearby home. I was expecting a midcentury-modern glass cube and found instead a large, gloomy-looking nineteenth-century Victorian manse. One gray afternoon, I stood on their portico and rang the bell for the first time. Inside, tiny slits of natural light illuminated corners and crevices, but the large center hallway was otherwise very dark. As my eyes adjusted, I could see small and curious objects, many with unusual shapes and textures, covering mantels and tabletops. At some point, as I was feeling both enveloped by darkness and overstimulated by my new surroundings, Ashbery appeared. In his late seventies, he was tall and broad, with very white hair. We toured the house, and he described some things that he particularly liked: a small ceramic plate, a William Morris wallpaper pattern, a Piranesi print. On that visit or another one early on, we sat across from each other on large upholstered chairs in the downstairs sitting room, waiting for David to return with the day's newspapers. The room was cool, shadowy, and quiet, and in my sense of surprise at the setting, I felt an inkling of "those things or moments of which one / Finds oneself an enthusiast," as Ashbery puts it in "A Wave."

Eventually, I spent a summer in the house cataloging objects. Each piece had a story about its provenance. Like the house itself, which Ashbery said closely resembled his grandparents' Rochester home, many objects were things he had saved or had replicated from his childhood. Curious about his past, about which very little had been written, I took a trip to Rochester and from there drove thirty miles east to Sodus, to see what remained of his family's farm. Although his mother, Helen, sold the seventy-five-acre orchard in 1965, the handsome Ashbery Farm sign that his father, Chet, made in the 1940s was still hanging out in front of the mostly unchanged farmhouse. Afterward, I visited nearby Pultneyville, the tiny, stunningly picturesque village on Lake Ontario. Young John Ashbery had spent his summers with his grandparents in a small house overlooking the lake. When I returned to Hudson, Ashbery asked me what I had thought. "Sublimely beautiful," I said. "Isn't it?" he replied. Soon after, he, David Kermani, and I drove upstate together, to walk around inside his grandparents' Rochester house for the first time since they sold it in 1942. Afterward, we drove through Sodus and Pultneyville, stopping to see inside the farmhouse and to visit other familiar streets and buildings.

One late summer's afternoon, I asked Ashbery if he had ever kept a diary in those early years. I was not expecting that he would hand me four small leather books containing about one thousand pages of writing, which he maintained assiduously from the ages of thirteen to sixteen. Started six months after his younger brother suddenly became ill and died, the diaries depict his life and family during a period of mourning. In the 1980s, Ashbery gave the four books to his analyst to read, shortly before the doctor unexpectedly passed away. Fifteen years later, a stranger spotted them among papers he had purchased at an estate sale and returned them. Since then, they had been sitting inside Ashbery's dresser, among socks and sweaters. I could peruse them if I wanted, he said, suggesting I just take them home for the weekend so I could see for myself that they were "silly and dull" and contained nothing of interest.[1]

The diaries were a revelation because the voice of the poet was so present already. In prose entries composed years before it occurred to him to start writing in verse, his wry sense of humor, patience, impatience, and attention to the experience of his experience are unmistakable. Without at first intentionally doing so, the diary also tells, in fragments, and fits and starts, the story of his gradual discovery of and growing excitement about modern poetry. This narrative is all the more moving because it occurred without fanfare in the course of his going to school, visiting grandparents, doing hated farm chores, getting haircuts, listening to the radio, seeing movies, and looking outside at views of lakes and orchards, shifting scenes in sun, rain, and snow. He vividly characterizes his ordinary days, his family and friends. He repeatedly expresses how strange he feels he seems to everyone, including himself. While he dreams of a future life in a big city, far away from the family farm, he also chastises himself for not fitting in better where he is. His likably earnest but self-deprecatory style chronicles in great detail meals, weather, school, reading, writing, painting, playing on the beach in the summer, and first experiences of falling in and out of love with local girls. He relegates important personal revelations, primarily his growing attraction to boys, however, into first Latin, then French, and later an increasingly cryptic language of indirection and absence. It took me a long time to untangle the way these private musings are equally present and bound up with his growing passion for poetry.

Several weeks after reading the diaries, I found, amid a pile of old newspapers on a shelf in Ashbery's downstairs sitting room, a very old typewriter-paper box marked "Private." Inside were handwritten and typed drafts of almost all Ashbery's adolescent writing: poetry, plays, and stories. Ashbery was shocked to see them, since he believed he had burned them, but they were entirely intact and in fine condition. The diaries talk about what he wrote; the manuscript pages show how. Together, they provide an astonishing record of his earliest creative life.

When I finally formally asked to write a biography of his early life, Ashbery responded that he assumed I already was. He telephoned four close friends and introduced me. Beyond that, he did not interfere. I forged my own relationships with Carol Rupert Doty, the daughter of his mother's closest friend; Mary Wellington Martin, his childhood playmate; Robert (Bob) Hunter, his Harvard roommate; and the painter Jane Freilicher, whom he met the day he moved to New York City in 1949. I visited and talked with each of them multiple times, often staying with Carol on my many research trips to the Rochester area. Their memories of events provided distinct perspectives on stories I already knew and new details to talk about in further interviews with Ashbery. They had all kept photographs and letters, invaluable materials in understanding events and recovering forgotten stories. Although I began with this close group of friends, through meticulous detective work I tracked down more than fifty classmates and acquaintances of Ashbery's. Among these were his first boyfriend, Malcolm White, whom he had not seen since 1943. I also found the cameraman Harrison Starr, who filmed Ashbery, James Schuyler, Frank O'Hara, and Jane Freilicher in James Schuyler's play *Presenting Jane* (1952). It turned out that Harrison Starr still had the film in his garage, a reel that had disappeared sixty years earlier.

Ashbery's recent poem "Queer Subtext" (*Breezeway*, 2015) begins, "I'm really not into the past, a zoo." The poem continues with this thought: "Really not. Why are you doing that for me? / Urinal my dreams, it seems. I could think of something, / the angle of his shirt, perhaps. The shatterproof screen door . . . // Elsewhere in real cities, a few biographies point, / postulate." When I first heard him read this poem, shortly after he wrote it in 2013, I felt that its playfully biting attack on biography reflected Ashbery's reservations at having become the subject of one. ("I *could* think of something," by the way, is a direct quotation from a few of our less successful interviews.) During much of his long and vehemently private career, it seemed extremely unlikely that he would agree to such an undertaking, and he outright refused several requests to write about his life during the decade before we met.

In the late 1960s, as he was becoming better known and his poetry was being read more widely, Ashbery stopped giving interviews or allowing ones he had given to be published. His anger at the process of being asked to explain himself and his poems had been growing for some time. When critics claimed that his poems were difficult or needed explication, he often seemed surprised, a reaction perceived as feigned or outright hostile. Repeatedly he responded to questions about his life and work by deflecting them back to his poems as containing the only thoughts about their potential meaning that mattered. When pressed, he argued that the creative process was always slightly mysterious, so that in attempting to explain it, he would also be obscuring it. He includes a version of this idea in the opening of *Three Poems* (1972): "I thought that if I could put it all down, that would be one way. And next the thought came to me that to leave all out would be another, and truer, way."

As a fifteen-year-old high school student, though, he was already deeply interested in the art of biography: "I'm toying with the idea of writing a fictionalized Biography of Caligula," he noted to himself (Friday, August 21, 1942). Although he never wrote it, his interests in biography as a genre (and a place to experiment in telling lives) continued to develop. In 1950, he discovered A. J. A. Symons's classic *The Quest for Corvo: An Experiment in Biography* (1934), which narrates the process of uncovering details of a writer's life and work as a kind of detective novel, an experience of learning as mysterious and as exciting as reading. By the early 1960s, Ashbery was corresponding with editors at Knopf about his planned biography of the French "pre-surrealist" poet, playwright, and novelist Raymond Roussel (1877–1933). Ashbery had already been working for several years on the project in France, first as part of a planned PhD in French literature at New York University, which he did not complete, and later on his own. In the late 1960s he applied for a Guggenheim Fellowship (which he did not receive that year) to complete "a critical biography" of Roussel. He had already tracked down and interviewed several of Roussel's very private family and friends, found his unlisted former homes, collected previously unknown photographs, and translated some of his most difficult prose into English. After spending so much time interviewing Roussel's circle, he felt even more drawn to know better the works themselves: "I feel I have a deep personal stake, since Roussel's literary interests closely parallel my own," he explained in his Guggenheim application.[2] Ashbery's curiosity and enthusiasm about biography were always at the service of his desire to become a better reader of writers he liked.

Studying Ashbery's resistance to and engagement with the biographical process deepened the ways I thought about the relationship between biography and poetry as I wrote this book. While spending over a year traveling often to Sodus and Pultneyville, seeing the landscape transform in all kinds of weather and talking with many people who had known John only in those places, I constantly read his poems. While not often overtly autobiographical, the landscapes he grew up with—the vast, pristine beauty of the lake and the trees and sky on the farm—and his joys and miseries as he looked out on these views are always present, a kind of background hum I learned to listen closely for in each of his poems.

The interviewing process also always led me back to Ashbery's poems. Anyone who writes a biography about a living person or for whom interviews are a significant part of the experience of learning about a life can attest that this process of discovery can be a tricky one. One is simultaneously a voyeur and a friend, an independent thinker and dependent on another's revelations. I went into every interview with two minds: one very open and one very skeptical. While I was simultaneously investigating all kinds of archives—and finding original letters, manuscripts, deeds, wills, school records, newspaper references, and so on—to corroborate and extend what I was hearing, my many previous research experiences had already taught me that documents lie plenty, too. The most powerful moments of discovery, as a result, tend to be unspoken ones. The past became very present in some of our interviews. On those occasions when I can reveal something someone else knows, and watch how that information causes a recalibration in the thinking of the person to whom I am speaking, I learn, I feel, a deeper truth than at any other time. One such moment occurred after months of interviewing Ashbery's relatives and friends, when I told John that not only did his father know he was gay (which John had assumed but had never known for sure), but also that Chet Ashbery knew this as far back as 1945.

Even in his earliest writing, Ashbery is drawn to specific moments when one's understanding transforms. His first poems about lonely men and women closely chronicle how a person thinks about his or her life while alone, and how that knowledge subtly but profoundly shifts around new people and new information. His developing appreciation for this drama of thinking and the poetic use he eventually made of it have produced some of the most sublime poems of his career. "Soonest Mended" begins: "Barely tolerated, living on the margin / In our technological society, we were always having to be rescued / On the brink of destruction, like heroines in *Orlando Furioso* / Before it was time to start all over again." The poem sympathetically traces how life's "early lessons" recur, a dynamic process of living and thinking.

John Ashbery's work has continued to reflect both directly and indirectly on the related practices of biography and poetry. The naturally probing nature of researching and writing about someone, especially one who is both observing and participating in that process, necessarily reshapes the thoughts of all people involved. Ashbery's newest poems offer the best indication of his current response to my completion of this biography of his early life, a book that documents the very artistic process it has further provoked.

The Songs
We Know Best

"My Grand Party"

Near midnight, Labor Day weekend, 1949: twenty-two-year-old John Ashbery holds court at his crowded basement sublet in Greenwich Village while the guest of honor, Frank O'Hara, sails confidently by, wearing a brightly colored scarf he has just acquired from somewhere in the apartment.[1] It is the first party John has ever thrown in New York City. About seventy people, everyone a writer, painter, or musician living nearby, spill onto the sidewalk, drinks in hand, talking loudly, taking advantage of one of the last warm weekends of the year. Their restless, dancing feet are the only part of their bodies visible from the street-level window inside. The packed apartment is hot and loud. A beautiful young musician John has never met, who arrived a few hours before on the arm of a former Harvard classmate, performs Francis Poulenc's "Perpetual Motion" brilliantly but also repeatedly on the piano. After an hour of nonstop playing, she collapses, exhausted, on the couch where John sits listening. She stares at him. John glances her way with a wry expression she reads as anxious. "It will be all right," she suggests helpfully.[2]

John isn't depressed, though, not tonight, at least; he's amused. Everyone he has met in the city and liked, and almost everyone he has wanted to meet or hoped not to meet again, have all come to his party. The mixture of attractive and plain, shady and sincere, men and women, gay and straight, drunk and sober, extroverted and shy, promising and successful, produces a strange and shifting mosaic inside his apartment.

It is well past midnight, and more people arrive. John has already had a good conversation with the poet Jean Garrigue, whose poems he has admired in Oscar Williams's anthologies since high school, and enjoyed talking with Emma Swan, a plain but poetically named woman, whose first book of poems is about to come out from New Directions. Both are very encouraging and say they like his poems. Emma and Jean, older than nearly everyone else, talk to each other seriously in a corner, and seem to be enjoying themselves. John sees the even older poet José García Villa, W. H. Auden's contemporary (and one of the shadier characters at the party), walk outside. John cannot remember where they met during the two months he has so far lived in New York City, and he has seen Villa only once since then. He is curious to know how the poet even heard about the party.

John gets off the couch in search of friends. Six feet tall and extremely thin, he is wearing his nicest sharkskin suit and tie, only slightly wrinkled from his sitting so long. He finds Jane Freilicher, who has become his closest friend in the city, talking animatedly with Frank O'Hara. Frank is asking her questions about her paintings with charming intensity. He has just returned from a jaunt to the Phoenix Bookshop, around the corner, on Cornelia Street, and John is eager to hear what Frank thinks of the place. The Phoenix has become John's new late-night haunt since his moving to Jones Street, for the bookshop stays open until well after midnight and is a gathering place for artists. He wonders who is running the shop right now, since the entire staff appears to be at his party. The owners, Adam and Virginia Margoshes, are drinking with John Lynch, a salesman, and talking to Ann Truxell, a painter with a charmingly foul mouth, who hangs out all the time at their store. Lately, Ashbery has been painting abstracts with her for fun, in a back room of the bookshop, which she helped set up as a studio. Painting is something John hasn't done seriously since high school, and the absorbing activity almost makes up for the fact that he hasn't written a single new poem since moving to the city.[3] How could he? He has already changed apartments three times, worked a full-time job at the Brooklyn Library, applied to graduate school, and visited nearly every bar on Eighth Street.

Thinking about not writing depresses him, though, so he goes to talk with Jane and Frank. They have clearly hit it off, which pleases him. Introducing Frank to his New York friends, and vice versa, is the whole point of the party. It is too bad that his two good friends, the poet Kenneth Koch, who only briefly met Frank while they were together at Harvard, and Jane's boyfriend, Larry Rivers, an excitable and exciting painter studying with Hans Hofmann, are out of town this weekend. John is sure that they will find Frank as celestial as he does. If it weren't for Frank, who materialized at Harvard just weeks before John graduated the previous June, his senior year would have been anticlimactic. During the last month of school they spent every day together, and John emerged from that intensely happy period thinking he had met not just a brother, but very nearly his "identical twin."[4] Frank and John do not look alike, but their flat, nasal accents—Frank comes from Grafton, Massachusetts, and John from far upstate New York—and even their off-the-cuff comments sound remarkably similar. Having served in the war, Frank is a year behind John at Harvard, but a little over a year older, and they regularly take turns in the role of the older, more experienced brother. John is proud to show Frank off to his new friends, and equally proud to show off his New York City life to Frank, who has traveled to the city to be with him, despite a beastly cold.[5] Seeing Frank and Jane together, though, already so close, John wonders briefly if these introductions might be working too well.[6]

He returns to the couch. The writer Pat Hoey and her current boyfriend, the painter Al Kresch, sit down next to John. Pat thinks John is a genius and, at every opportunity, tries to get him to talk to her about poetry. She asks him a lot of questions, which he answers patiently. She asks him to write a poem; a piece of paper is obtained, and he obliges. Pat thinks the poem is the best thing she has ever read, but it gets lost almost immediately after he writes it.[7] Frank sails back into the room and tells John an amusing story of what happened during his walk to the Phoenix Bookshop. The story seems to involve a young mother, her young son, and Frank's eye-catching scarf, but John isn't listening carefully, and the spirit rather than the details of the story penetrates his consciousness.[8] Al, however, listens closely to Frank's tale. He has never before met anyone with Frank's social charm, and he wonders if John, whom he likes very much, feels jealous at how quickly Frank has won everybody over.[9] John is elated that Frank is having such a good time at the party. Pat mentions that the poet Allen Ginsberg is outside in a suit and tie, regaling several people with his thoughts about poetry. Someone wonders aloud if this is possible, for Allen is apparently under house arrest uptown. Later, when John goes outside, Ginsberg isn't there. He also looks for the poet Delmore Schwartz, whom he is told is talking outside with other members of the *Partisan Review* staff, but he cannot find him anywhere.

It is after two in the morning, and the party is slowing down. Jane Freilicher tells John she is leaving. She kisses Frank good-bye. It is unlike her to be so positive, but she thinks Frank is "a special breed . . . so charming."[10] John usually likes her ability to zero in on any strange or awkward behavior and skewer it. She often says what he is thinking but is too polite to say aloud. She doesn't do that now; she is in too good a mood. It is disconcerting. She tells him he has thrown a grand party. He has merely tried to throw a decent party, but he is glad it has gone off so well. He begins to think of it as "my grand party."[11] The party is nothing like the already-famous event Robert Motherwell presided over in Provincetown a few weeks earlier. All the New York abstract expressionist painters were there, and Motherwell declared that together they made up a New York School of painters. The stories already circulating about Motherwell's speech make his pronouncement sound very serious and auspicious.[12] John is satisfied that his casual party of paper cups and cheap beer, Poulenc and late-night visits to bookshops, is nothing like that. He is equally pleased that he is in New York City, which is clearly the place to be for an artist at this moment, the city that John has felt certain he should live in, ever since he was a young boy on his family's upstate New York farm.

The party is over. As John and Frank climb into his twin bed, intimate but never romantic for them, dawn appears aboveground. In the agreeably dark and cool underground room, still delightfully buzzed from the evening's frivolities, they go to sleep.[13]

1

"The Pleasant Early Years"

1927–1935

Shortly after Christmas 1935, Helen Ashbery relayed some astonishing news to her elder son. His short poem about a snow fight that he had composed for fun a few weeks before had been read to acclaim at the New York City apartment of the famous novelist Mary Roberts Rinehart.[1] The crowd of publishers and writers found the work delightfully clever, and they applauded its eight-year-old poet.[2] Hearing the story of his first poem's journey from his family's fruit farm in the tiny upstate village of Sodus, New York, all the way to Fifth Avenue, a place he had seen only in movies, John Ashbery felt awakened to new ideas about poetry.[3] He had written the poem to amuse himself; the idea that it might also amuse others, even older artists he had never met or seen, seemed extraordinary. Feeling full of energy and suddenly capable of great things, he tried to write something new, but he could not revive the combination of instinct and concentration that had led to his first poem's composition. The longer he thought about how he had written "The Battle," the more utterly mysterious writing poetry suddenly seemed to him, and he gave it up. An unarticulated hope remained within him, though, that words and ideas might one day provide him with an escape from his current existence, which he felt was dull and discouraging.

By any measure, his life in 1935 was ordinary. He was a fourth-grader at the local public school and lived in the family farmhouse with his parents, Helen and Chet Ashbery; his paternal grandmother, Elizabeth;

The Ashbery farmhouse in Sodus in the 1940s. The Ashbery Farm sign is in front, by the road.

John Ashbery at six weeks, with his parents

The Dartmouth Street house

and his four-year-old brother Richard. The only unusual thing that had happened in his life so far was that he had skipped third grade at the recommendation of his second-grade teacher. He had never traveled farther than a one-hundred-mile car trip west to see his father's relatives in Buffalo. His life was circumscribed by a ten-mile radius between farm, school, and the neighboring village of Pultneyville, where his maternal grandparents, Henry and Adelaide (Addie) Lawrence, lived. He had few school playmates and no close friends; the local kids with whom he most often played were the children of his parents' friends.[4] During long winters, especially with the excessively cold and snowy local weather, he found little to do at home but read, listen to the radio, draw, or bake with his grandmother on Saturday mornings. He also started to take piano lessons from a local teacher, practicing on the upright in the living room. All day long, his neat and quiet mother cleaned the house or cooked, though she sometimes surprised everyone with pointed remarks at supper. Once, John overheard her refer to his left-handedness—"at least he eats right-handed!"—suggesting, he thought, that she found him slightly odd.[5] He tried to keep out of the way of his father's temper, and to steer clear of his noisy, athletic, energetic brother. Whenever he could, he stayed with his grandparents in Pultneyville, for he preferred their peaceful house with its rows of books, grand views of Lake Ontario, and doting grandfather.

Addie and Henry Lawrence's 1926 passport photo, taken in preparation for their first and only trip to Europe and the Middle East

Since the fall of 1934, when the Lawrences retired to Pultneyville, John had hardly visited Rochester, which was thirty miles away, and had until then provided him with some excitement.[6] He had spent much of his early life in the city, and he missed it. Born at Rochester General Hospital on July 28, 1927, he initially stayed with his mother and her parents, who then lived downtown, at 69 Dartmouth Street, in the middle-class home where Helen and her younger sister, Janet, had grown up. His grandparents encouraged visits, and John's father was preoccupied in Sodus, for the busiest time of year on the Ashbery Farm occurred during the height of cherry season, in mid-summer. John instinctively enjoyed staying with his grandparents in any case, not only because of their affection, but because he loved their house. Well built in the late 1890s, the modest, Victorian-style house, which smelled of his grandfather's pipe smoke, had back and front staircases, stained-glass windows, wooden trim, floral wallpaper, built-in bookshelves, and mantels and shelves crowded with knickknacks, including collections of ceramic dogs and miniature shoes. Most were collected from his grandparents' 1926 trip to Europe and the Middle East, their only trip abroad. Even before he could read, John liked to run his fingers over the textured

John at about a year old, with his grandfather Henry Lawrence

Chet Ashbery in 1915, on the Ashbery Farm in Sodus

Mary Elizabeth Koehler (Ashbery), John's paternal grandmother, known as Elizabeth, in the 1880s, before her marriage. Her parents, Ferdinand Koehler and Elizabeth Thomas (Koehler), emigrated from Germany to Town Line, a suburb of Buffalo, in the 1860s.

Henry Charles Ashbery, John's paternal grandfather, in his stenciling and rubber stamp business in Buffalo, around 1900. He trained as a stonecutter. Henry, born in Buffalo, was the eldest son of John Aschbery (b. 1835) and Mary Hatfield, both from England, who arrived by boat in 1855.

spines of his grandfather's collection of leather-bound volumes on the shelves downstairs and imagine their contents.[7]

From early on, John's predisposition for his grandparents' company created tensions with his father, an estrangement that only deepened as he became more vocal about his distaste for the farmhouse and farm life, which were his father's proudest achievements. The elegant, black-and-white Ashbery Farm sign, which Chet Ashbery made himself and hung by the road in the front of the house, testified to the care and attention he lavished on the house and farm. His own parents, Elizabeth and Henry C. Ashbery, had purchased the seventy-five-acre property in 1914, after twenty-three-year-old Chet discovered the extraordinary land about a mile from Lake Ontario, an area that benefited from the wet and windy weather produced by the lake. He spearheaded the acquisition and convinced his parents and older brother, Wallace, to move from Alden (a suburb of Buffalo), New York, where the family had lived

for more than a decade and where they had community roots, to Sodus, where they knew no one.[8] He personally completed most of the
renovations on the primitive house and innovations on the orchard,
teaching himself woodworking and new agricultural techniques.[9] Over
the course of a decade, the Ashbery family became integral to the community, and Chet a sought-after local bachelor.[10] Charismatic, athletic
(he played catcher on the local semipro baseball team), and passionate
about farming, he married a college-educated city girl on September 5,
1925. Reporting on Chet's marriage to Helen Lawrence of Rochester,
at St. Paul's Church on East Avenue (the stunningly beautiful location
of many high-society city events, including George Eastman's funeral
in 1932), the *Sodus Record* noted warily that "one of the best known
young men of Sodus" and "a leading young farmer and fruit grower" had
married a woman "not well known here."[11] The community's guarded-
ness about the city equaled John's later resistance to the farm. When
he ventured out into the orchard, as he sometimes did alone, even as
a young child, he explored the landscape, talked to farmhands, and
played with family dogs. On one solo walk, he saw a bag filled with crystals
that looked like candy. A farmhand encouraged him to taste it. His par-

Chet and Helen on their wedding day, September 5, 1925

ents were frightened and furious later, when they realized he had eaten fertilizer, a detail of farm life he later invoked in "Popular Songs" to describe "the guano-lightened summer night landscape," a phrase that sounds romantic but is not.

John's dislike for the farm was not only a preference for other ways of living, but a reaction to familial stresses that developed not long after he was born. When John was three months old, Chet's sixty-one-year-old father died of a sudden heart attack in his bedroom. Chet and Helen immediately moved from their own apartment in the village to the farmhouse to live with Chet's mother. Helen did not know her mother-in-law well, and though sensitive to her grief, she was taken aback by the woman's imperious, uneducated manner. There was an immediate loss of privacy and more demanding physical responsibilities from living on a farm, and Helen escaped so often to her parents' house in Rochester that it became something of an Ashbery family joke, though a bitter one for Chet.[12] During the first two years of John's life, he had few intimate moments with his father.[13] Chet had been extremely close to his father, and the day-to-day work of running the farm by himself (his brother had long since moved back to Buffalo to marry), compounded by the financial stressors of the Depression-era years, wore him down. With financial anxieties mounting, his already short temper became explosive.[14] His father-in-law, whose respected and stable career as a physics

John with horses on the farm, about 1930

John with baby chicks, around 1929

John and "Pal," around 1931

John on his tricycle in back of the Dartmouth Street house, around
1931

professor and chair of the department at the University of Rochester had spanned nearly forty years already, proffered a $4,500 gift so Chet could pay off his parents' mortgage.[15] This money gave Helen immediate financial independence from her mother-in-law, but it also placed Chet in a new and financially dependent position, which was uncomfortable for him, and he took his frustrations out verbally on Helen.[16]

John gathered and stored impressions—first, of what he saw and, later, of how he felt. In his earliest memory, a black car zoomed by on the road in front of the farmhouse.[17] Sometime later, he walked through a field of tall grass across from the house on a calm summer evening, and he felt a sensation that he could only later articulate as peacefulness.[18] Shortly after his brother, Richard Seeley Ashbery, was born on March 12, 1931, John watched his parents arrive with the new baby at Dartmouth Street. His mother felt so faint walking up the path to the house that Chet scooped her up and carried her upstairs to bed, and John suddenly experienced a tremendous surge of tenderness toward them both. John followed them to his mother's room and did "a funny little dance" to try to make her feel better, but she was too exhausted to enjoy it, and his father and grandparents ushered him out.[19] A few weeks later, the family sat together in the front pew at St. John's Church in Sodus to celebrate Richard's baptism. The Reverend John Williamson called the family forward, but added, "No, not you, John."[20] Rebuked, he sat down again, embarrassed. One afternoon not long afterward, he was standing next to his father in the barn at the farm when Chet asked him whom he loved more, his mother or father. John thought of his gentle, pretty mother and responded quickly, "Mother, of course," and immediately felt ashamed because he had spoken the truth and disappointed his father.[21]

Helen and her two boys continued to stay in Rochester as she recovered her strength, and since John was expected to stay out of the way, he learned to entertain himself. One afternoon, he rummaged through a handsome green rectangular box from the B. Forman Co. department store, which his grandparents had kept to hold memorabilia from their trip abroad, the year before he was born. It was a treasure chest containing postcards, pamphlets, maps, and menus, with tiny reproductions of paintings, sculptures, pyramids, churches, and gardens. For weeks he studied the box's mysterious contents without being able to read a word, yet the pictures and writing, much of it in foreign languages, fascinated him. When he exhausted that amusement, he left the house by himself without informing anyone and took his tricycle out for a ride around the block, a mild act of transgression that felt thrilling.[22] A neighbor alerted his mother, who went to collect him, but not before his brief adventure gave him a first, delicious taste of independence, an experience he alluded to in several published and unpublished poems: "Take out my tricycle for a spin and return it / before anyone missed me" (*Flow Chart*, 1991); "I ride my tricycle of thought / Along their sparkling sidewalks, remarking the uneven places" ("The Children").[23]

Soon it was time to attend school, but the Sodus school system did not have a kindergarten. John's parents and grandparents decided that, beginning in the fall of 1932, just after John turned five, he would move to the Dartmouth Street house to attend Francis Parker School No. 23. Henry Lawrence made arrangements, and Chet went along with his plan, even though it meant being separated from his elder son for nearly a year. Chet later described his father-in-law as "very interested in John's education."[24] John felt overjoyed with these plans but sensed enough underlying tensions to keep his feelings to himself. Once the school year began, he walked two blocks every morning to the same highly respected public school on Barrington Street that his mother and Aunt Janet had both attended, and where the bell still rang sonorously from the bell tower at eight each morning. Inside, dark wood paneling, transom windows, and polished oak wood floors made the two-story structure seem much more like a school*house* than a public school.[25] John liked his teacher Miss Austin and was excited that many children whom he had met on Dartmouth Street were in his class.[26] His personal goal for the year was to learn how to read.

On most days after school, he played outside with other children on Dartmouth Street until his grandparents called him home. His favorite imaginative game was to "make up" and "perform plays" with Evelyn Weller and her older sister (who lived in a Victorian mansion at 95 Dartmouth), using the Wellers' big backyard.[27] Once back home, John was expected to remain quiet and occupied. Even before he could read well, he liked to pore over his grandparents' enormous set of *The Book of Knowledge* volumes, studying colorful drawings and deciphering some of the words in his two favorite sections: "The Child's Book of Poetry," which included hundreds of Romantic and Victorian poems, many of which he soon memorized, and "Things to Make and Things to Do," which described a series of often complex steps for building things and playing games.[28] On some special afternoons, he accompanied his grandfather on errands in his grandparents' newest Ford. They drove to Wegman's grocery store on East Avenue, which had just introduced the first "vaporized spray" to keep vegetables moist. As his grandfather shopped, John stood still, waiting for the water to mist the greens, a vision he found "beautiful."[29] Other afternoons, Addie hosted one of several women's groups, including the Rochester Poetry Society, the Hakkoreoth Reading Club, and an outreach committee for the nearby Memorial Art Gallery. She was neither an enthusiastic nor an accomplished cook, but for these afternoons, she made such delicate and delicious finger sandwiches that John's mouth watered in anticipation.[30] He would not dare take one until she offered, though, for his grandmother disciplined him so frequently for small infractions at home that he wondered if she disliked him.

Addie was strict, and John learned to be polite and careful. Her home was a place primarily to instill manners and morals in children.[31] Once, when John was about three years old, he yelled "Wipe!" from the bathroom upstairs while she was in the backyard hosting a garden party for professors' wives, and she harshly punished him for it.[32] A book that Addie kept called *The Child at Home; or, The Principles of Filial Duty* (1833) encapsulated her approach to child-rearing. The gentler end of this view toward correcting childhood behavior included social advice at the heart of the proverb "Least said, soonest mended," the phrase that Ashbery shortened in the late 1960s as the title for a poem that chronicled the "early lessons" of growing up.[33]

John absorbed a feeling and a mood while living with his grandparents that he connected to their nineteenth-century American values and beliefs. Henry Lawrence was born in 1864 at the Sodus Hotel, which his entrepreneurial parents briefly owned during its heyday.[34] The sudden death of his young father less than two years later, however, changed Henry's fortune.[35] By sheer force of his intelligence, discipline, and thriftiness, he finished his PhD by the age of thirty after doing research in the new field of X-ray technology (then called Roentgen rays) at both the University of Rochester and Cornell. Though he chose to study science, he was equally adept in languages and business, earning extra money tutoring students in Greek and Latin and, later, in buying and selling stocks.

John's grandmother Addie, three years younger than her husband, grew up on a family farm just outside Pultneyville and trained to be a schoolteacher (though she never worked), excelling in multiple subjects and performing in plays before marrying.[36] They were both products of the American Victorian age, a period marked by "the rise of capitalism" and the dominance of "the individual," which Ashbery describes in the opening of "Definition of Blue" (*The Double Dream of Spring*, 1970). His grandparents' lives and attitudes profoundly shaped this "definition." They took pride in their new home, in their downtown neighborhood of professional men, in their smart investments, their new car, their family, their church, and their nation. They believed in public school, shoveling one's own driveway in the snow (which Henry Lawrence was still doing at ninety when he passed away), and Republican presidents. They were against the New Deal and "that man," President Franklin D. Roosevelt.[37] Optimistic and modest, they lived and spoke with a clarity—on

Edmund Wilson Lawrence and Ruth Ann Holling Lawrence Owen, Henry Lawrence's parents. Edmund Lawrence died of "congestion of the stomach" a few months after Henry was born. She remarried an Englishman, Samuel Owen, "a renowned Glass Blower," who opened "Owen's Crystal Museum" on Jay Street in Pultneyville. Samuel's adult daughter married Ruth Ann's brother, Captain James Holling, in 1868, and the local Commercial Press gleefully reported on the resulting complex family relationships.

behavior, morality, and individual responsibility—that appealed to John.

Attentive to the exactitude with which they spoke (and lived), John became very alert to new sounds and meanings of words as he was learning to read. In the evenings before bed, his grandfather read stories aloud. He began with fairy tales, then read *The Heroes*, Charles Kingsley's popular children's adaptation of Greek myths, which John loved, and later Johanna Spyri's *Heidi*. His grandmother also introduced him to new words. She used the term *vestibule* to refer to the tiny tiled room between her two heavy wooden front doors, where the mail landed with a satisfying thud each day after it passed through the brass mail slot, a word that John enjoyed repeating. During kindergarten that fall, he had his own unexpected encounter with a word: "I sat alone at school on the second-floor landing looking down . . . and thought, *I regret these stairs*." He had no idea why the phrase came into his mind, for it was unlike anything anyone had said to him, but he liked it. He understood how *regret* was usually used, but the oddness of the phrase suddenly expressed the precise shape of his melancholy mood sitting on the steps in the afternoon light.[38]

John often stayed with his grandparents on weekends, even when he could have returned to the farmhouse. One spring weekend in 1933, his grandmother took him downtown to see his first movies, an excursion that felt very grown-up. They saw the animated short film *The Three Little Pigs*, followed by Frank Buck's live-action *Bring 'Em Back Alive*. The following winter they also went together to see the new live-action version of *Alice in Wonderland*, featuring Gary Cooper. By then, though, he had moved back to the Sodus farm and was missing his life in the Dartmouth Street house.[39] In the prose poem "The Lonedale Operator" (*A Wave*, 1984), Ashbery compresses his memories of these separate outings into a reflection on first experiences and the confusion one feels as one's tastes change. He sees *Alice in Wonderland* as an adult and wonders how he could have ever liked the film as a child:

> Years later I saw it when I was grown up and thought it was awful. How could I have been wrong the first time? I knew it wasn't inexperience, because somehow I was experienced the

first time I saw a movie. It was as though my taste had changed, though I had not, and I still can't help feeling that I was right the first time, when I was still relatively unencumbered by my experience.

He feels upset, even becoming terrified at his new thoughts, because he clearly remembers his first few experiences at the movies and his delighted reactions to what he saw. He asks, rather incredulously, "How could I have been wrong the first time?" He has trusted his first impressions, which he must concede are incorrect in this case. He concludes, however, that his initial judgments have value to him as "unencumbered" responses to art. These memorable first impressions provide a foundation from which he can test his future feelings and opinions.

John contrived to stay with his grandparents even after kindergarten ended, traveling with them to their summer home in the tiny village of Pultneyville, on the shore of Lake Ontario. He was forestalling the inevitable return to the farmhouse, which was going to happen by the end of the summer. He had been happier in Rochester than in Sodus, but he was even happier in Pultneyville. The view of the lake from his grandparents' living room window was so marvelously beautiful in the summer that he felt a joyful sensation of having "what I wanted."[40] Adding to this ecstatic feeling

The side porch of the Pultneyville house, which looks out onto Lake Ontario, early 1930s

Mary Wellington in Pultneyville, age five, just before John remembers meeting her. She lived in Rochester and stayed, along with her two "very pretty" older sisters, at her grandmother's house for the summer.

was a new friendship. One day, he discovered six-year-old Mary Wellington collecting shells on the beach across from his grandparents' house. Her grandmother had recently purchased a summer home a few doors down from the Lawrences'. Mary was an ethereal, fine-boned, graceful creature with light blond hair and blue eyes. She did not look at all like the irreverent tomboy she actually was, and John was smitten.[41]

They sought each other first thing in the morning and, for several summers, were inseparable during the day. Together they combed the beach for treasures, made up new stories, climbed trees, and sprinted from one backyard to another. John's favorite summer uniform was either a bathing suit or a one-piece romper with green shorts that buttoned into a polka-dotted top and felt like no clothes at all; Mary wore light summer dresses, which John worried were transparent.[42] They designated an area full of willow trees behind Pig Lane as their official hideout. On hot days, they sat on the Wellington dock with their feet dangling in the lake. When they felt hungry, they bought five cents' worth of candy at Fred Hart's store or ate Fig Newtons at the Lawrences'. On rainy days, they played cards on the enormous couch in the Wellington living room. At night, John lay contented in the twin bed in his second-floor bedroom, with the window open, smelling the lake and listening to the hum of wind and water. Later Ashbery described how deeply he absorbed the sounds of this melancholy water music: "the plaintive sound / of the harp of the waves is always there as a backdrop / to conversation and conversion, even when / most forgotten."[43] John's initial associations with waves were connected to his new friendship and the stunning location, more pleasurable than "plaintive," except in worrying about his move back home.

For a sixth-generation Pultneyvillian, John carried his legacy lightly. There was almost no area of the tiny village he explored on which his ancestors had not planted roots, in the form of a house, memorial, or tombstone. Some relatives, such as his grandfather's cousins Paul (1872–1957) and Lillian (1864–1953) Holling, unmarried siblings who stayed across the street, retained distinct Victorian sensibilities, styles of dress, and mannerisms, and seemed like living relics. Nearly every villager displayed ancestral objects of some historical interest in their homes, a practice that led to an annual show-and-tell in the town hall on May 15, the anniversary of the Battle of Pultneyville (1814) during the War of 1812, when British gunboats fired cannons briefly at the shore, a minor historical footnote confirmed when Henry Lawrence and several other neighbors dug up cannonballs in their yards. John's grandfather kept other historical artifacts, including a "green wooden slab" that had been a ship's cabin door his great-uncle Horatio Throop allegedly used to swim five miles to safety when his boat sank in 1820.[44] John could trace his lineage, issuing from a long line of sailors, through objects dating back to the late 1700s.

John learned most about his past by rummaging around the Lawrences' frame house, which sheltered the detritus of more than one hundred years of local work and family life. His great-great-uncle Washington Throop built it in the early 1830s to provide his daughter, Sarah, with a clear sight of ships arriving and departing the busy port, a view of the lake John also appreciated. (Herman Melville described Lake Ontario befittingly as one of "those grand fresh-water seas of ours," which "possess an ocean-like expansiveness, with many of the ocean's noblest traits.")[45] Sarah gave the house to Henry and Addie Lawrence in 1916, along with remnants of her family's sailing life. Her scrapbook chronicled the family's successful nineteenth-century steamship business, and

Sarah LaPlata Throop Miller (1838–1915) left her Pultneyville house on Washington Street, overlooking Lake Ontario, to Henry Lawrence. Sarah's father, Washington Throop, built the house in the early 1830s, next door to his brother Horatio Throop's house. Sarah died in the living room in May 1916, leaving a diary of the final six months of her life, which John Ashbery found and read as a child. His poem "Cousin Sarah's Knitting" alludes to details of her life.

her diary illuminated her daily view of Lake Ontario out the living room window during her final bleak and lonely winter.[46] Both scrapbook and diary became cherished objects in the Lawrence household, and a source of curiosity and entertainment for John. Years later, when Ashbery dramatized and memorialized Sarah's romantic view of the water—"So many brave skippers / such a long time at sea," in "Cousin Sarah's Knitting" (*Wakefulness*, 1998)—he channeled that combination of history and melodrama he encountered first through seeing her scrapbooks and diaries lying on bookshelves. Ashbery captures his curious and whimsical attitude toward the past in "Fragment": "Thus reasoned the ancestor, and everything / Happened as he had foretold, but in a funny kind of way."[47] Surrounded by venerated objects and ancestors, John Lawrence Ashbery was also in a "kind of way" the future that their myths, histories, and prophecies "had foretold," an idea that struck him as "funny."

John dreaded the end of the summer and the move back to the farm. He felt isolated, restless, and unhappy there, and he was much more aware of his feelings by virtue of the comparison with his more peaceful and interesting life the previous year in Rochester. The smell of his father's Chesterfield cigarettes pervaded the house, much less appealing to John than the aroma from his grandfather's pipe.[48] He had not

Richard, about 1933

seen his father on a daily basis for over a year, and the awkwardness between them intensified into regular conflicts. It seemed as though Chet spanked John for even the tiniest misdeeds, and scolded him more often and more harshly than Addie ever had. At the farm, "Richard ran everywhere and got into everything," and John "started to think of him as a pest."[49] In John's absence, Richard and Chet had bonded. Their exuberant, outdoorsy, athletic personalities were very similar.[50] John felt like an outsider and unconsciously retaliated by actively seeking out quarrels. He complained about the foul-smelling chickens, which ran around right outside the kitchen. One afternoon, he let the water pump run and then rolled around in the mud pile he had created. Another day, he turned a hose on one of his father's uncles who had been unfriendly, soaking him. These infractions resulted in a "walloping," lightly by his mother and much more severely by Chet.[51]

John felt solitary and unhappy. His parents and grandmother were busy trying to make ends meet on the farm, and there were very few objects or books around the house for him to explore. When he looked out the front or the back of the Ashbery farmhouse, he saw vast swaths of land and no other houses, a stark and lonely view. In the winter, for months on end, the land was covered in deep snow. In the late spring, nearby Lake Ontario intensified weather patterns so that it was often very blustery and wet, though John began to like that kind of unsettled sky most of all, for it fit his unhappy mood. The farmhouse was also literally a colder place to live than the Dartmouth Street house had been. It had lower ceilings and less natural light, and its furnace blew heat directly into the living room, which was so far from John's bedroom in the upstairs back corner that the warm air could not reach it.[52] On Saturday mornings, John warmed up in the kitchen while his paternal grandmother baked küchen and bread, recipes she knew by heart from her German-born parents.[53] She would affectionately scold John and "grab and wash his ears."[54] He enjoyed these mornings most of all, but he missed his home with his other grandparents.

He felt no more comfortable at school. Despite the advantage of his year in kindergarten and the benefit of knowing already how to read and write, he received his lowest grades during all of primary school at the beginning of first grade in Sodus; a B in reading, C in writing, and B+ in drawing.[55] His poor grades were especially disappointing because he naturally gravitated toward reading, writing, and drawing. Still, the marks did not bother him as deeply as his lack of friends. He did not have much in common with his Sodus classmates, whose interests generally leaned toward hunting, sports, and farming.[56] In the afternoons and weekends, the primary social events took place at high school basketball games, community pastimes in which John had neither talent nor concern. He quickly gained a reputation for being "smart, quiet, and different," and even schoolmates who were the children of family friends were not especially nice to him.[57] Chet arranged for his friends Art and Castelle Boller to drive John to school with their daughters on some mornings. Mary Ann, who was also Chet and Helen's goddaughter, liked to bet her sister that John would trip as he walked from his door to their car.[58] Some classmates were even more direct about their dislike, calling him "a sissy."[59]

The quickest way to escape in Sodus was through movies, and John enthusiastically went to see any film with anyone. Any theater would do, but the grandest ones, which he liked best, were in the bigger cities of Newark and Rochester. He went with his Ashbery grandmother to see *Flirtation Walk* (1934) because her nephew Dutch Koehler, then a West Point cadet, had a cameo in it. She yelled "There he is!" at the screen, to John's amusement. He went with his parents to see the new Busby Berkeley films at the grand theater in Newark, including *Dames* (1934) and *Gold Diggers of 1935*, for musicals were his father's favorite, and John, too, became a fan. He went with them to see the movies of the Ritz Brothers, a slightly "more evil version of the Marx Brothers," who had several popular films during the mid-thirties.[60] While watching the trailer for an upcoming film *The Night Is Young* (1935), John heard the song "When I Grow Too Old to Dream," which he felt was "too wonderful" and immediately afterward bought the sheet music and learned to play the song on the piano.[61] Even scary films were worth seeing because they were entertaining, although when his mother took him to see an adaptation of Charles Dickens's *The Old Curiosity Shop* (1934), the tense scenes with Quilp terrified him so much that she had to take him out of the theater.[62] He saw movies without his parents, too, beginning with Laurel and Hardy's *Babes in Toyland* (1934), a comedy with a very dark sense of humor that his friend Buddy Gaylord unwittingly chose for his seventh birthday party outing.[63] John found the film's "very funny" rapid-fire dialogue, which included puns, double entendres, and other "verbal pyrotechnics," "exciting."[64]

The more John saw and heard, the more he sought ways to get others to hear and see him. During the winter, his parents invited Miss Chadwick, his second-grade teacher, over for dinner one evening. There had recently been a very popular song that played on the radio called "Throw Another Log on the Fire." Toward the end of the meal, as the fire in the fireplace was dimming, John said, "So shall I throw another log on the fire?" Everyone laughed uproariously, which he loved.[65] At school, he often made witty remarks, but he also tried to stand out in other ways. Although the youngest student in the fourth grade, he volunteered to perform Alfred Lord Tennyson's "The Eagle" in the auditorium at an assembly for the entire school. He had discovered the poem while perusing a children's poetry textbook at school and liked how "short and dramatic" it was. The description of the eagle enjoying its high perch and its ability to fall "like a thunderbolt," allusions to Zeus that John knew from reading about Greek mythology in Kingsley's *The Heroes*, also appealed to him.[66] It took him only a few minutes to memorize the poem, and he recited both stanzas perfectly:

> He clasps the crag with crooked hands;
> Close to the sun in lonely lands,
> Ring'd with the azure world, he stands.

The wrinkled sea beneath him crawls;
He watches from his mountain walls,
And like a thunderbolt he falls.

No parents or grandparents were invited to (or even knew about) the recitation. John's performance was for classmates, teachers, and him only.[67] His voluntary decision to take on the challenge of performing poetry suggested a willingness, even a desire, to behave in ways utterly independent from others in his school and town. No one around him explicitly connected the image from the poem of the lonely bird soaring above and looking down at a world "beneath him" with the voice of the eight-year-old boy speaking those words, but his classmates intuitively sensed his ambition and lack of interest in them.

His grandfather also recognized John's desire for escape and encouraged his sense of independence. His grandparents had been away for several weeks on a series of car trips, to visit John's aunt Janet and her husband, Tom Taft, and John was eager to have them home. Henry had written him an official-looking letter from Ohio, on "Mansfield-Leland Hotel" stationery, promising a visit to Pultneyville soon: "When we come home I will come down and get you to spend Saturday and Sunday."[68]

They picked him up as promised, to see a movie in Rochester.[69] Planning to watch the new adaptation of Shakespeare's *A Midsummer Night's Dream* (1935), starring Mickey Rooney as the mischievous forest spirit Puck and Olivia de Havilland as Hermia, John read his grandparents' copy of Charles and Mary Lamb's *Tales from Shakespeare* (1807) and his grandfather's 1864 edition of the *Comedies*, though he made little headway at first.[70] The film opened with a performance of Mendelssohn's entire *A Midsummer Night's Dream* Overture, a piece that John had never heard before. Directed by Max Reinhardt and William Dieterle, the film received mixed reviews, but to John, who discovered both Shakespeare and Mendelssohn in the same afternoon, the combination of words, ideas, humor, and music was unequaled by any previous experience of art.[71]

When they arrived home in Pultneyville the evening of the movie, John went directly upstairs to his grandparents' bedroom, sat at his grandfather's desk with its even then old-fashioned Remington typewriter and composed his first poem.[72] He titled it "The Battle":

The trees are bent with their glittering load,
The bushes are covered and so is the road.
The fairies are riding upon their snowflakes,
And the tall haystacks are great sugar mounds.
These are the fairies camping grounds.

Their swords are made from glittering ice,
They sparkle and shine and look very nice.
But Mother Earth's soldiers—they're bushes and trees,
Then there are some rabbits who would venture out.
But that all depends on what they're about.

The battle's beginning! It's a fight to the end.
The rabbits pitch in! Some help they must lend.
The bushes are conquered! Well that was short.
How shall they celebrate their victory?
Well, my dears, that's a long story.

They celebrated their victory with a feast,
With turkey and dressing and cakes of yeast.
But let us get back to the trees and the bushes.
They are weighted down with snow that pushes and pushes.

But who should come along then little boy Ned?
With muffler of blue and mittens of red.
He freed them from their tiresome load
And then was off again down the road.

BUT—when the fairies came out again they were angry, every
    one!
But burst out in laughter at having such fun.
They vowed they would never again have a battle
That was so much ado about nothing.[73]

John's story of a fight between fairies and bushes was humorous and
clever, but even more amusing was his invention of the whimsical, wry
narrator (a Puck-like character, though one slyer and less devious) who,

in a series of highly comical asides, describes the escalation of anger, the battle itself, and its aftermath. For two stanzas, tensions between Mother Earth and fairies build until an eruption at the beginning of the skillfully written third stanza. The narrator expresses his excitement: "The battle's beginning! It's a fight to the end." Given the announcement, one expects an epic struggle to follow, but the poem compresses the action, and a mere two lines later, the fairies triumph and the narrator returns to comment wryly on this remarkably speedy coup: "The bushes are conquered! Well that was short."

If that were all, the poem would have been clever enough, but there was more. Battle over, the narrator addresses his curious audience and becomes gently coy: "How shall they celebrate their victory? / Well, my dears, that's a long story." Adopting this cozy, old-fashioned tone, the savvy narrator with a sense of his audience's limited tolerance for dull details appears to launch into the "long story" of the celebration, a "feast, / With . . . cakes of yeast," but interrupts himself to "get back to the trees and the bushes," the main action. Again the description of this battle is compressed and quick. Anger escalates, until they "burst out in laughter at having such fun" over "so much ado about nothing," the narrator's witty allusion to another Shakespeare play. From beginning to end, the narrator maintains a tone of distant, lighthearted mastery over the story, a complex good humor that is the poem's most impressive and sophisticated feature.

Up until the evening he typed out his poem, John had amused only himself with his active imagination. The urge to write, however, was something extraordinary and new. Inspired by his excitement about Shakespeare's play and Mendelssohn's music, he expressed his feelings in his own style, transforming the season from the play's enchanted summer to a Rochester winter and replacing the marriage drama with a snow fight. Although written for fun, John's first poem demonstrates a prodigious talent. There had been few signs up until this point that he could write such a poem (or any poem). Yet his deft, instinctive delight in the film had built upon a foundation of knowledge about poetry that he had gained in such ordinary ways that he hardly knew he had it. Some of what he knew was merely obtained from observing his grandfather, who often picked up a favorite volume of Percy Bysshe Shelley's *Minor Poems*, or *Selections from the Poetical Works of Robert Browning*, or Cowper's *The Task*; or from his grandmother, who cut Edgar Guest poems out of newspapers. Henry and Addie also wrote poetry, usually to communicate something amusing or special to each other or their friends. Ten years before he wed her, seventeen-year-old Henry turned a sentence into two neatly composed lines of verse for Addie in her high school autograph book:

> Drop one pearl in the
> Casket of memory for me.
>   Henry E. Lawrence P'ville February 23, 1882[74]

For her garden parties, Addie sometimes wrote out place cards that rhymed a person's name with a witty compliment about his or her personality.[75] John spent so much time reading poems from *The Book of Knowledge* that when his grandparents moved permanently to Pultneyville, in September 1934, they gave him their complete set to keep with him at the farmhouse, where he had few other books of his own. Those volumes included many ballads, stories in verse, and other short, rhymed witty or sentimental poems. John knew well William Allingham's "The Fairies" ("Up the airy mountain / Down the rushy glen / We daren't go a-hunting / For fear of little men" . . .), which helped to inspire his first poem.

"The Battle" drew from this natural exposure to poetry, but in its exuberance demonstrated an inclination to write independently from any tradition he had so far encountered. John had no formal training, but he did have an intuitive sense of rhyme, rhythm, and irony, and no inhibitions about relying on or breaking rules. Stanza lengths, metrical and rhyme patterns, and narrative perspectives shift throughout. The final line, a pun on Shakespeare's *Much Ado About Nothing*, is one of the only perfectly pentameter lines (a combination of iambic and trochaic beats), a meter of which he certainly had never learned, though he had heard it spoken in Shakespeare's play. He demonstrated, above all else, a quick and naturally musical ear.

In playfully composing the poem, John also documented his earliest ideas about art, thoughts he would deepen and rediscover in the future. In "The Battle," the fairies' short-term memory is one of their most charming features; it means that they cannot remain angry for long, and it allows the poem to shift from one emotion to another very quickly. This technique was John's adaptation of one of the most moving aspects of Shakespeare's play, the sense that anything can happen in a dream and the uncertainty one feels, at times, not knowing whether what one remembers happened in a dream. When the young characters awaken in the forest in act 4, having recovered their personalities and natural desires, they deliver the play's most memorable and moving poetry through their collective confusion about what they dimly remember of their other desires. Demetrius describes his dreamlike memory of the eventful night as "small and undistinguishable, / Like far-off mountains turned into clouds."[76] The young characters' confusion between dream and memory allows them remarkable freedom to forget their painful romantic longings quickly and move on to adapt to happier feelings and ideas. Almost every character in the play discovers that to dream and to forget are equally crucial ways to learn, an idea that would become a hallmark in many of Ashbery's mature poems.

John wrote the poem for himself only, so the swift and positive reaction from members of his family to his tiny tour de force took him completely by surprise. His father laughed. His grandparents praised it. His mother, who never bragged to others about her son and who had no interest in poetry, copied the poem into her own handwriting several times to preserve copies, and shared it with her sister. His aunt Janet was so proud of her nephew that she showed the poem to her cousin Elizabeth Sherwood Rinehart, who in turn gave it to her mother-in-law, Mary Roberts Rinehart. After John was informed of his poem's journey to New York City and told that it had received great acclaim, he felt inspired to write more. He planned an entire volume of poems and drew a cover page in crayon entitled *Poems for Boys and Girls*. He placed typed drafts of "The Battle" between the covers, but he could not write a new poem.[77] He tried to fall back into that focused, clear state of mind in which he had composed his first poem, but he could not figure out how to make it happen again. The process of writing a poem felt as mysterious to him as if he had never done it, and the more he tried and failed, the more frustrated he grew. He thought about his poem's success in New York City and could not imagine anything better: "I didn't think I'd ever be able to pull off another coup like that one. There seemed to be nowhere to go but down."[78] Since he understood that he was never going to be able to write another poem as fine as "The Battle," he decided to quit writing poetry altogether. Feeling disappointed, but relieved to be rid of the pressure to write, he abandoned his new volume and eventually forgot he had begun it.

Only Addie noticed that John stopped writing poetry after "The Battle." She encouraged him to coauthor a brief poem on the subject of spring flowers in early 1936. The resulting five couplets, however, beginning "Yellow daffodils, bright and gay / Greet with joy the new born day," sounded much more like her voice and her taste in poetry than his.[79] Working on the composition with his grandmother did not inspire John to want to write any new verse on his own. It would take another seven years before he sat down again to write a new poem.

Blue Mountain

1936–1940

Gradually, John began to cultivate an identity as a quick wit. He honed his comic persona in the company of family and friends. If he said something funny enough at home, his mother would look up from her housework long enough to say, quite seriously, "Oh, John, you are such a card."[1] He was bored in school and irritated by chores at home, but he discovered there were funny ways to protest what he did not enjoy so that no one, least of all his father, who would have spanked him for it, could tell he might be complaining. He also continued to study music and painting, and privately read about new developments in the history of art. Although he had given up writing poetry, he could not rid himself completely of the idea that maybe someday, as unlikely as it seemed, he might become an artist.

In July 1939, John attended sleepaway camp for the first time. He did not want to go; he had successfully avoided being sent there a year earlier.[2] Despite his efforts to resist, his family drove him to Camp Cory, a YMCA camp on Keuka Lake, near Rochester, and left him at the boys' dorm for nearly two weeks, the longest period the eleven-year-old had been away from home. His parents felt that two weeks spent out-doors with other boys his own age would be good for him. He hated the place, particularly the daily schedule of recreation: sailing, canoeing, and making jewelry in the craft shop, which many boys called "The Crap Slop"—activities he took great pains to avoid.[3] At the beginning

of his second week, he wrote a letter to his grandparents (who had paid
for the experience):

> July 12 1939
>
> Dear Grandpa and Nana: I am having a nice time at camp. I
> sleep in a top bunk from whense [*sic*] I am writing you. The food
> is very good more so than at home. To-morrow we are going on
> a canoe trip. The counselor and boys are nice. Much love to
> everybody.
> John[4]

In its six laconic sentences, the missive was more deadpan and
parodic than anything he had ever written before. Suddenly, he made
some creative use of his misery. Even the inclusion (and misspelling) of
the archaic "whence" suggested his arch approach to composing not just
any letter home, but the most quintessentially dull letter from the most
average camper of all time. He embellished the letter's lack of detail,
emphasizing its absence of substance by repeating even nondescript
phrases, a technique that heightened the missive's manufactured bland-
ness. He also imaginatively rendered a first-rate mealtime to get a rise
out of his audience.[5] In fact, by the end of the session most campers
were confined to the infirmary after rancid butterscotch pudding sick-
ened nearly everyone, which confirmed what John had already strongly
suspected about camp food.[6]

During the following fall, in eighth grade, he wrote another, even
more substantial parody.[7] He composed the "fake report" in his English
course during an especially dull class period. When his kind and tedious teacher, Mr. Klossner, asked each student to write a true story and
then read it to the class, John invented a fictional story in the form of a
newspaper account:

> [T]he school children in Mansfield [Ohio] were all very civic
> minded. . . . [T]here had been a lot of traffic accidents involving
> children and so they decided to form their own police force for
> pedestrians and helping people across the street and stopping
> cars and everything.

He had never been to Mansfield but had been hearing about the city for years, from his grandfather's letters on Mansfield-Leland Hotel stationery and from his mother and grandmother, who "were always talking about how nice the tourist hotel was." He simply wanted to be able to express his dissatisfaction—with his small-town American life and its inanities, sentimentalism, boring school assignments—without getting in trouble for his critical views. Throughout an otherwise fabricated account, John sprinkled bits of local lore he had picked up. As soon as he read his piece to the class, Mr. Klossner "became very excited" and went "running up to the front of the class and said, 'Isn't that fantastic! Listen kids, if kids can do that in Mansfield, Ohio, then they can do it in Sodus!'"[8] John was shocked that his "fantastic" story seemed believable to his teacher and classmates.

He had recently performed in the school play, learning to sharpen his delivery to get bigger laughs. The seventh-graders put on Louise Saunders's slight and witty one-act verse comedy, *The Knave of Hearts*, and despite John's inexperience, Miss Florence Klumpp, a new teacher and the young director, assigned him the starring role of "the knave."[9] His mother helped him by sewing, at his request, a ridiculous red suit with an "eighteenth-century doublet," through which to enhance the buffoonish nature of his character. He gleefully prepared his part by practicing exaggerated gestures and mispronunciations, behavior and speech that Miss Klumpp directed him to heighten even more (saying *pomp-de-belly*, for example, instead of *pompdebile*), in order to make his performance as funny as possible.[10]

After the success of this production, John started to write his own material. The first one-act play he wrote, which he entitled *Ye Gods*, was a religious parody. The title of the lost play suggests that it drew on his knowledge of Christian education and his enthusiasm for Greek mythology and other pagan myths. On June 6, 1937, he was confirmed in front of his entire family at St. John's Church in Sodus, an event he viewed as a public occasion much more than a religious one. Afterward, Addie gave him an inscribed Bible to commemorate the event, and he read the book carefully and skeptically over the next few years.[11] He described his work-in-progress in one of his first letters to Mary Wellington—"P.S. No. 3 I am writing a play called "Ye Gods." Its [*sic*] a scream to say the least"—extolling its possibility as a witty vehicle for his friends to perform together over the summer in Pultneyville.[12] Despite his initial enthusiasm, he never mentioned it again. As was the case with many other plays he would begin over the next few years, he probably did not finish writing it. Ideas took hold of him, and he worked intensely until he did not know how to develop them further.

He was constantly swept up by new ideas, especially during sixth grade, when an illness gave him time to read and learn whatever he wished. For most of sixth grade, from October 1937 to April 1938, John and Richard (who was in first grade) stayed home together with scarlet fever and then whooping cough.[13] Although neither boy felt terribly ill, the doctor prescribed extensive bed rest. Staying inside to read and listen to the radio was what John already liked to do best anyway. For seven months, he easily avoided his three least favorite activities: chores, exercise, and outdoor recreation. He also had his own room once again, after his mother temporarily moved Richard down the hall, and he enjoyed his privacy. She placed the big family radio in the hallway between them for entertainment. The primary drama of the day involved arguments about which radio programs to play. Richard loved *The Lone Ranger*; John preferred soap operas such as *Ma Perkins* and *Pepper Young's Family*, and liked the ads. One afternoon when his mother came to his bedroom to do her daily cleaning and disinfecting of the space, he made up a new joke, punning on a disinfectant and sung to a popular tune: "Lysol you last night and got that old feeling." His mother looked up briefly from her work to laugh.[14]

The radio show that John could not bear to miss each day, however, was *Vic and Sade*, a fifteen-minute program written by Paul Rhymer that chronicled the average life of the Gook family. Mr. and Mrs. Victor Gook (Vic and Sade) and their son, Rush, live in a small, cozy house in a small town. A revolving cast of friends, including "Smelly Clark" and "Bluetooth Johnson"—names John loved—stop by to chat. Often the story begins with a simple family conversation, for example:

> RUSH: . . . Nicer Scott claims he can unfry an egg.
> VIC: I bet he can't.
> RUSH: Ain't it ridiculous a guy claimin' junk like that?
> VIC: How does he go *about* unfryin' eggs?[15]

The Gook family would find these sorts of nothings to talk and squabble about, seemingly desultory conversations revolving around bland subjects such as weather or housekeeping that John thought were "brilliant."[16] Listening every day for months, he memorized snippets of the show, absorbing its combination of slowly unfolding conversational rhythms, its dry sense of humor, and its piercing observations about family, education, and culture in American small-town life, delivered with a sweet understatement that made their sardonic intent easy to miss.

Shortly after the boys finally returned to school for the end of the year, Helen celebrated their good health by taking them to see Errol Flynn's new Technicolor film, *The Adventures of Robin Hood*, in nearby Newark. They thought Flynn was just the right mix of irreverent and heroic, an excellent Robin Hood. John began addressing Richard as Sir Richardson. As soon as they arrived in Pultneyville for the summer, he came up with the idea to open a "Knight Club." He invited all the children spending the summer in the village to join the club, where they discussed their exploits and addressed each other as "Sir" this and "Sir" that. Among the new group of children were several whom John especially liked: Eleanor "Barney" Little, a dark-haired, serious girl and a voracious reader, and her cute, vivacious younger sister Joan (Jo).

Richard, Carol, and John on the swings in Pultneyville, 1936

Carol Rupert, the daughter of Ottilie (Teal) Graeper Rupert, Helen Ashbery's best friend from college, stayed in the house next door to the Lawrences'. Along with her younger brother, Pede, she lived all summer at the home of her maiden aunts, three beloved and intelligent sisters (Emma; Carolyn, known as Connie; and Olga) whom everyone in the village called the Graeper girls. Carol had a "deep timbre voice" that made her sound mature, but she was a year and a half younger than John and treated him as an older brother.[17] Her cousin Billy Graeper, a year older than John, stayed in a rental house a few doors down with his parents and also began to play with the group.

John and Mary Wellington led the Knight Club together. In the film, Olivia de Havilland played Maid Marian, but none of the children cared for the role of the damsel in distress. Seamlessly blending the legends of Robin Hood and King Arthur, John spoke to everyone in an imaginative version of medieval English, and everyone took turns playing a knight of the forest, an outlaw, King Arthur, or Robin Hood. The area of willow trees became an amalgam of Sherwood and Windsor Forests, described with a smattering of history and myth added and invented as needed. John advised each of his friends to choose a tree (and surrounding grounds) that would serve as his or her castle.[18] There were occasional insurrections, such as when Richard and Carol pulled away the ladder that John was using to survey the scene from a barn roof.[19]

The following summer, the "knights" picked up right where they left off, and their histories grew even more elaborate, expansive, and wittier. The children spent more time in their imaginary "kingdoms, empires, domains, dukedoms, and marquisdoms . . . and—oh yes! Duchessdoms," and talked for hours about what to name their castles and realms.[20] Years later, Ashbery wrote several poems that directly alluded to the Robin Hood story, his connection forged in earnest through his frolicking childhood games. In "Meditations of a Parrot" (*Some Trees*, 1956), the parrot repeats "Robin Hood! Robin Hood!" while looking at the sea. Twenty years later, the title "Robin Hood's Barn" (*Self-Portrait in a Convex Mirror*, 1975) invoked both the idiom "to take the long way around" and his childhood memory, as the speaker reflects on an experience of growing up, as ". . . your young years become a kind of clay / Out of which the older, more rounded and also brusquer / Retort is fashioned."

This period in Pultneyville was a particularly rich source of "clay."

He memorialized his affection for Barney Little, for instance, with a reference to the race car driver Barney Oldfield in *A Nest of Ninnies* (1969), the man after whom she earned her nickname to mark her very speedy birth. Many of Ashbery's later poems also invoked the transient feeling of summer, a mood that John identified early on as school and farm life loomed ever closer in August: "Alas, the summer's energy wanes quickly, / A moment and it is gone" or, even more wistfully, "a hint / of fall in the air, soggy and bored."[21] The happiness John felt in Pultneyville served as a kind of armor to help him withstand any unhappiness he felt during the rest of the year, and it protected him from other sorts of pain as well. In *Flow Chart* (1991), Ashbery's sophisticated reflections on the past briefly slide, for a moment, into the language of childhood retorts: "I'm rubber / and you're glue, whatever you say bounces off me and sticks to you," since the "words have, as they / always do, come full circle."[22] In the later "Episode," he describes how dramatically social culture shifted from the beginning to the end of the 1930s, crucial changes that, as a young boy, he noticed from the sidelines without understanding what such shifts in taste might mean:

> In 1935
> the skirts were long and flared slightly,
> suitably. Hats shaded part of the face.
> Lipstick was fudgy and encouraging. There was
> music in the names of the years. 1937
> was welcoming too, though one bit one's lip
> preparing for the pain that was sure to come.[23]

In the mid-thirties women's "lipstick was fudgy and encouraging" and "music" could still be heard and felt. By 1937, a feeling of optimism was giving way to something darker, but John did not connect Lillian Holling's often repeated remark around Pultneyville that "what can't be cured must be endured," or his mother's "life is a funny business," with worrisome radio reports about Nazi Germany, Adolf Hitler's increasing power, or the likelihood of another war.[24] These world events did not interrupt his imaginative playtime in Pultneyville's lake and trees, but shadowed it, forming pieces of the "clay" he would dig up and sift through later.

Ever since his failed attempt to write a second poem after "The Battle," John had pushed aside thoughts about writing poetry. In late December 1936, however, he picked up *Life*, the new magazine his grandfather subscribed to, and read a feature article on an art exhibition, "Fantastic Art: Dadaism and Surrealism," opening at the Museum of Modern Art in New York City, and he was swept up again in thoughts of art and artists. He had never heard the term *surrealism*, but the magazine's definition of surrealist art as "no stranger than a person's dream," was both completely understandable and very appealing to him.[25] The article included photographs of objects from the exhibition: Meret Oppenheim's now famous fur-lined teacup; paintings by René Magritte, Salvador Dalí, Giorgio de Chirico, and Pablo Picasso that used images of clocks, trees, houses, and chairs, but their shapes and colors altered in such a way that they became slightly stranger and more menacing in the process. Here were examples of ordinary objects that John saw and used every day presented as art, and he found that in their transformation, they became more compelling. To see objects from his dull world tweaked slightly, just as a dream might do, and in that process of transformation becoming something new, vivid and exciting, thrilled him. Seeing the strangely beautiful examples of surrealist art consciously rekindled his former desires to become an artist.

John wished to go see the exhibition in New York City, but since that was impossible, he asked his grandfather to take him to the Rochester Central Library downtown, which was a beautiful "art-deco gem" he liked to visit, to learn more about surrealism.[26] He found Julien Levy's new volume, *Surrealism* (1936), on the shelves and sat down at a table. The text, a combination of history, analysis, and artistic examples of the surrealist movement, was both dense and playful, certainly not written for a nine-year-old boy, even a precocious one. Yet the young Ashbery at once responded to the rebellious, critical, energetic spirit of the artistic movement.

As he flipped through the images of surrealist art at the end of the book, he felt a jolt at the sight of Joseph Cornell's *Soap Bubble Set* (1936), which resembled a child's homemade diorama, containing bits of a clay pipe used to make soap bubbles with "marbles, and toy birds," but put together in such a way that their very ordinariness seemed "dazzling."[27] John felt "astonished" to see these ordinary toys and bits of unimportant things he had enjoyed as a young child transformed by Cornell into something so strange, extraordinary, and beautiful.[28] Looking at the photograph of Cornell's box triggered a nascent thought that other things from his own "dim, dopey" life might also have the potential to become art.[29]

He began to learn much more about art. After Sodus schools dropped their art program in 1938, his grandparents arranged for both John and Richard to begin Miss Rebecca Cook's painting class every Friday afternoon at the Memorial Art Gallery on University Avenue in Rochester. The weekly trips to Rochester alone gave him something to look forward to, but he also felt stirred by the stunning museum, and by the chaos of the basement art rooms, with their "smell of paint . . . the floor wax, and the mess."[30] For his mother's forty-sixth birthday, on August 15, 1939, and to commemorate the end of his first year of study, John presented her with "a copy of a crayon drawing of Anne Cresacre by Hans Holbein [the Younger]." Holbein was famous for his portraits, and his intimate, psychologically probing, and very mysterious portrait of Anne Cresacre, completed in 1527, was considered one of his best.[31] It was also the painting John knew most intimately, for a print hung in the Ashbery living room, a wedding gift to his parents and one of the only pieces of art in the farmhouse. In his rendering, John carefully and successfully captured Anne Cresacre's gaze, the very aspect of Holbein's

John painted this copy of Hans Holbein the Younger's Anne Cresacre for his mother.

portrait that made it so mesmerizing. His father helped him fit his finished work with a frame.

John was in the midst of a period of remarkable physical and personal growth. He had become exceptionally gaunt and tall. A photograph taken in August 1939 showed him towering over Richard and their two-year-old cousin Larry Taft. He was also (as were his friends) beginning to experiment sexually in ways that were changing his feelings about others and himself. On one evening over the summer, he kissed Mary Wellington after walking her home, but her surprise seemed to him a brusque rebuff, and it never happened again.[32] On another afternoon, at a picnic, he shared a flirtatious kiss with Jinny Gilbert, the daughter of one of Helen's college friends, who promptly told Carol Rupert all about it.[33] Carol's cousin Billy Graeper, who was visiting Pultneyville for several weeks of the summer as usual, slept over in John's room on several nights, and they sometimes kissed and touched, though they never mentioned what happened between them, either to each other or to anybody else. John could recall feeling attracted to boys as far back as kindergarten, but he was conscious of this strong feeling now in ways he had never been before. He kept this knowledge secret, for he "didn't know there was such a thing as homosexuality" and worried he might be "the only one so afflicted."[34]

John and Richard had enjoyed the summer so much that by January

Larry Taft on Helen's lap, John (standing), Richard (in front), Henry Lawrence, Addie (standing), and Janet Taft (holding Sheila), 1939

John, Larry Taft, and Richard, August 1939

John and Mary Wellington at the Pultneyville Firemen's Fair photo booth, summer 1939

Chet and Richard, Ottilie (Teal) and Carol Rupert, and Henry Lawrence in Pultneyville, 1939

Richard and John "clowning" with Chet, 1939

1940, they were already beginning to plot activities for the next one. Their idea, which John shared in a letter to Mary Wellington, was to mount a full performance of *The Knave of Hearts* for the village. He would star as the knave, since he already had the costume and knew the part. Mary would play Violetta, the other lead. He assigned Richard the part of a herald and doled out other roles to all the children. He planned to ask Pat Brownbridge to direct.[35] Pat was a stout, swarthy, middle-aged man who lived in Pultneyville with Henry Lawrence's cousins Lillian and Paul Holling as their "manservant," and went to every family function with them. Everyone accepted him as the elderly Paul and Lillian Holling's butler, though John eventually understood, about a decade later, that Paul and Pat were, in fact, lovers.[36] He was a jovial extrovert who often mentioned that he had done some theatrical training early in his life in Ireland, and John thought he might be interested in helping to put on the play.

Preparations for the summer accelerated even as John began to mention to Mary in passing that Richard was home sick. In February, he wrote that Richard had been diagnosed with "rheumatic fever," and John had stayed over at Carol's in Rochester for three days to see the "swell" *Pinocchio*, not realizing that the two events were connected. His parents had sent him to the Ruperts because Richard's illness, which

Paul Holling (son of Mary Sheffield and Armine Andrew Holling), Henry Lawrence's first cousin, at age twelve in 1884

began around Washington's Birthday and was initially diagnosed as grippe, had continued to worsen.[37] Helen and Chet were trying to determine what was wrong with him, but the doctors' diagnoses kept changing, and no one wanted John to worry unnecessarily. John stayed very busy, starting a new stamp collection, attending art classes at the Memorial Art Gallery and writing long, amusing letters to Mary about her pet duck, which she had originally believed was male, rechristening it "Lady Jamaica Wallingford Featherskirts Daffodilia Wellington Duck" ("Daffy" for short).[38]

As John focused on casting the play, his parents grew increasingly worried about Richard, but they shielded John from knowing anything more. On March 8, Chet Ashbery bought Richard a two-wheel bicycle as a present for his upcoming ninth birthday, on March 12. Just before his birthday, Richard's health deteriorated and he was admitted to Strong Memorial Hospital for more tests. After three weeks in the hospital with a series of shifting diagnoses, doctors were still uncertain but suggested probable leukemia, at that time a fatal disease for a child. Out of a combination of their feelings of protectiveness and uncertainty, John's parents continued to keep him quite ignorant of what they feared was the severity of his brother's illness. He visited Richard in the hospital only once, finding him more sleepy and confused than ill.

John attended school and continued to do well in his classes. He and Richard had both stayed home before with childhood diseases. John supposed, and no one corrected him, that Richard had the same sort of illness. Even the fact that Richard was staying in Strong Memorial Hospital was not necessarily alarming, since John had also stayed there once, to have his tonsils removed, and Addie and Henry went frequently for appointments.

By early April, however, doctors had diagnosed Richard conclusively as suffering from "acute lymphatic leukemia" with "secondary anemia."[39] John's parents informed him of the name of the disease without explaining its prognosis. Richard's health was deteriorating very rapidly, and no medicine yet existed to stop it or slow it down, as there would be less than a decade later. Richard returned home from the hospital to Sodus and seemed to improve with regular blood transfusions, but there was nothing else doctors knew to do to save him. Many of Chet's and Helen's friends donated blood.[40] John knew very little of what was happening because his parents had sent him to stay with his grand-parents in Pultneyville. He was told only that Richard was home again from the hospital, and he assumed that his brother was improving.

From Pultneyville, John could properly prepare for the summer, and he wrote Mary about his solo explorations of their willow tree kingdom, which had been completely flooded in early spring rains. In passing, he mentioned that Richard had "Lukemia" [sic], but the letter contained no other discussion of what that meant. His parents were not telling him anything, and indeed, they were probably frightened and confused themselves, for not much was understood yet about childhood leukemia. The letter to Mary contained a detailed account of the state of their re-spective castles and a playful plea not to "get all quacked up"—not to worry about the flooding—"cause the same thing happens almost every year, and next summer you won't know the difference." It was a statement likely as much for himself to keep at bay his general anxieties about Richard's strangely lengthy absence, of which there was still no word, as it was to her about the imminent destruction of their kingdom.[41]

By the end of April, John was back in Sodus and Richard had moved to Pultneyville for more transfusions. Carol, too, was sick, with scarlet fever, and her house had been quarantined; John believed both would recover. His immediate concern was to figure out how he and Mary could best protect their kingdom from the danger of potential invaders once summer began:

> We shall take our cups, saucers, winebottles, and even wrigley vines. We shall have a hidden garrison where everyone (of us) will run for when the alarm sounds. It shall be camouflaged, of blackberry bushes, grass, and vines. If the marauders get to [sic] daring, we shall bombard them with deadly mudballs. It shall be a secret kingdom, with a secret entrance. No one but we four or perhaps our parents shall no [sic] about it.[42]

John created "a book of magic recipes" using ingredients they could procure by the creek. They would be able to write secret notes to each other using lemon juice and heat, a "wonderfully spooky" trick he had recently learned from *The Book of Knowledge*. He was looking forward to lemonade and hot dogs at Pultneyville Firemen's Field Day, swimming in the lake, and especially their "secret kingdom." With such extensive forethought, John presumed this summer was going to be their best ever.

He sent no more letters that summer. In early June, Richard worsened, and Chet Ashbery bought him a "wheel about chair," as he was too weak to walk.[43] While John finished school in Sodus, Richard received regular transfusions from blood donated by friends in Pultneyville. These transfusions seemed to help the secondary anemia, and reports trickled in that Richard's condition was improving. John finished eighth grade by winning the district spelling bee, the only student with a perfect score.[44] He then won the county spelling bee in Palmyra, the first Soduskan to do so. This county victory meant that the bee would be held in Sodus for the first time the following year. At Class Day, John received $2.50 as the student with the highest average in school and a special award for winning the county bee.[45]

When school ended, Helen sent him to stay with his "aunt" Aurelia and "uncle" Sandy at their comfortable home in Greece, New York, just outside Rochester. Aurelia Hillman Sanders had been one of Helen Lawrence's dearest friends in her sorority at the University of Rochester, and John was fond of their adopted son, Dick, who was about the same age. John always looked forward to visiting them at their pretty home. He was told that Richard, who had always loved the Fourth of July, planned to watch the fireworks, encouraging news that suggested he was becoming healthier. No one told him what they must have known by this point: that Richard was dying.

"Uncle" Sandy (George Sanders) with John Ashbery and Dick Sanders, about 1930

A few days before July 4, Carol, who had finally fully recovered from scarlet fever, went to stay with her aunts in Pultneyville. Richard was staying in a bed in the living room at the Lawrences' house, next door, and she went over to visit him. He lay in bed and looked so pale and weak, so extremely ill, that she felt incredibly scared for him.[46] She had not understood until that moment how seriously ill he really was. A day or two later, his doctors said that there was nothing more they could do. Richard was brought home to Sodus on July 3. He seemed to rally the next day and recognize the holiday, but the following morning he was not doing well. Chet and Helen sent for John. It was Friday morning, July 5, and the fastest way to return home was by car. Aurelia drove John to Rochester. Carol's aunt Connie met him there and drove him back to Pultneyville so that his grandfather could take him home to Sodus to see Richard.

When John reached Pultneyville, just after three in the afternoon, his grandfather told him his parents had phoned; Richard had just died. John was confused and shocked. He had no idea what his grandfather meant. He still had not grasped that death was even a possibility for his brother. He walked into the backyard and saw Carol's little brother, Pede, and told him that Richard was dead. Pede was so upset that he ran back into his house. Carol heard the noise of the banging door, looked out her bedroom window, and saw John in his shorts and shirt, knocking the rolled-up comic book he had brought for Richard against one hand and wandering around alone in Henry Lawrence's vegetable garden, waiting for his grandfather to drive him back to Sodus.[47]

◄─❄─►

The funeral for Richard was on Monday, July 8, 1940, at two thirty in the afternoon at Ashbery Farm. Reverend John Williamson arrived from St. John's Church to conduct the service. "There were banks of Easter lilies," sent by local families, the smell of which overpowered all others and lingered for days.[48] John's parents arranged for Carol and her aunt Olga to take him on a picnic in Pultneyville during the service, but just as they were leaving the house with their picnic basket, John saw the funeral procession, with the hearse carrying Richard's casket, as it drove down Washington Street toward the Lakeview Cemetery. The Lawrence family ancestors, including all the Throops and Hollings fam-

ilies and their direct descendants, were buried there, on plots of land
that bordered Lake Ontario and offered to the grieving the most magnificent views of the lake imaginable. As John recognized the procession
passing the house, Olga hurried him back inside under the pretext that
they had forgotten some essential item for their picnic, and he pretended
not to have seen anything.

Later that night, John returned home to Sodus. Over the next few
days and weeks, the family did not say much to one another, but they
each made some small adjustments. Chet began reading the Bible every
night, staying up late and studying the Christian Scientist Mary Baker
Eddy's testimonials on the power of faith. He framed a photo taken the
previous fall of Richard throwing a football, his young son's athleticism
and charm fully displayed. Chet had finally taken the old roll of film to
be developed on July 1, 1940. Helen, Chet, and Elizabeth worked on the
farm, for it was nearly cherry season and there was a lot to do. Richard's
twin bed was removed from John's bedroom.[49]

Each family member kept to himself. John roamed about, and one
afternoon, in the back of a closet, he discovered piles of unopened gifts
Richard had received while he was ill. He left most of them alone, but
he took a few books, including Marie-Catherine D'Aulnoy's translation
of *The White Cat, and Other Old French Fairy Tales*, which his parents'

Richard playing football, fall 1939

friends had given to Richard not knowing he was too ill to read it.[50] A half century later, Ashbery would translate the bittersweet tale of "The White Cat" from French.[51] John's parents sent him to visit his aunt Janet, uncle Tom, and three-year-old cousin Larry for a few days in their new house in Elmira, New York. John sent his parents a postcard, noting that he was having a nice time and had purchased some new "songlasses" [sic]. When he returned home, his parents remarked on his poor spelling, which he found insulting.[52] Only much later did it occur to him that they were suggesting he had been thinking of Richard.

The Rupert family arranged to take John and his parents on a trip at the end of July. Although they grieved for Richard, they worried even more about the impact of his death on the rest of the family. Carol's father, Philip, who had been Chet's best friend in the 1920s and who had been responsible for introducing him to Helen, drove the car. Ottilie "Teal" Rupert was still Helen's closest friend more than twenty years after graduating from college. They traveled first to visit Teal's sister, Alma Dandy, in Ogdensburg, two hundred miles northeast.[53] Alma and her husband, Howard, were committed Christian Scientists, and they talked with Chet about faith, conversations that John overheard and found strange and upsetting. The next day, they continued on to visit Paula Grant, another of Teal's sisters, who lived one hundred miles farther east, in Plattsburgh, on Lake Champlain. A photographer snapped a stark picture of the group in matching touristy hats and strained smiles on a boat trip down the St. Lawrence River. After Plattsburgh, the group drove to Blue Mountain Lake, which was meant to be the highlight of the trip.

The two families arrived in Blue Mountain, checked into their hotel, and walked down to the lake. John had stayed there overnight once two years earlier, on the way back from a brief genealogy mission to Vermont with his mother and grandparents. At that time, everyone had felt lighthearted. His mother, especially pleased with a tourist hotel they stopped in near Ticonderoga, had declared its floor "so clean you could eat off of it," an expression John had never heard before and which delighted him.[54] In his grief, John found that everything that had happened before, especially those fleeting, pleasant memories, had taken on a different valence and color, as though the memory itself had changed. To add to his confusion, it was his thirteenth birthday. Much

Philip and Carol Rupert with Helen, John, and Chet on the St. Lawrence River, July 1940

The Rupert and Ashbery families on the top of Blue Mountain, July 1940

later, in *Flow Chart* (1991), Ashbery could describe a version of how it felt to be "handed a skull / as a birthday present":

> Early on
> was a time of seeming: golden eggs that hatched
> into regrets, a snowflake whose kiss burned like an enchanter's
> poison; yet it all seemed good in the growing dawn.

The breeze that always nurtures us (no matter how dry,
how filled with complaints about time and the weather the air)
pointed out a way that diverged from the true way without
        negating it,
to arrive at the same result by different spells,
so that no one was wiser for knowing the way we had grown,
almost unconsciously, into a cube of grace that was to be
a permanent shelter. Let the book end there, some few
said, but that was of course impossible; the growth must
        persist
into areas darkened and dangerous, undermined
by the curse of that death breeze, until one is handed a skull
as a birthday present.[55]

The image Ashbery paints in his poem brings to mind Frans Hals's
painting *Boy with Skull*: the open curiosity and energy of a young boy
"undermined / by the curse of that death breeze" that thrust a skull
into his hands one afternoon and required him to carry it up a mountain. A group photograph at the summit documented the grief-stricken

John and Helen (and Sheila),
August 1940. Photograph taken
by Chet Ashbery.

families. That night, they went to eat supper at a diner in the village. The place had a jukebox, and Carol asked John to dance, to help make the dinner feel more festive. When they stood up, John spotted a very elderly couple sitting alone in a booth. They were storekeepers he had seen earlier in town. He thought they looked terribly frail and tragic, and he started sobbing. His family comforted him, assuming that his grief was for his brother. He kept trying to explain to them that they were wrong, that he felt sorry for the elderly couple at the other table.[56]

The summer had never happened, yet it had also felt so long already, and it was only the beginning of August. Back in Pultneyville, Carol's mother suggested that the children put on a play. It was an activity that she thought might cheerfully occupy John. They had already started work on preparing *The Knave of Hearts*, but no one wanted to perform it anymore, perhaps because it had so many parts, one of which had been assigned to Richard. Instead, Carol's mother suggested they learn *The Princess and the Robber Chief*, a short, four-character play loosely based on the King Arthur legend that she had seen in a book during college. She told John about it, and in a few days he had written it out in his own hand. Carol was to play the Princess; John the King; Mary would be the Robber Chief. The children found old costumes, sold tickets, and performed in the barn behind Carol's house. The play concerns a melodramatic love story between the Princess and the Robber Chief, for which the King finally sacrifices himself. His last speech:

> Soon your wicked blood will flow
> And the whole wide world shall know
> That I, though, old and weak and sad
> Yet a lion's courage have.[57]

The Robber Chief then stabs the King to death, and afterward explains to the Princess why he must run away and hide. She is so moved by his words that they fall instantly in love. The play ends with the Princess's surprisingly optimistic statement: "Love doth conquer all."

The performance was a great success. Someone took a photograph of the actors in their costumes, to mark the occasion. Mary stands in her Robber Chief's attire hugging Carol, the Princess. John, kingly in robes and a crown, surveys the scene wisely. In the background: a lovely

Carol, Mary, John, and Carol's brother Pede after the performance of *The Princess and the Robber Chief* in Pultneyville

summer's day in Pultneyville with a bevy of relatives and other elderly neighbors milling about. The production had done what Teal intended. John did not know at the time that the suggestion to put on a play was meant to distract him from his grief, but it had temporarily worked. He had focused his attention on wittily adapting four pages of rhyming verse, and this work brought friends and a community together and entertained them. This experience demonstrated, in a way so natural that it remained an unarticulated insight for many years, a communal value to the work of writing. The performance of the play remained the highlight of the summer for audience and performers alike, referred to as a special event by those involved, ultimately separated in their minds from the tragedy that preceded it.[58]

In September, after John's first week of high school, his parents took him on another short trip to Blue Mountain Lake with the Ruperts. John and Carol answered every question the adults asked them with "I durnt want to," a phrase they thought fantastically funny.[59] The trip was less sharply painful than the one of six weeks before, yet John always associated Blue Mountain with the shock of his brother's death and his family's pain and grief. Later the word *blue* invoked for him, among its many other associations, those trips, too, and the loss of his brother: "the blue snow"; the "steep blue sides of the crater"; the "blue cornflakes in a white bowl"; and "the extra worry began it—on the / Blue blue mountain."[60]

In the weeks that followed, John pretended not to see his parents grieve. Chet was very quiet, turned inward; he had stopped drinking, and tried to find comfort by studying the lessons of Christian Science. He had already developed and framed the photograph of Richard throwing a football, and now he placed the picture, which was exactly the image of what John believed Chet most desired in a son, in the living room, on a side table just beside his reading chair.[61] Every night, Chet sat down next to it and read Mary Baker Eddy's testimonials of the miraculous recoveries of believers, stories he had not read early enough to save Richard.[62] Chet's sense of loss was irreparable, and it magnified the sense of isolation he had felt due to earlier losses, beginning with his father's death in 1927 and compounded by his older brother Wallace's sudden death from a heart attack the previous year. John felt guilty that he, the less athletic, less "normal," less good son, had survived.[63] Both John and Chet felt a powerful sense of guilt after Richard's death, but they were unable to share it, retreating into their private thoughts in different corners of the house.

Without directly mentioning any of the details of that time in his life, John offered an image of his feelings at the very end of "Definition of Blue." The poem offers an intensely personal description of a process of growing up, of coming to grips with one's survival, one's disappointments and feelings of guilt:

> And yet it results in a downward motion, or rather a floating
>   one
> In which the blue surroundings drift slowly up and past you
> To realize themselves some day, while you, in this nether world
>   that could not be better
> Waken each morning to the exact value of what you did and
>   said, which remains.[64]

What "remained" for John and his parents was a stunned feeling, as though they had been knocked to the ground by a giant wave. They were reeling from the aftereffects of a storm so fierce and fast in its destructiveness that it had changed the entire landscape of their family. In "A Wave," Ashbery continues the thought he begins in "Definition of Blue" to a more mature emotional reflection: "What is restored / Becomes stronger than the loss as it is remembered; / Is a new, separate life of its own. A new color. Seriously blue."[65] In this later poem, the difficulty of surviving and recovering from loss lessens over time, and eventually the blue hue one once knew is more than "restored," becoming "stronger," a "new" deeper, warmer, "seriously blue" color.

Shortly after returning to Sodus, Helen and Chet drove John to the New York State Fair in Syracuse to compete in the state spelling bee. He had been invited as a result of winning the county bee in June, an event that felt as if it had taken place in a different lifetime. For a few days at the end of September, John lived in a dorm on the grounds and was able to go on rides and enjoy the fair with other county winners from New York. There was a lot of activity, things to see and do, and the anonymity of being among crowds of other schoolchildren provided an unexpected reprieve from the intensity of the summer. The bee began, and John spelled D-E-S-P-A. He knew immediately he had made a mistake. He corrected himself, but it was already too late. He was out on D-E-S-P-E-R-A-T-E-L-Y, and his parents drove him home.[66]

3

Quiz Kid

1940–1941

The Ashbery family's communal grieving had begun with their two trips to Blue Mountain, but back in Sodus for the school year, each member of the family coped with Richard's death alone. They could not talk about what had happened, in part because they had never talked freely about their emotional lives before. Each member of the family felt inexpressible thoughts and feelings. For most of the fall, they stayed together inside, skipping church, community basketball games, and movies, venturing outside only for work or school. Chet's suddenly introverted behavior and total silence on the subject of Richard's death shocked even his closest friends.[1] The small community observed the withdrawn family anxiously and sympathetically, aware of how deep a wound Richard's death had left on them all.

About five months after Richard's death, this period of isolation began to end, and the family resumed some community activities as the holidays approached. In some raw, instinctive way, John's mother must have understood her son's need to—or she needed him to—communicate, and she gave him a handsome leather diary, his first, for Christmas. His initial reaction upon discovering the blank diary was disappointment, for he had hoped for art books, puzzles, and games. For a few days, John left the book alone, but before the end of the year, he began to write in it. On the "IDENTIFICATION" page, he responded to every one of the book's questions with a joke:

John in a new suit, fall 1940

Residence <u>5th Avenue</u>
My weight is <u>400 lbs</u>.
Height <u>4½"</u>
Color of Hair <u>greenish-blue</u>
Color of Eyes <u>bright orange</u>

Under "RECORDS":

<u>Jimmy Dorsey and Glenn Miller</u>

There was no sense from these responses that he had any designs on the book (or use for it) beyond amusement.

The silliness of his responses belied the seriousness with which he was simultaneously conducting his life as a thirteen-year-old high school freshman. At the start of the school year, he had ambitiously registered for five rather than the required four courses, choosing Latin as an elective. He immediately preferred that small course (only eleven students) to any other, borrowing books from his teacher and his grand-parents' friends; teaching himself Roman history and additional vocabulary and grammar; and spending hours learning how to read and write the language on his own. He had always been a stellar student without much effort, but in high school he was surprised to discover there was actually more work required, and he had to adjust to the schedule and make himself work harder, particularly in algebra, which he hated. He was very busy with school and had no interest in keeping a diary, since he felt there was nothing of note to report, but the blank book, with its daily page quota, intrigued him as a potential challenge. Despite his initial hesitation, he added to his other tasks the exercise of writing a daily entry.

In part because he felt embarrassed by how little he had to say, even his first entry, on January 1, 1941, already established a wry, intimate tone that he would cultivate in offering an account of his day. He managed to fill out the entire page with details, suggesting he was quickly becoming more eager than resistant to the project:

> January 1. Wednesday Wea. fair—not a snowflake. Ther. 29°
>   After going to bed at 1 am last night I arose this morning at 20 after 8. Jinny [Gilbert] and I played "Easy Money" this morning and I won. Mother and daddy came from Ruperts earlier than I expected and we left for Pultneyville . . . had dinner with Aunt Janet and Uncle Tom . . . mother and I went for a walk. We (mother, Nana, Grampa and me) played a new game that Nana got for Christmas called "Town Hall." A very pretty little game which forms the pattern of a town. It's only a little before nine, but mother wants me to go to bed, so adieu. Seemed like Sunday.[2]

While the entry diligently transcribes what had happened in his day, with very few embellishments or indications of how he was feeling— "Seemed like Sunday" as his first and only expression of opinion—it also snuck in humorous asides. For example, he added seemingly extraneous details about the weather, "fair—not a snowflake," or informal asides such as "So adieu" at the end of his entry, which also added a sense of intimacy, the casual civility with which one says good-bye to an old friend.

John continued his conversational style for several "uneventful" school days, then reread what he had written and decided it ought to be better.[3] He already felt a powerful sense of duty toward completing his daily entry, but he also wanted to improve it. He had before seen only two examples of diary writing, both by ancestors, and neither, he felt, fit his own life very well. One was a short diary by Samuel Throop, Henry Lawrence's great-grandfather, who kept his account in a logbook on a sailing trip to Cape Horn in 1800, shortly before he settled in Pultneyville. The Graeper girls found the book stuck in the rafters of their attic, and John and Carol read the diary together one rainy afternoon. John found Throop's combination of detailed nautical notes and travel narrative (some parts written in rhymed couplets) fascinating but also inimitable.[4] The other diary John knew well was equally foreign. This one was the book Sarah Throop Miller kept in her Pultneyville house in 1916, the year she died, which his grandparents had saved in a small tin box in their living room. John read its opening page: "I am all alone; no one to love me, none to caress," a captivating phrase, with words so doleful and direct that he memorized them.[5] He did not want his new diary, however, to sound like either of these ancestral examples, and decided "to get the diary of Samuel Pepys from the library, so as to inspire mine."[6] His assumption that he ought to look at a published model indicated an unconscious view of his blank volume as a writer's book even before he thought of himself as a writer. After spending a few days composing entries in Pepys's voice—"Rose this morning and donned my new Christmas shirt and blue pants. Scalloped tomatoes for dinner (ugh!) Social Studies test. I do not think I erred"—he again grew impatient.[7]

John concluded the problem was not the form but the material. He felt an aggravated sense of his life as very boring, with dull, eventless days. In each entry, he tried to be thorough and honest, including such details of his day as "at home the stove was being dismantled and the house was brrrr," but when he reread those remarks a few days later, he felt acutely self-conscious about what he judged his "silly" life in a small, rural village.[8] Sometimes he chastised himself directly: "wrote in my diary (silly)," he concluded one entry in frustration.[9] Sometimes he would simply stop writing: "Nothing worth the ink, so good night."[10] In the absence of significant events to report, however, and so far unwilling to give up the diary project entirely, he developed a wittier, more ironic approach to narrating his ordinary experiences. One evening he described himself as "doing nothing vigorously."[11]

John hoped for more exciting news to report, but when he finally had some, he was not sure how much detail he could or should trust to the page. One afternoon in mid-January, at his Memorial Art Gallery class, he fell in love with a new student; perhaps even more important, he discovered over the next few months that she did not love him back. He started to write about his new feelings, but he had recently discovered that his mother sometimes secretly read his diary (which was, perhaps unconsciously, a reason for purchasing it). Irritated by his lack of privacy but determined to record the most noteworthy experience he had so far had, he considered how to write it. John noted in his diary in the evening after class, "Scis pulchra puella—amor Frances Grant" (You know, the love of a beautiful girl—I love Frances Grant).[12] When the class went outside together later in the period, John wrote, "Shot snowballs and feasted eyes." Frances was actually rather simple looking, with "dark brown hair and ordinary features," but John felt an intense sensation when he looked at her, a feeling so powerful that he repeatedly tried to explain it.[13] His choice to express his reaction to her in Latin suggested that for him, the language of love was not English, and it also provided him with a way of keeping his revelation private.

FRANCES RELYEA GRANT
ROCHESTER, NEW YORK
English

Frances Grant in her Goucher College (class of 1950) yearbook photograph

He could not wait to see Frances each Friday, and when he did, the renewal of his original sensation at the sight of her only excited him further. This secret feeling that "I can't put F.G. out of my mind" gave his week a focus and a shape that were vivid and new.[14] In *Three Poems* (1972), Ashbery describes how even a brief sight of beauty can serve as a source of renewable artistic energy, a seemingly impersonal description that actually closely follows what he experienced that afternoon in Rochester when Frances Grant entered his art room and he felt an "electric shock" at the sight of her.[15] Ashbery writes, "[A]s the artless gestures of a beautiful girl surround her with nobility which may never be detected, the fountain of one's life."[16] After meeting Frances, John noticed that time seemed to alter so that Friday appeared painfully far away and then thrillingly close. When he finally told Frances how he felt about her, her reaction was decisive and negative, but she somehow also communicated to him a sense of hope—or he heard hope in what she said—that they would talk more about it the following week. He felt miserably happy and "lay in bed—thinking" during the week.[17] All winter what he felt about her shaped his other thoughts. Sometimes he did not mention her for an entire entry, but then printed her name on its own line at the bottom of the page, as though to indicate that everything he had written until then was colored by her constant presence in his mind—or, more precisely, what her presence in his mind did to shape his other thoughts and emotions.[18]

As John gradually understood that no actual relationship was ever going to occur with Frances, he began to change the way he described his feelings about her, at first mocking himself for his foolish devotion. After a clumsy weekend, nearly setting St. John's on fire by toppling a lit candle at a church dinner, John concluded that his mistakes were the result of his being "possessed" by his love—"mea amor Francescae," he wrote with wistful self-deprecation.[19] At a dance they both attended several weeks later, her coldness left him feeling "heartbroken," a "plight" he described as a stronger feeling of disappointment than he had ever experienced before.[20] Although distressing, this heightened emotion made even his most ordinary, dull days seem tinged with new shades of color and feeling. In *Three Poems*, Ashbery articulates the question he learned to ask and answer through this early, intense, and chaste romantic episode: "Is there something intrinsically satisfying about not having the object of one's wishes, about having miscalculated?"[21] John discovered that the answer was yes. Petrarch's "Laura" and Dante's "Beatrice" would remind John again in college of what he absolutely understood that winter: unrequited love was good for his writing.

As the intensity of his feelings gave him access to some new ways to express his experience, his confidence in imagining how he might transcend the diary page grew. He began to envision his future as an artist, an idea he initially declared softly (in parentheses) to himself in his diary:

> February 20 Thursday Wea. Same Ther. 14° Overslept this morning as usual. This noon the wind blew a veritable gale but I braved the storm. The class discussion of the Social Studies chapter turned out to be a dizzy review of the first few pages. I am writing a theme on my future occupation. (artist). It must be at least 1,000 words long. I must have nearly 1,000 already. In Latin, I seem to be the only one who understands the pronouns and the i-stems.
>
> I got a painful scratch on the writer (pardon, listening to the radio) I mean a scratch on the finger. It hurts me terribly. (oh quite) I had no homework. I am making more Poe's illustrations and I think I shall show them to Miss Cook tomorrow.

"I got a painful scratch on the writer," he wrote nonsensically, distracted by the radio, but then left in the happy accident. Although he was not sure what kind of "(artist)" he might become, painter or writer, the slip suggested at least a subconscious preference. The declaration also underscored his combination of ambition and self-deprecation. He could state quite seriously that he would become an artist (though in parentheses) and make fun of himself simultaneously.

The more important entry in terms of his future as a poet actually had been written the day before. John's diary entry for Wednesday, February 19, offered evidence of wit, focus, and self-awareness, hallmarks of what would become his best poems. Although the entry was in his diary, it also read like a prose poem, a form he did not directly know:

> Wednesday (written on Wednesday). February 19. Wea. Blizzard-
> ous Ther. 16° Today (Wednesday) the weather was extremely bliz-
> zardous. The day seemed so much like Wednesday. In English
> we are reading poems. At noon I walked uptown even though
> the weather was blizzardous (I think I mentioned that before). I
> made up the Social Studies which was given on the Friday I was
> absent. 92%. The marks in the Latin test yesterday were very
> poor, but I managed to get 100%. For dessert tonight we had a
> sealtest ice cream cherry pie, a rare treat. After supper I started
> to illustrate Poe's "Hop-Frog" But I did not get on very well. I
> listened to Eddie Cantor and Mr. D. A. Wednesday. Wednesday.
> I am feeling silly today. Blizzardous. Written (oh definitely) on
> Wednesday.

His frustrations with the limitations of the diary form were spurring stylistic inventions. Diary entries were, by nature, tedious and repetitive, but by duplicating words so boldly, he gave wit and rhythm to the fact of repetition (the way, in the future, he would do in the highly repetitive "sestina" form). He felt a stubborn sense of discipline carrying him toward consistency and completeness; yet he also resisted these same conventions. By honoring the diary form, however, or at least trying to while also making fun of it, he was unearthing original sounds in his own voice.

At the same time, though, he started experimenting with other forms of writing, especially short stories and plays. At night, just before bed, he kept his commitment to writing in his diary, but during the day, he found loose-leaf paper or Ashbery Farm stationery to imagine dialogue, plots, and characters.[22] He even used the diary as a tool to trick himself into having greater self-discipline: "[Today I rose at 6:30 to begin working on my play.] Note—I put this in last night in order that it might spur me to rise early, but it didn't."[23] He composed "The Rug," a play about two adult brothers who try to outmaneuver each other to save an old family house, and the beautiful but manipulative servant who overhears their machinations.[24] After handwriting four incomplete acts, he stopped. In early March, he began "Sertus," a play set in about 57 BC, when Switzerland was coming under the control of the Roman Empire. He felt the opening was the best thing he had written and worked so intently on it, actually waking up early to write it before school, that his mother became worried that his devotion was unhealthy and insisted, much to his annoyance, that he return to bed.[25] He developed a practice of combining classical characters and contemporary language, a technique that would reach comic perfection a decade later, in Ashbery's one-act retelling of Homeric epics and Greek drama, *The Heroes* (1950). In "Sertus," Roman warriors threaten the established lives of a noble family, resulting in painful but also comical squabbling. Opullo, an "old and trusted servant" of Sertus, the Consul, gives the first speech:

> OP: (*sharply*) Partia . . . I do not like traitors. Traitors who, for a few pieces of gold, or for a place in the army of the enemy, deliberately betray those friends who trusted and believed in [*sic*]. Misdoings such as these cannot be justified from any viewpoint. A traitor is as a purple cloak—when its folds embrace the shoulders of a chief, it flaunts its proud colors to the sky and revels in its reflected glory. But when it is discarded and it hangs on a peg in the corner, then it loses its pride, a whim of its owner, to be forgotten now that its purpose has been fulfilled.
>
> PAR: (*rather startled at this unprecedented outburst*) What . . . ?[26]

The serious tone of Opullo's romantic image of a rich cloak hanging listlessly alone on a peg juxtaposed against Partia's seemingly guileless, concise attack on its pretension demonstrates Ashbery's earliest intuitive experiments in mixing highly literary and colloquial language for humorous effect. John did not know how to continue these early plays beyond a first act, however, and each one stops abruptly.

He stayed very busy, focusing on "making several literary attempts at self-culture," rather than dealing with tensions at home.[27] One night, Chet was angry at the way John played a card game and threw the deck of cards all over the room.[28] When his father had to wait in the car too long for him after school one day, "he exploded like an arsenal." Yelling provided an outlet for Chet's distress, but John protected himself from thinking more deeply about what was causing it by concluding that his father was simply a "cranky and ill-tempered . . . grouch."[29] Rough winter weather continued through early spring, and John remained in his room reading and writing as "the worst blizzard in history" kept the area frozen and isolated until April.[30] When the ground finally began to thaw, he looked forward to a rainy Easter Parade, where he planned "to exhibit my common sense and my new coat," and he felt lonely that no one around him shared his excitement about the holiday. Implicit but left unsaid was that had Richard been alive, *he* would have shared John's excitement. John played alone in Pultneyville, building "the ruins of a magnificent castle on the beach" and inspecting his flooded castle grounds, which looked like "a raging torrent" from the wet weather.[31] Back home in Sodus on Easter Sunday, John noted that "the whole afternoon seemed to be pervaded by gloom."[32]

The weather finally began to cooperate, and John had more events to report. First came late April's unseasonably warm weather, and he immediately began to plan activities for the summer, borrowing one-act plays from the library "in hopes I could find one for this summer's performance."[33] In early May his aunt Janet gave birth to a baby daughter, Deborah Whittier Taft, an occasion that John, echoing his mother, found miraculous. Soon after, trees and flowers bloomed in a marvelous profusion of colors and smells. John's spirits soared as he went for a walk in the woods one afternoon in search of wild flowers. He returned with a splendid bouquet of "Trillium, Jack-in-the-Pulpit, and most of all pale lavender violets and saffron colored ones" for Addie, with whom he was staying while his mother helped Aunt Janet with the new baby for nearly a month.[34]

While living there, he learned that his grandparents were finally selling their 69 Dartmouth Street house after renting it out since 1934. The finality of this revelation, seven years after he had last been inside the house, took him by surprise and stirred his former longings for the place. After art class one afternoon, he walked the few blocks from the gallery to Dartmouth Street to meet his grandfather and tour his old home's empty rooms, which "did fill me with such sad memories." He wished to keep a souvenir and chose "a paneled iron parrot" knocker.[35] That night in Pultneyville, he attached it to his bedroom door.[36] The following Friday, on the last day of art class, Rebecca Cook, who was moving away, asked John what had happened to Richard. He had never come back to class, and she had always wondered why. When John told her that Richard had died, she was so upset that she kept handing him tubes of paint to take home, a moment that John only tacitly alluded to in his account of Miss Cook's attention to him during the final class: "[M]ade a quite good picture of a lady in an Empire-Period white gown with a green shawl [that] Miss Cook kept. She will not be back next year and so, since this is the last class, I shall probably not see her again."[37] Even to an audience that consisted of only him (and often his mother), he would say he felt "sad" only about losing the old Dartmouth Street house.

The complexities of what he felt he could or could not write about only intensified. John looked forward to a visit from his friend Dick Sanders. Just after final exams, in late June, which John easily aced, Dick arrived in Sodus. They played miniature golf, read comics, went swimming, and then "talked (when in bed) until all hours of the night."[38] Not only was Dick sensitive, compassionate, and very fond of John, but he also knew intimately and without being told how painful Richard's death had been for the Ashbery family. The three-day visit with Dick was cathartic. He and John talked, and they also touched. The summer before, Billy Graeper had told him about this thing that could happen to him if he held his penis. He said that white stuff would come out, an image offered without explanation and one that John found "rather alarming."[39] In bed together, he and Dick Sanders hugged, kissed, and fondled each other, and John ejaculated for the first time. In the context of their closeness, the experience felt more wonderful than frightening. When Dick left a few days later, John wrote a poem-note in his diary made up of phrases from their conversations that he did not want to forget:

> tulip garden
>   old dutch
>   home all our own until
>   recall once more
>   fashion in shows
>   dog cast in
>   days before
> were almost learning to forget

happy   fear came from
                          a trough
     kin[40]

John wanted to remember what had happened, but he also did not want anyone else to know or find out. He used fragments and lowercase letters, added white space, and took out all punctuation, mechanical changes but ones that condensed his experience into its essence and retained the substance of his feeling. All his conflicting emotions were present in the cryptic, moving note he wrote to himself about Dick's visit. His diary entry had to occur in a form that would render its importance legible and memorable for him without illuminating for anyone who found and read it exactly what had happened. The note was John's first original modernist poem, written as a way to remember and record his private experience. It was composed for the occasion without any sense of imitation, especially since he had yet to read anything it might have resembled.

After Dick left, John returned to Pultneyville. He reopened the "Knight Club," shuttered since 1939, adding new details, using adventures discovered through reading Tennyson's *Idylls of the King*, *King Arthur and His Knights*, and *Le Morte d'Arthur*. On the anniversary of Richard's death, John went swimming and completed crossword puzzles with Barney Little, and Chet played tennis all afternoon with Uncle Tom, an ordinary summer's day indicating that the family was beginning to recover. All month, John explored the old mill and the little old schoolhouse with friends, performed in several plays for other children, and swam in "MONSTROUS" and "MONSTROUSER!" waves. John, Billy Graeper, Mary Wellington, and Carol Rupert posed in Lake Ontario, smoking corncob pipes, for a photograph—an idea they borrowed from the comic strip *Li'l Abner*, which they pored over at Mary's house with other comics every Sunday morning. For several weeks, the group spoke only cockney, pig Latin, or the "ops" language (in which "op" is added after every consonant) to one another, effectively and joyfully excluding anyone over the age of fifteen from their conversations.[41] John "said good-bye to everybody" on September 1 before packing up his things to return home.

His days immediately resumed their dull and eventless shape, which he bemoaned in his diary. "I have often observed that nothing ever seems to happen to me on Tuesdays," John noted a few weeks after beginning his sophomore year in high school.[42] The remark "nothing" on Tuesdays had already become a refrain the year before.[43] Latin II (with Miss Copeland) was all right, and his new English and beginning French classes were both taught by the "extremely young and pretty"

Barney (standing) and Jo Little in Pultneyville, early 1940s

Billy Graeper, Carol Rupert, John, Mary Wellington, and Janet MacKay standing on the Wellington Dock, which they jokingly referred to as "much used rotten boards," during the summer of 1941, "the last, great Pultneyville summer"

Miss Case, whom he liked.[44] Those courses constituted the high points of his school day. He was nominated for president of the student council, but he lost the election. He watched helplessly as his new friend John Anson, a quiet, kind boy whose family had recently moved to Sodus, was bullied and then unfairly sent to the office as the instigator. John was cast in the small but witty role of Professor Bean in the senior play, *Spring Fever*, but sorry not to get the larger role for which he had auditioned. Most frustrating was that apple season was an especially busy time on the farm, and now that John was old enough, he was expected to help pick, sort, pack, and ship the fruit.[45] His father grew five different types—Greenings, Golden Delicious, Baldwin, Northern Spy, and McIntosh—and John developed a distaste for them all. He had so many required chores around the farm that he often had to postpone his own plans because he "packed apples all day." He was always relieved when some chore was canceled: "There was no apple packing today," he wrote with evident relief at the extra time he had gained to write and draw. He tended to notice sympathetically anyone who felt similarly glum about farmwork, observing "a whole band of sullen negro apple pickers" as he and John Anson walked back one afternoon from the nearby Cohn farm.[46]

John felt a restless desire to make something out of the ordinary happen, and so he was constantly motivated to learn new things. He started a Latin newspaper, translated *The Princess and the Robber Chief* into Latin, and Latin texts into English.[47] Other afternoons, he painted or studied art: "I drew an excellent picture of a lady lying supine amidst her billowing skirts and powdered hair. She has just fainted because a man shot her in the arm with a pistol." During afternoons in Pultneyville, he spent time reading at an elderly neighbor's house. Mrs. Merrell—years later Ashbery realized she was his image of the calm and spiritual Mrs. Moore in E. M. Forster's *A Passage to India*—had amassed an impressive art library, especially on French painters. He discovered two favorites, Jean-Honoré Fragonard and Jean-Baptiste Greuze, borrowed books and "examined" their paintings, especially *The Swing* (Fragonard, 1775/1780) and *The Broken Pitcher* (Greuze, 1763). He used *The Broken Pitcher* as a model for several drawings "reminiscent of Greuze," including one of "a young lady with a basket of apples which I called *Les Pommes*" and another with "a buxom maiden showing more of her charms then [sic] is normally considered decent." When he and Carol found a print of Greuze's *The Milkmaid* in an old trunk, he hung it over his bed in Pultneyville.[48] He found books on *French Painters and Their Paintings* and *French Painters of the 19th Century* at the Rochester library. To understand "classic paintings" more thoroughly, he borrowed Thomas Bulfinch's *The Golden Age of Mythology and Fable* (1913) from the Sodus library. He also started art class again with a new teacher, Mr. Bennett, who was "tall, thin, and wears slightly foppish clothes, conservative, and knows his bus[iness]."[49] At Friday's session, John had his "picture complimented by can't you guess?"[50] Frances Grant had returned to class, and he looked for new ways to attract her attention.

In late October, he discovered an ingenious method. Sibley's department store sponsored a local competition to win a coveted spot on the extremely popular *Quiz Kids* national radio show, which taped in Chicago. As soon as John learned that the show was auditioning in Rochester, he went to the store to fill out the extensive questionnaire, which included queries "about school activities, hobbies, ambitions, and favorite books . . . also . . . a 250-word essay on why I should be a Quiz Kid."[51] He learned a few days later that his essay was marked "excellent," and had been chosen from hundreds of applications, and he would get the chance to compete against other winners of the written portion of the test in three rounds of verbal quizzes.[52] Whichever student won would be named "Rochester's Quiz Kid" and then sent to Chicago to play the game on air. The opportunity to audition for the show was the most exciting thing that had ever happened to him. Ever since *Quiz Kids* had begun airing from the Merchandise Mart on June 28, 1940, starring a genial host, Joe Kelly, and five bright, charming local children under the age of sixteen, John, like many other children his age, wanted to be on it. The show had become so nationally popular that *Life* magazine had just featured a current champion, seven-year-old Gerard Darrow, on its cover.[53]

John, in fact, had been harboring a wish to appear on any quiz show for a long time. Every evening, he listened to radio quiz shows with his parents in the living room. He shouted out many of the correct answers before the contestants, and Chet liked to try to stump him by pulling out his copy of *The Century Book of Facts*, which he kept by his living room chair, to test John's knowledge of state capitals and other statis-tics.[54] When John got the right answers, his mother would look up and say, "Oh, John, *you* should be on a show." For months before the Quiz Kids opportunity arose, John had been trying to get his name read on air. He had sent in several biographical sketches to another quiz show (for adults), *Dr. IQ*, including one piece on Marie Antoinette that he was particularly proud to have researched and written. More recently, he had mailed a suggested quiz question, "identify schoolmasters of literary fame," to *Quiz Kids* and was disappointed that it also was not used on the show.[55] Chosen to audition, though, John worried that he was not *Quiz Kids* material—neither as worldly nor as smart as the chil-dren on air seemed to be. He did not realize that his background and interests actually fit the show very well, for he had a modest upbringing, a remarkable memory, several esoteric interests, including knowledge of obscure pieces of classical music and nineteenth-century French painting, and was deeply self-motivated and curious.[56] He was lucky, though, not to understand. The best part of appearing on *Quiz Kids* was the chance it presented to escape Sodus and see new possibilities for his future, yet to have this experience occur in such a compressed period of time that he never altered the very "dull" life that had actually provided the means, and would continue to prepare him, for a real escape.

John recognized this opportunity as unique and was extremely mo-tivated to win. It was late afternoon on the last Wednesday of October 1941 when he arrived on the third floor of Sibley's department store "scared" and "ecstatic" for round one. He donned the cap and gown provided to each contestant, and was seated at a long table with micro-phones in front of an audience, which included his parents and grand-parents.[57] Homer Bliss, a local radio announcer in Rochester, asked the children questions for a half hour, which felt like a minute to John as he easily vanquished the competition. His competitiveness was evident not only in his glee at winning, but in his pleasure at so solidly beating his opponents: "I do feel sorry for the other contestants, especially the little girl, sniff."[58] In a ceremony afterward, he received a *Quiz Kids* gold key and was invited to a semifinal round the following Saturday. The next round went even better because it was more competitive. "O sanctissima O thou joyful day," he wrote in his diary, elated and exhausted, soon after he arrived home and was interviewed by the local press.[59]

John enjoyed the week leading up to the final competition. He felt that his participation had already improved his social status: "People are getting very cordial all the time!" he remarked, especially pleased that Frances Grant had demonstrated some new interest in him. His parents were behaving especially nicely, too. They bought him a new "pork-pie" hat and a "reversible" coat. Adding to the festive feeling, his cousin Wallace Ashbery Jr., John's favorite relative and the only son of Chet's older brother, had arrived from Buffalo. Five years older than John, Wallace was a passionate student of politics, music, and literature, and the two had a great time talking and listening to Tchaikovsky together all week. Wallace had brought along a recording of *The Nutcracker Suite*, which John heard for the first time and loved. He listened to it repeatedly until he could almost play "The Dance of the Reed Pipes" by ear on the piano. His mind felt sharper because he was so nervous and excited about the upcoming competition, as though he were gaining new powers of observation as the finals drew nearer.

Because his mind remained so clear and focused on what was about to happen, he became unusually attuned to the ordinary minutiae of his daily existence. Time seemed to slow down, and as he wrote in his diary, "my mind began to take a morbid interest in details."[60] He attended his piano lesson, which was terrifying because "a fierce dog [who] barked at me, bared its teeth, jumped up and clawed me," a scene he would later include with strikingly similar clarity in his novel, *A Nest of Ninnies*. Waiting in the wings of the Palace Theater in Rochester for the competition to begin, he peeked out at the audience from behind the curtain and spotted his parents and many classmates and friends, though he did not see *her*. He sat down onstage in cap and gown, and the curtain parted. The quiz began, and John answered several questions on music, correctly identifying the composers of "Danse Macabre," "Finlandia," and "Valse Triste." By the middle of the quiz, he was trailing one boy, but then he surged ahead by naming the face on the one-hundred-dollar bill. Helen, who was trembling, leaned over to Mary Wellington and said, "But John has never *seen* a one-hundred-dollar bill, I'm sure."[61] A few minutes later, the score was again tied. Then John broke the tie by correctly stating that the "Battle Above the Clouds" took place during the Civil War. He had to answer one more question correctly to win.

He quickly named three presidents with the same first and last initials: "Which means I am Rochester's Quiz Kid!"[62]

He was "glad that was over," and remained giddy all day. "Nana said it was my day," he wrote happily after his family took him out to his favorite restaurant, the Manhattan, a huge space decorated in art deco style, for his favorite meal, chicken à la King. At home in the evening, John read the newspaper's account of the competition, "a sight to see!": "Blue-eyed, shy, slender farm youth wins Quiz Kid title and other such." By the next morning, John discovered he had become a local celebrity: "Everybody's asking me when I'm going on the air [and] I got a letter addressed to the Quiz Kid." He also received "a letter from Jinny [Gilbert] in the most endearing terms." Even Frances Grant admitted that she "saw the audition." His Sodus classmates treated him better, too, generously voting to give him the top-of-the-line radio that *Quiz Kids* had donated to his school. John could clearly hear New York City stations with it and began listening to the Metropolitan Opera broadcasts every weekend. He decided to start a scrapbook about his win (though he ended up using it to document the actors, composers, and writers he admired).[63] The praise that meant most to him, however, was the least public: "Grandpa is so pleased," he wrote simply.[64]

Over the next few weeks, John enjoyed his new public status. Storekeepers and families he did not know recognized him and wished him luck for his trip to Chicago. He prepared for his appearance on the *Quiz Kids* show by studying in the Rochester Central Library's reference section and reading about obscure composers and painters. Then, suddenly, on December 7, 1941, his thoughts, which had been exclusively focused on the upcoming national broadcast, shifted. He was playing at Carol Rupert's house when he heard that Japan had bombed Pearl Harbor: "Japan declared war on the U.S.!!" he wrote, adding that he had "listened to the news reports" all day with Carol and Billy Graeper. He recognized that a major international event had occurred but wondered what to report about it in his diary, since his external life had not changed at all. The entry he scribbled at the end of the day suggested the news unnerved him, for it was an unusually scrambled paragraph, which included a postscript note that "my little fish is dead," and a full signature.

Over the next few days, he wondered if he would still get to go to Chicago. He assumed and calmly accepted that his *Quiz Kids* broadcast would be canceled because of the war. On the other hand, he still hoped to leave, for when he heard news reports of blackouts in big cities, he worried that they would "have one in Chicago while I am there."[65] On December 9, when he learned that he would in fact travel to Chicago that night, he was relieved and thrilled. Friends and family made a fuss over his departure. John Anson gave him some Peppermint Patties, and the Graepers and Ruperts threw an afternoon send-off party. Reporters accompanied John, Helen, and Addie to Rochester's Union Station for photographs. The station's gorgeous architecture—its high ceilings, brick-and-wood interior, and arched windows—gave John, as well as lending to the proceedings, a feeling of dignity and grace.[66] He waited and watched as

> Fred and Esther Radcliffe were there to see us off. He printed my name on a thing in a machine and bought me a *New Yorker* and a Fritzi Ritz comic book. We hurried onto the train and were shown our drawing room. I am in the top bed. Nana in lower, and Momma in other lower. Oh! boy what fun to have the wind outside. Momma and I went down to the lounge and I read my *New Yorker*. I feel quite distingué with it under my arm. We came back and I undressed and am now in bed. The train sways quite a lot and I keep thinking its [*sic*] going to tip over. Very good night.

The next morning, when he woke up as the train approached Chicago, he felt already older and more mature. He watched "scenery" from the "club car" and ate "a delicious breakfast" in the "dining car."[67] The *Quiz Kids* broadcast, which was scheduled for later in the day, became suddenly less important than the thrilling experience of seeing new things.

John felt ecstatic traveling. He took his first-ever cab ride to the grand and elegant Palmer House Hotel and walked through the lobby with its high, ornate, and enormous arched ceiling mural and Greek and Roman statues decorating each alcove. The family's eighteenth-floor rooms were "very nice," John wrote twice. They took another cab to the art gallery, where he swooned over the Thorne Miniature Rooms, re-creations of period rooms in exquisite miniature detail, which he had wanted to see since reading about them in *Life*.[68] He visited Marshall Field's, the department store, with its gorgeous Tiffany ceiling, glittering even more than usual as a backdrop to a spectacular fifty-foot-tall Christmas tree. John loved the architecture of Chicago's aquarium. By the late afternoon, when he "cabbed to the studio," he was no longer a taxi or city neophyte.

At the studio, he met the regular contestants, including Dick Bannister, Joan Bishop, Richard Williams—"(he's swell!)"—and Ruth Duskin, and felt secretly disappointed to learn, now that the hour had finally arrived, that the broadcast would be delayed by a special news report on the war. He answered several questions very well in a practice round, but as soon as the show started, he raised his hand too slowly, only in time to answer one question, about French artists. Afterward, he was uncharacteristically gentle toward himself: "Oh, I did all right."[69] The trip had nonetheless far exceeded his expectations. "Oh! but I am sorry its [*sic*] over! I hope I come again. . . . Happily good night!"[70]

After he returned to Rochester, he tried to retain that rapturous sense of adventure he had felt while traveling. He threw himself into

John on the *Quiz Kids* set at the Merchandise Mart in Chicago, December 10, 1941

various intellectual and social projects: he wrote an essay on Molière for French class, finished Dickens's *Oliver Twist*, and began Thackeray's *Vanity Fair*. He drew for hours every day and created a miniature ancient site: "[M]y History of Bublio. It's coming along swell!"[71] The level of detail he added to his big world writ small was directly inspired by his having seen the Thorne Miniature Rooms in Chicago. He helped trim his grandfather's tree and shopped for Christmas presents, finding for himself "an interlocking *Laughing Cavalier* Puzzle for only $.10."[72] A *Quiz Kids* fan sent him a reproduction of Honoré Daumier's painting *The Third Class Railway Carriage* (about 1862), "in honor of the question about artists on the quiz kids," which John affixed to his Sodus bedroom wall. As holiday noises drifted upstairs one evening—the Ashberys had invited the Buckmans, Hollings, and Bollers over—John stayed in his room to write and draw.[73] He overheard someone remark, "John seems to carry his applause along with him," which suggested to him that others found him much more confident and self-sufficient than he generally felt. Because of his public achievement, classmates and acquaintances began to replace their view of John as "different" with a perception that he was a "genius," an epithet that remained permanently attached to him locally.[74] Only his father did not seem to share these positive feelings, which reinforced John's sense that "they would never be close."[75] On returning home from Chicago, John noted how moody and unhappy Chet seemed in the days before Christmas, and then he accidentally "smashed the car. The front end anyway," while driving alone. Chet was unhurt but enraged, and John chose to escape his wrath by staying in Pultneyville.[76]

As 1941 came to a close, John took stock of his year. He had accomplished, even exceeded, his goal of making something exciting happen in his life, but he had discovered in the process that he still felt lonely. Looking forward to Christmas Day, he also found himself looking backward: "I am happy with anticipation but should be happier if Richard were here. Christmas Eve is one of the happiest times but also the saddest." More than a year after Richard died, John expressed his grief. The uncommonness of his admission of feelings about Richard's death, however, also reflected the magnitude of the loss, sadness that would dissipate over time but never fully disappear. Nearly sixty years later,

Ashbery composed "The History of My Life," a dark, fable-like poem that addresses his brother's death directly, with unusual candor:

> Once upon a time there were two brothers.
> Then there was only one: myself.
>
> I grew up fast, before learning to drive,
> even. There was I: a stinking adult.
>
> I thought of developing interests
> someone might take an interest in. No soap.
>
> I became very weepy for what had seemed
> like the pleasant early years. As I aged
>
> increasingly, I also grew more charitable
> with regard to my thoughts and ideas,
>
> thinking them at least as good as the next man's.
> Then a great devouring cloud
>
> came and loitered on the horizon, drinking
> it up, for what seemed like months or years.[77]

In its spare lines, the brief lyric suggests that the speaker's identity as a "brother" shaped his life. Beyond that implication of supreme loss, however, the poem, despite its clarity and control, does not venture. Even after so much time has passed, the narrator is still at a loss for words. He can intimate that his brother's death left an open wound that just preceded the narrator's adolescence, and provoked, as the poem harshly expresses, his life as "a stinking adult." He can also suggest that Richard's death effectively marked the end of "the pleasant early years," an earnest phrase tinged with ironies amassed through time—"months or years"—and through the mists of memory, age, and alcohol.

In 1941, John understood that the pleasure he had come to experience through winning a spot on *Quiz Kids* and discovering the joys of traveling did not erase the pain he still felt. Nor, though, could such an immense loss eliminate his chances for feeling happy. For the time being, those realizations were enough, and he had nothing more to say about his grief. It had taken him the entire year to articulate his sorrow, and those two carefully controlled sentences about his feelings for Richard were, in their own way, a culmination of his process of mourning. On Christmas Day, he simply listed his presents—no new diary for 1942—and left the rest of the pages blank.[78]

4

The Art of Self-Education

1942–1943

John felt energized in the early days of the New Year. His first order of business was to go buy a new diary. The previous Christmas, he had been disappointed to receive one during his family's traditional afternoon present exchange; this year he was sorry his mother had not purchased another. He narrated his jocular hunt for a new book:

> Dear Diary: I bought you in a Woolworth 5 and 10 on January 2, 1942, after looking all over town. You were not exactly what I wanted, but I am satisfied.[1]

He felt upbeat and promised to "get in a few good pages as with last year."[2] Already by January 7, he was "planning my new novel, as yet unnamed." By August, he admitted that he had purchased the diary specifically for "literary practice."[3] He wondered if it could provide raw materials he might draw on at some point in his future, though how and when these dull, seemingly unusable pages might become art he had no idea.

One of his early entries in his new diary included the first poem he had composed since 1935. After writing a "long" thank-you card to his cousin Wallace Jr., who had sent him some Christmas presents, he added a poem, "Miserere," for fun, as a postscript. He jotted it down as easily as if it had been only yesterday that he last wrote a poem. After sending the letter, though, he decided the poem was too "dolorous," and rewrote it "with an absurd ending," copying only this stranger version into his diary:

Miserere

Canto first
Ah! Bleak and barren is the moor
The orphan girl she sheds a tear
And thinks of home, her parents dear
Departed from the worldly sphere
Full seven months ago!

Canto second
The wind doth blow, the snow doth pelt
Unmerciless against her brow
Her footsteps falter; her progress slow
Becomes. She sinks into the snow.
O cruel fates, supreme!

Canto third
From yonder cot a light doth gleam
If she can reach it—but, alas!
She sinks again upon the grass.
The dawn hath come; a stiffened mass
Lies dead upon the moors!

Canto fourth
The cottage folk, they found her there
A hapless child, sweet life so near!
They put these words above her view:
"Ye stranger, ye may well despair
She died in agonee!"

Prologue (should come first)
Hear my tale, ye maidens fair
Take counsel by my song

Thine honour pure is better far
Than wicked lies, so wrong.[4]

The poem begins with an interjection, "Ah!," that introduces the archetypal Victorian, sentimental narrative poem on which this short work is modeled, and serves equally as a shrewd if affectionate critique of this kind of poem. The first stanza demonstrates the requirements of this genre in quick, broad, and also deadpan strokes: "the orphan girl," "the bleak and barren . . . moor" she walks upon, and the sad tale of the death of "her parents dear." Young Ashbery hits every compulsory note of the many nineteenth-century poems—from Eliza Cook's "The Old Armchair" (Ashbery later described this poem as "a sort of leading with your chin") to Thomas Hood's "The Song of the Shirt," to Arthur Hugh Clough's moving "Say Not the Struggle Naught Availeth," among others—that he had read often in *The Book of Knowledge*.[5] While the tone of his poem remains serious and sorrowful throughout, tiny details underscore its parodic elements: the shift from sinking "into the snow" (Canto second) to sinking "again upon the grass" (Canto third); the blunt description of the girl's dead body as "a stiffened mass"; and the use of overtly formal ("Canto first") and archaic ("agonee") language, and British ("honour") spelling. In the final stanza, he highlights his poem's absurdity by ending with the Prologue and a pun, a humorous choice that undercuts the poem's sentimentality and turns the sorrowful tale into something clearly different. The last phrase—"so wrong"—suggests the author's sharp awareness of the original tone this new poem has achieved in its subtle shifts between melancholy and wit.

Stormy weather insulated John from many of his usual chores, and he reveled in the extra time he had to do what he liked for most of the winter. He read enthusiastically and eclectically, finishing Thackeray's *Vanity Fair* (1848), Fielding's *Tom Jones* (1749), Du Maurier's *Rebecca* (1938), Wharton's *Ethan Frome* (1911), Dickens's *Hard Times* (1854), McKenney's *My Sister Eileen* (1938), the *Arabian Nights*, a book on surrealism, one on home decoration, and biographies of Thackeray and Van Gogh. He loved *Rebecca* for its exciting plot; *My Sister Eileen* for its sense of a free life in downtown New York City, one he hoped for himself in the future; and *Vanity Fair* for its lessons on how to manipulate people to reach one's own ends. He used his *Vanity Fair* education to practice getting around his parents' demands, so that, "through dexterous handling" of his father, John "stayed at Pultneyville" as often as he wished.[6]

From his perch in Pultneyville, he sent more than twenty letters—and almost every one also contained an original story or play—to amuse his summer friends. He shared a new short story, a burlesque in the style of Arthur Conan Doyle, with Billy Graeper. Mary Wellington, however, became his primary and most enthusiastic muse, and over the winter he wrote a long play for her, which he parceled out over nine letters so that she would respond to each installment. He set the drama in an old mansion full of collectibles, which included an entire room of antique teapots, playfully adding new details each week to please her: "I have been writing a play called *Twelve Nights in a Barroom*. It is a nice, doleful mellerdrammar but there is so much slapstick in it you may not like it. Or is that what you do like?"[7] Since Mary had the only copy of a previous scene, John could never remember title, characters' names, or plot from one letter to the next, a situation he exploited for comic effect. This exaggerated forgetfulness exempted him from any responsibility to continue the plot from exactly the point at which he last left off the story. As the work developed, he also shifted its genre from horror to mystery, to melodrama, to romance, adroitly exaggerating these frequent shifts in tone.

He could not wait to see his summer friends again, but as warm weather approached, he was distressed to discover that almost no one would be returning to Pultneyville. Only Carol would be around the entire summer, but when he tried to interest her in collaborating on a play, as he had planned to do with Mary, she showed no interest. He played croquet and badminton with Carol, Pede, and Billy Graeper, but their games often ended in accusations of cheating and a fight. One morning, they began to build a medieval French town out of sand, but the others lost interest, and John finished the work alone. Even his fifteenth birthday party—which he had looked forward to celebrating at Emma Graeper's "Woodshed at the Captain Throop House," a charming tea shop she had recently opened in the rear of her home to make extra money—felt sad.[8] In August, there were a number of chores his father required him to do on the farm, and he frequently had to return to Sodus to empty garbage pails, rake grass, and pick beans, cherries, and tomatoes. He had to entertain his difficult young cousin Larry, who was visiting, and, worst of all, manage his father's roadside fruit stand, a task he especially hated because he imagined everyone he knew drove by and saw him standing there alone.

By August, John's writing began to provide the primary, sometimes the only, escape from feeling miserable. As he explained to Mary, who was at camp in Canada: "I would doubtless be bored to death were it not for my occasional literary attempts."[9] Writing stories replaced his previous adventures in willow trees, though he still sent nostalgic letters about those days. He stayed in Sodus alone to read, write, and listen to Offenbach's *Orpheus* overture on his new phonograph (a birthday present from his parents). It was a period he recalled later as listless and disagreeable. In Ashbery's "Syringa," the narrator's bitter memory at being stuck in some small town "one indifferent summer" ends the poem:

> "But what about
> So-and-so?" is still asked on occasion. But they lie
> Frozen and out of touch until an arbitrary chorus
> Speaks of a totally different incident with a similar name
> In whose tale are hidden syllables
> Of what happened so long before that
> In some small town, one indifferent summer.[10]

In late August, John took the bus by himself to see Disney's *Fantasia* in Rochester.[11] He was looking forward to walking in the city and then seeing the film, for he had heard that the music in it was wonderful. He took a seat in the nearly empty Capitol Theatre, one of the more rundown of Rochester's movie palaces and the only place where the film was still playing, but he was surprised and disappointed by the wooden, uninteresting images that accompanied and dulled the music. He felt irritated at having wasted an afternoon. On the way out, he stopped by the theater's basement restroom. A man materialized next to his urinal in the poorly lit space, "asked if I needed help," then reached over and grabbed his penis. John panicked, rushed away, and did not stop or look back until he was safely on a bus. When he arrived home, no one asked him where he had been, and he told no one what had happened, leaving those "hidden syllables" out of even his diary, waiting to be formed into words and phrases later on, if he could only figure out how to write them down.[12]

The new school year provided some unexpected encouragement for his "literary attempts." Initially his junior-year courses were unpromising. World History, he complained, "covers the world from antediluvian times to the present, and I don't quite see how it's going to do that."[13] Intermediate Algebra involved "mysterious rites concerned with finding the square roots of numbers."[14] Latin III (again with Miss Copeland) and French II and III, which he planned to take in one year with quirky Miss E. Wright, a "not very pretty but good teacher," would be acceptable. Miss Wright liked to sing "Deep Purple" in French, and John loved the puzzle surrounding her first name; it took him eight months of sleuthing to discover, to his delight, that *E* stood for "Emogene." The high point of his day, however, was English class with "clever" Miss Florence Klumpp, the same teacher who had directed his performance of *The Knave of Hearts.* A tiny, plain woman who believed poetry was the highest art and who idolized Robert Frost, Miss Klumpp was a 1937 graduate of the College of Wooster with a degree in education and diverse interests in classical music, religion, and the French language.[15] She was considered a hard grader who was not easily impressed. John confided his literary ambitions to Miss Klumpp and a new classmate, Betty Lou Burden, who admitted she was also writing a novel.[16] One afternoon, Betty gave John her novel-in-progress to read. That night, in apologetic

Florence Klumpp (later Anson) in her graduation photo from the College of Wooster, 1937, shortly before she became a teacher in the Sodus public schools

and small handwriting in his diary, he criticized it harshly. Appreciating Betty's ambition but disliking her work motivated him to improve his own. When Miss Klumpp offered to give him regular feedback on any extra writing he submitted, he redoubled his efforts.[17]

He began to work on his novel and stories more consistently. To have such a critical new reader inspired John to become more rigorous and analytical about his own work. He had been keeping a diary for almost two years, but when he lost the book for nearly a month that fall, jotting entries only irregularly on loose-leaf paper, he reveled in the additional time he had to write other kinds of things.[18] He wrote several episodes for "my new novel." After a few weeks, he came to the conclusion that "one of the things wrong with my writing is that I don't enlarge on things enough."[19] This problem was one of length as well as depth, for he abandoned works-in-progress and started new stories whenever he felt stuck. The twenty-two pages he had written of his novel, *Deborah Payne*, constituted, by far, the longest he had been able to sustain a story; yet what he had written did not reassure him. He felt he could envision what and how he wished to write, but these lucid ideas seemed to disappear as he tried to wrestle them onto paper: "I have such wonderful thoughts but when I try to put them on paper it just won't come right," he wrote irritably.[20] He was increasingly critical of how he used language. One morning, he described lovely weather:

Today was nicer than yesterday, a typical fall day—crisp blue
sky and clouds and a cold wind scattering myriad leaves—

He stopped himself there because "I'm beginning to sound like one of my short stories."[21]

Even when he finally "finished for the first time" a new story, "Episode in the Public Library," he felt that it did not satisfactorily communicate his character's interior emotional life, which is what he meant to do.[22] The story's plot was inspired by his reading Poe and Hawthorne stories and his job volunteering at the Sodus town library: Miss Covell, a woman self-conscious about a large birthmark that covers half her face, forgets her shame while busy with her library tasks, but when a young girl innocently asks her about the mark, she feels so embarrassed that she cannot wait to return to her cluttered, homey nineteenth-century apartment to read alone. John worked on several drafts over two months before typing up what he believed was a polished 1,250-word version to show Miss Klumpp. She criticized the latter half, saying that "it let her down at the end."[23] John agreed; on rereading it, he felt that the story's conclusion seemed closer to melodrama than the reality he had intended in the depiction of Miss Covell's sense of pride and shame. He could not get close enough to the character or write well enough yet, he mused, to reveal how much more interesting Miss Covell's experience of her life was than what people noticed about her.

His struggle with the story was similar to his frustrations with keeping his diary, though at Christmastime he still purchased a new one for 1943. The sheer amount of "nothing worth tabulating," however, that cluttered each page irritated him.[24] Entries seemed full of repetitive and unimportant details: a nosebleed; seeing neighbors; drawing class with Mr. Bennett; air raids, which required all children to disperse to specific homes in town and sit still; classes; chores; movies. One day could stand in for countless others. He knew how different each day was, yet he could not describe his thoughts in a way that captured distinctions that mattered most to him: "Today—as usual. And yet, each day is not the same. They are not monotonous in their sameness since each one has one hundred minute details."[25] He kept recording, even when his entries annoyed him, because he wanted to use these "details" in the future: "(You may wonder why I have put down such seemingly idiotic details. It is because I wish to recreate this day every time I read these pages.)"[26] He amused himself only by varying the way he described "nothing": "Packed apples toute la journée or til 4:15 o'clock thene eye soone wente toe bedde, wheyre eye redde variouse and sundrye bookes. Nowe eye am goinge toe wrighte, eye thinke."[27] As he drily concluded on another day, "Got up, went to school, walked uptown at noon, came home, read, went to bed. What more is there to say?"[28] Much later he would find ways to express this experience of "nothing" as the something he instinctively felt it also was, writing in *Three Poems*: "How like children in the way of thinking that some beatific scrap may always fall and as time goes by and *nothing* ever happens one is not disappointed but secretly pleased and confirmed in one's superstition: the magic world really does exist."[29]

He searched for writing advice, studying old and new texts at the

Rochester Public Library. He discovered and read poet Margaret Wid-
demer's *Do You Want to Write?*; Carolyn Wells's *A Parody Anthology*;
Horace's *Odes and Epodes*; and Sherwin Cody's *How to Write Fiction*,
but found no answers to his questions in these works. He studied contemporary writing in the *New Directions Annual*. In the 1942 edition, he
discovered an excerpt from Alvin Levin's novel-in-progress, *Love Is Like
Park Avenue*, a work that, though its story bore no relationship to John's
own life or thoughts, began to suggest to him ways to forge a relationship
between both. He felt Levin's stories, in which "stream-of-consciousness
narrators, often women, reflect the yearning of lower-middle-class New
York," achieved greatness by using language that reflected the characters' struggles to express their thoughts.[30] He could see the difference
between Levin's insightful complexity in fiction and his own, where the
feelings and thoughts he most wished to express were absent.

It was not until the end of February that it occurred to him to try
poetry once more instead of prose. One afternoon, he "consoled" himself by "the thought of the new poem which I am writing. I must get at
it now":[31]

Miss Rachael Pym

Rachael, our governess, always wore
A dress of blue-black, watered silk
That touched the pavement when she walked
Between the banks of melting snow
A blue-black stain upon the snow.
Beneath the narrow strip of white
Around her throat, she wore a brooch
Of imitation onyx.

Each night we children used to sit
Beside the coal-fire in the grate
And look at picture books,—while she
Sat on the straight backed, haircloth chair
And made her knitting needles click
And flash before her silent eyes.
But when the sluggish, iron clock
Behind her chair boomed half-past nine

She rose and took a candlestick
And swept before us up the stairs
In frigid majesty.
One night when she had tucked us in
And was about to turn and go downstairs
Ann asked her daringly
"Rachael, kiss us good-night.
We want you to."
She kissed us hurriedly and haughtily
But just before she blew the candles out
I saw a single silver tear
Poise for a moment—and race down her cheek.[32]

The poem's subject (similar to his short story) is a young woman with a sorrowful secret. This story, however, is told from the perspective of the child for whom she cares, a voice limited by its access to knowledge and its youthful tone. As a result, "Miss Rachael Pym" managed to give a greater indication of the governess's melancholy interior life than his story had, and without completely resorting to melodrama. The poem retained its understated, mournful tone throughout and hinted at thoughts unsaid. John was pleased with his work, but he was not sure if it was good. He left the poem at school for Miss Klumpp to read.

Even before she responded, he felt inspired to write more poetry. He stayed in Pultneyville all weekend, describing "wonderfully rough" waves in short poems he reread critically. When he arrived at school on Monday, Miss Klumpp had read "Miss Rachael Pym" and thought it was "very very good," the highest praise she had yet given. She was much more excited about the poem than she had been about any of his stories with similar themes, and announced that she would send it, and another short poem he had written, "Night Song of the Ocean," to *Scholastic* "with a letter telling about me," because the magazine printed works of young writers. "They may publish it!" After this, John went right back to work: "I'm going to write another one tonight." He composed a formal poem called "Sea-Voices," in which every other word rhymed, but he was unsure if that technique worked well and decided "to write it over in verse less exact."[33] For several weeks he composed many new poems and experimented with forms: "a poem a day seems to be my average," he noted proudly.[34] Soon, however, he began to worry that despite multiple new works with varied titles, all his poems sounded the same.

After his art class the following Friday, he went straight to the Rochester Central Library to peruse its poetry section for the first time. He took home Edgar Lee Masters's *Spoon River Anthology*, "which I like *very* much," and Amy Lowell's imagist poems.[35] Imagist poetry, a concise modernist form that Ezra Pound defined and promoted at the end of World War I, in which a single, vivid image was illuminated in precise, condensed language with no formal meter or rhyme, intrigued him for its brevity and vividness. Part of what John admired about these poems was how deftly words painted an intense, clear picture. He discovered the poet H.D. (Hilda Doolittle) and loved her imagist poems included in Louis Untermeyer's five-hundred-page *Modern American Poetry, Modern British Poetry: A Critical Anthology* (1942). He enthusiastically copied "Oread" into his diary:[36]

Whirl up, sea—
Whirl your pointed pines
Splash your great pines
On our rocks.
Hurl up your green over us—
Cover us with your pools of fir.

He liked the poem's energy and familiarity. The subjects of imagist poems were often (but not always) found in nature, materials, such as waves, trees, and rocks, that John was surrounded by in his life. Had he written them in verse, his diary descriptions of weather—"A sort of a freezing fog was falling all day, coating everything with ice," for example—would have come very close to imagist poetry.[37]

He began writing imagist poems almost exclusively. He cut short his novels, stories, and diary entries because he felt that "I must try to finish another poem."[38] He understood better how to complete a poem, even though he usually ended up spending more time writing a short poem than he had ever done on a much lengthier piece of prose. He stayed home from school, ostensibly with a sore throat, but actually to try a concise five-line form called the cinquain (an example of which he had seen by Adelaide Crapsey, a local Rochester writer, in Untermeyer's

Anthology). In his cinquain, "To Rosa," he attempted to combine a natural image with a complex feeling about a person:

> You came
> To me like vines
> Reaching up to strangle
> An abandoned house with quiet
> Sureness.

His poem was an ambitious attempt to create a gothic, unsettled feeling in few words. Although pleased to write a concise new poem, he was also critical of his full day's work, which he declared his "not too satisfactory cinquain."[39] As soon as he finished copying the poem into his diary, he was already exploring other forms and ideas, for he wanted to write poems that were more elegant. He studied Untermeyer's selections of works by Elinor Wylie, Conrad Aiken, and John Gould Fletcher. Especially thrilled by Wylie's poetry, which he thought "very elegant," he discovered her "Venetian Interior" (a poem that Untermeyer had not included in his anthology) and copied it into his diary.[40] By the time Miss Klumpp told him that his poems had been rejected by *Scholastic* magazine, he had already dismissed them in his own mind, declaring especially "Night Song of the Ocean" "a putrid thing . . . that I shudder to recall."[41]

He was so engrossed in his new literary work that he had no idea that forces had been at work for several months to change his life. Margaret Hubbell Wells (Mrs. Lyndon Wells), whose summer property across Lake Road was about a mile from Ashbery Farm, had set these new plans in motion. An intelligent, vivacious, determined woman, Wells had grown up in a mansion known as "the old Hubbell House"—her father was George Eastman's lawyer, and her mother a society woman—on the grandest stretch of East Avenue in Rochester.[42] She was the mother of three boys, and her youngest son, Donnie Wells, was the same age as John, and they occasionally played together on the beach. She was extremely fond of Helen Ashbery and had been so impressed by John's performance on *Quiz Kids* that she had long harbored a wish to do something for him. Her two older sons had attended Deerfield Academy, a boarding school in Massachusetts, and she decided that John ought to finish his high school education there.

On February 6, she sent a long handwritten letter to Deerfield Academy's legendary headmaster, Frank Boyden (who had been running the school already since 1902).[43] She explained her idea to him:

> Do you ever offer scholarships to boys who are fine students— really brilliant—yet do not meet the qualifications of well-rounded boys? I would be so glad to gamble five hundred dollars on a boy by the name of John Ashbery, if you would be willing to have him at Deerfield for one year (1943–4) with the promise that you would keep him for one more year—gratis—if you thought he were worth it.[44]

She offered additional details about John's family that she felt would attract Boyden's interest. Helen was "one of the saints of the earth"; Chet was "a moderately successful farmer" with "only a high school education." Neither could help their son get the kind of educational opportunities he needed. She felt that John was "not a well-rounded boy," but "holds great promise" and, under Mr. Boyden's tutelage, "might amount to something really important." Boyden wrote back immediately, offering John an interview and a potentially significant scholarship.[45] In April, John mentioned Deerfield for the first time in his diary, noting that at the end of Easter vacation, his father and grandfather were driving him three hundred miles away to see a new school to which "we think I'm going" next year.[46] A week after the visit, he remarked only that "We went to the Academy. I was petrified. I don't know how I like it."[47]

Chet was much more unequivocally enthusiastic about the school. Shortly after returning home, he sent a handwritten letter to Boyden on Ashbery Farm stationery, explaining "how much we enjoyed our visit to Deerfield . . . Its atmosphere is so friendly, wholesome and understanding."[48] He had not expected to, but he had liked Deerfield and, especially, Frank Boyden, tremendously. Chet was surprised to discover that Boyden genuinely sought out his opinions. The headmaster had recently started a program requiring Deerfield boys to help local farmers whose supply of farmhands had been depleted by the war, and he and

Chet discussed related agricultural issues as enthusiastically as they discussed John's future.[49] Boyden responded to Chet's letter warmly and immediately. He would charge only $500 per year for John to attend (though a significant expense, the amount represented a huge scholarship, for the annual cost had recently risen to $1,700). He also sought Chet's ideas on proper farm equipment, soil, and other farming matters.[50] For the first time during John's years of education, Chet felt that his knowledge and skills had made a powerful difference in his son's future. Henry Lawrence had also accompanied John to the interview, fully expecting to use his position as a college educator to help arrange his grandson's future, but Boyden did not respond nearly as warmly to him.

Henry Lawrence had been favorably impressed by the school as well, and he believed that attending Deerfield would be a good opportunity for John. He also thanked Boyden in a letter soon after returning home, writing very affectionately about his grandson:

> About John: He is very dependable. He is somewhat shy but has faith in himself without conceit. He has unusual capacity for amusing himself but enjoys social contact; if left to himself, he would take to your school library which, I must confess, I found very attractive. He has large intellectual curiosity, enjoys music and dramatics.
>
> He is clumsy at boy games; his shyness has kept him from getting interested in these sports. I am sure that a wider association with boys of the sort we saw at Deerfield will lead him to take interest in this direction. He has a remarkable memory and naturally takes to study. I am sure you will like him.[51]

Boyden took several months to respond to Henry Lawrence's warm letter extolling John, making it very clear through both his long delay and his clipped but professional tone that they would not be corresponding further. It was Chet Ashbery whom Boyden had enjoyed meeting most.

John, in the midst of an emotional crisis, remained subdued and distant throughout the negotiations. His reaction to this opportunity was muddled because his mind was still at the Memorial Art Gallery, where he had fallen completely in love with a man he had met there the weekend before leaving for Deerfield. On that Friday afternoon, John finished his painting and left art class early to wander through a new exhibition of paintings by men in the army and navy. As he studied the works, "the most beautiful man I had ever seen then or since," John Lewis, a twenty-year-old sailor stationed in Rochester, introduced himself. They began talking about the paintings, then walked together to the museum's art library to look up other works, whispering together in a quiet, intimate conversation about themselves and art. Afterward, Lewis suggested they go to the men's room together, where they entered a stall, and "he felt me, caressed me," an experience simultaneously ecstatic and unnerving because "I didn't know what to do, what I was supposed to do."[52] John lost track of time and suddenly heard his grandfather, who had been waiting in the car, enter the bathroom in search of him. John exited the stall and went home in a daze, his emotions such a volatile mixture of excitement and longing that he could hardly think.

That night, buzzing with memories of the afternoon, he wrote in his diary, subtly preserving a record of what had happened, in case his mother read the entry: "I . . . went to look at the exhibit. It was things by men in the army + navy. Then we went downstairs. Looked at paintings of 4 freedoms in art library and other things." Only the discreet shift from "I" to "we"—a technique barely noticeable but that produced a sense of private mystery and intimacy he would employ in future poems—and the reference to "other things," which in context seemed to refer to other paintings, signaled what he most wanted to remember. Alongside the diary entry, in very small letters, he wrote in his high school French: "à m'etait point un rêve" (to me was not at all a dream).[53] He was in agony to see John Lewis again, to recapture a trace of that afternoon. He phoned the number Lewis had scribbled down for him, but there was no answer. With no word yet from him, John traveled to Deerfield and back in a fog. When he arrived home, he called, wrote, and returned to the exhibit repeatedly, in case Lewis visited again. A few weeks later he received a cold note from Lewis and never saw or heard from him again.

He had no one to talk to about Lewis's silence, and felt wrecked by it. He became irritated by every facet of his current life: "How sick I am of afternoons in this drab, hateful school and going to the library, walking uptown with Betty and all the rest."[54] Every day seemed even more the same than it ever had before: school, library with Betty Lou Burden, and home where his father "bellows" constantly.[55] Even his mother had recently refused to allow him to take out a library book he wanted to read (B. A. Williams's *The Strange Woman*, 1941) because it was considered somewhat racy, a position that enraged him.[56] He summed up his disdain for his present life in a five-word diary entry: "School, uptown, library, home, bed."[57] Worse than just his usual wry complaints about his life's dull monotony, he felt angry—"I hate it all the same . . . I'll be glad to go away next year."[58] He was too "petrified" about the future and emotionally overwrought in the present to embrace enthusiastically the gift of escape from Sodus and the farm that he had been handed after wishing for it so long.

He climbed out of his depression slowly and through writing. His new poems were only one quatrain, but they were filled with excitingly strange and vivid images. Up until then, the one element that linked almost every character in John's stories or poems was a sense of secret shame that left each feeling lonely and separate from others; a character tried to voice her—his characters were almost always spinsters—"hidden syllables," but could not, or did not know how to, form them into words and sentences. Two years earlier, John had composed a modernist-like poem as his diary entry after spending the night with Dick Sanders; he had expressed his emotional and sexual feelings in the form of white space, extra empty places to indicate where those missing syllables would have been arranged if he had felt safe writing them out. In the wake of his present turmoil, his imagination for how to account for his crucial experiences seemed to stretch in new ways. In "Winter Dusk," he describes the eerie dancing shadows of "leafless" trees:

> Now, in the windy sunset-glow
> The leafless maple trees join hands
> To dance demented sarabands
> And weave strange patterns on the snow.[59]

These "demented sarabands" create unusual, even beautiful new "patterns." In another quatrain, "It Seemed As If the Devil Himself," written the same day, he addressed his own feelings and thoughts almost allegorically. John Lewis, "the devil," had provoked in John such searing and bewildering pain by opening him up and shutting him out within such a short period of time, and the poem seethed with rage:

> It seemed as if the devil himself looked down
> His face contorted in a lecherous grin
> And laughed and shouted till he shook the town
> "Strive, strive, you little innocents, to sin!"[60]

The poem accuses the devil of defiling the pure and of leading "innocents" to "sin." This traditional accusation is only one aspect of the poem's narrative. In both "Winter Dusk" and "It Seemed As If the Devil Himself," however, trees "weave" "strange patterns" into the snow; "little" ones are pushed by a man with a "contorted . . . grin" to "strive" and get on with it. The poems reflect John's complex thoughts about his situation. He felt a sense of guilt about his attraction to men, about leaving Sodus, his family and friends, and his childhood for a brighter future far away, but he wanted to "strive" anyway. He well knew—he had recognized it about himself when he read *Vanity Fair* and identified most with Becky Sharp—that, though "innocent," he could also be "the devil" when he chose, as cold and calculating as Lewis had been toward him. He hated Lewis, but he also identified with him.

John reluctantly started his summer job in late July. From seven in the morning to six at night, with an hour off for lunch six days a week, he hammered covers onto cans of cherries at the Sodus Fruit Farm, a big farm and canning facility directly across from the Ashbery Farm, on Lake Road. He hated the job and never lost his distaste for the work: "I'll be back in August, / after the cherries have left. / How motivated is that?" ("In the Time of Cherries").[61] The job at the Sodus Fruit Farm was tedious, but he began to look forward to seeing a new friend, Malcolm White, each morning. Malcolm was a thin, artistic, seventeen-year-old high school graduate from Amherst, Massachusetts, who had been invited, through church connections, to spend the summer living and working with the Buckman family, who ran the Sodus Fruit Farm.[62]

Within days of their meeting, John's crush on Malcolm had developed into musing in his diary about ways to seduce him. The young daughter of a neighbor visiting the Ashbery family one evening announced that she had a boyfriend; John wrote in his diary "Comme je veux . . ."[63] It was what he wished, too. By the evening of his sixteenth birthday, he had decided to take action: "Demain j'ai l'intention de séduire le beau gar qui travaille à la ferme de fruit" (Tomorrow I plan to seduce the handsome boy who works at the fruit farm), he wrote in slightly fractured French.[64] He invited Malcolm to meet him after work, and reminded himself—quoting Emily Dickinson, whose poems he was reading—not to rush: "Come slowly, Eden." They listened to some of John's records and talked about art, music, poetry, and life without any awkwardness or hesitation. Malcolm was interested in drama, poetry, and French literature. He had appeared in several plays in high school, had published a poem in his local paper, read voraciously, and was about to begin Amherst College in the fall.[65] They discussed the poet Arthur Rimbaud, especially "O saisons, o châteaux," and Hart Crane's passion for Rimbaud's *Illuminations*.[66] When it started to get late, John walked Malcolm home. The next day, they walked uptown: went to the library; had root beer floats at Knapp's; talked more, about movies, books, poems; and listened to records. In the evening "after supper we walked down to the lake and back, avidly discussing literature."[67] The next night, they sat together under trees and talked about their lives in ordinary and artful ways: about their families, about becoming artists, about books and ideas they wished to explore. In Malcolm's efforts to educate himself beyond the provincialism of his small town and his family's limited means, John heard echoes of his own history. He felt that they "were both great talkers" and understood each other.

Their friendship soon turned romantic. They went to the movies and came home late, holding hands as they walked alone. Cousin Wallace, who was visiting, told John that his grandmother "suspected us of having some girls along (!)."[68] They went to the beach and read together "under beach umbrella No. 28." At night they returned and, under a shared blanket, kissed and masturbated each other. "Joie," John wrote in the upper right-hand corner of his diary. "X-tz," he added at the bottom of the page, hiding but noting his pleasure.[69] (He carefully hid Malcolm's gender by leaving out the word *garçon*, in case his mother knew it.) The next night, they went to the Sodus theater to see *Action in the North Atlantic*, with Humphrey Bogart, a lousy movie made exquisite because they sat close to each other in the dark theater balcony holding hands, and kissed. A few nights later, John treated Malcolm (or "Mac," as he now called him) to dinner in Rochester, and then Malcolm treated John to the movies: "Mac bought my movie ticket; the show being *The Constant Nymph* at the Palace and excellent!"[70] For twenty days, until Malcolm took the train home, they were together. They promised to see each other in the fall, since Amherst and Deerfield were not too far apart.[71] From his home, Malcolm immediately began a correspondence, and John studied his letters, even borrowing a book on handwriting analysis from the library, concluding that Mac "is practically a saint."[72]

John had begun the summer with ambitious plans to prepare for Deerfield. He assembled a challenging reading list, including "Voltaire, Rousseau, Hazlitt, Addison and Steele, Montaigne, Browning and Kant," declaring: "I am trying to educate myself to a high point."[73] Instead of reading these philosophical texts, however, he borrowed "the *Life of `Hart Crane . . .*" from the library.[74] He added ellipses to indicate that his interest in Philip Horton's *Hart Crane: The Life of an American Poet* (1937) was in its depiction of life as much as art. He read at the beach, absorbing the book's mostly sympathetic portrait, though one shaped by the prevailing language and attitudes of the time:

John and Malcolm White in
Pultneyville, August 1943.
Photograph taken by Chet Ashbery.

[W]hatever the causes of his homosexuality . . . [t]he investigations
of this field of sexual pathology are at best experimental. . . . The
psychoanalytical explanation of Crane's homosexuality would
probably be that it was due to an Oedipus complex, the fixation of the love impulse upon the mother with a correlative
antipathy towards the father. . . . But it is . . . more human,
to consider the conditions rather than the causes of his aberration, and to understand clearly that when he arrived at
the threshold of maturity, his nervous system was so inflamed
by years of constant strain that he was probably incapable of
sustaining any satisfactory relationship whatever, even of an
abnormal kind.[75]

By fifteen, John had indirectly imbibed Horton's assertion that homosexuality was "abnormal" and an "aberration"; he viewed his attraction to men as his secret "affliction."[76] His experience with Malcolm
directly countered those ideas, and John expressed his joy in their intimacy: "Ce que nous avons fait cette nuit est trop belle du dire" (What
we did last night is too beautiful for words).[77] As he and Malcolm dated,
John gained a brief, private vision of a loving homosexual relationship.
He carried this experience forward, and it became part of powerful armor
he did not yet realize he was amassing for himself, even though he never
spent time with Malcolm again.

Alone after Malcolm's departure, he suddenly realized his summer
was about to end, and he chided himself for not having accomplished
more: "I lay in bed all morning, big lazy horse that I am."[78] He began
to read again, first Robert Frost's and then Edna St. Vincent Millay's
poems. He arranged to meet with Dr. Katherine Koller, a well-known
and respected English professor at the University of Rochester who
was "very well read in the field of poetry," and had a summer house
in Pultneyville.[79] She looked over his poems and encouraged him to
keep writing, and he listened closely to her suggestion that he read
carefully the works of W. H. Auden, excited that she knew the poet
personally.

John felt more mature, as though he knew his childhood had already
ended. He stared at the view of Lake Ontario from his grandparents'
window and saw something new:

Right after supper—"There fell red rain of spears athwart the sky" [from "The Last Judgment," by John Gould Fletcher]—well, not exactly but the wind blew terrifically hard for a few minutes and the lake turned the weirdest color—deep green turning to dark blue and millions of bright white-caps—and you could clearly see the piers and submerged rocks for quite a distance out.[80]

He noticed the lake's slight shifts in color and light and felt increasingly nostalgic about how far away he was going to be and how much more would change in his absence. He visited Mary Wellington in Rochester, and they looked through their old letters, amazed at how just three years before they had still felt unselfconsciously like children. A few weeks later, he copied out parts of his 1941 diary to share with Mary:

Looking through my diary for 1941 I find that two years ago today, in the morning, you and Anne and your grandmother and I played Michigan poker. After lunch we played Michigan at the Little's [sic], then you and Joan and I went in swimming amid "monstrous" waves. . . . Remember? Gee we had fun that year.[81]

When Billy and Carol came to Pultneyville, they all played together in their old trees. John had not visited the "Castle of the Slopshire" in years, and it felt bittersweet: "We lay underneath our cherry tree and Billy and I took turns dropping blossoms down on the other two. Gee it was beautiful up in our tree."[82]

At night in his bedroom in Pultneyville, John felt most acutely that his childhood days were over: "I am sleeping in the back room at Pultneyville. I love it here in this room," he wrote, thinking about the sounds and smells of the waves that drifted through his window.[83] Even when he returned for vacations, the room was not going to be his any longer. Aunt Janet's husband, Tom Taft, had decided to volunteer for the navy, and Janet was moving to Pultneyville with her two children. Six-year-old Larry would live with Helen and Chet during the week and attend school in Sodus for the next three years. Henry Lawrence had agreed to pay two hundred dollars a year for Larry to board with them; this amount would help offset the cost of Deerfield, which Chet had decided to pay without Mrs. Wells's help, though John knew nothing of these financial arrangements.[84]

In the last few days before he left, Chet insisted John pack apples on the Ashbery farm, exhausting chores that drove away his nostalgia and about which he fumed that "nothing more need be said."[85] Larry began first grade in Sodus, and since John no longer had to attend, he indulged in late nights of reading, feeling older than he ever had before. He had a great sense of anticipation: "Tuesday—Think! Just a week from tonight I'll be going up to the Wells [sic] to spend the night and the next day—School!":

> This morning I worked packing apples. This aft I went uptown, got a haircut and went to see the teachers. I saw Miss Wright Miss Lawrence and Miss Copeland but no Miss Klumpp. . . . Nobody seems to realize but me anyway this is the ending of an era—my childhood. I will never really <u>live</u> in this house again, only visit here.[86]

The next morning in Pultneyville, there were "tearful farewells from both Grandma and Nana and Grandpa. I am rather pleased to see I can cry after all." Attached to his home, yet already detached enough to gauge his emotional investment in what was quickly becoming his past life, John left for Rochester. In the afternoon, he went for a final trip to the library before arriving at the Wellses' house to sleep, for he was to take the train from Union Station the next day with Donnie Wells, who was also beginning Deerfield. Lying in a strange bed that night, he felt a tremendous sense of excitement: "To bed now, up early tomorrow."[87]

5

Self-Portrait at Deerfield

1943–1945

After arriving at Deerfield Academy on a "very crowded" shuttle from Greenfield train station, John and Donnie Wells parted.[1] John headed to his assigned address, Delano House, which was one of Deerfield's most remote residences. To anyone who saw him setting off alone, he looked neat and composed, a self-possessed 5' 10½", 135-pound figure whose angular face resembled Frank Sinatra's. That night, he described the long walk even more dramatically: "I nearly died carrying my heavy suitcase way down here."[2] His strange new surroundings interrupted the familiar rhythm of his thoughts, and the life he had known intensely for sixteen years receded. Reading, writing, piano practicing, radio shows, Saturday opera, movies, Carol, Mary, his grandparents, his parents, the farm, Lake Ontario, the waves—all felt unreal to him. Even his reveries about Malcolm White, which had enjoyably occupied his mind for the past two months, ceased.[3] Delano was a quiet, pretty house, a home he would have welcomed except that the four other boys who lived there were all on scholarship, certain that everyone else at Deerfield knew, and instinctively wary of one another as outcasts.[4]

"I wish I was home," he wrote in his diary on Sunday, September 26, his fourth day at Deerfield. He had already performed abysmally on athletics program placement tests, witnessed a student collapse in an epileptic fit, and contracted such a bad cold that he felt "too stupid to write another word." After mandatory church service, he wandered over to inspect the school's new art studio, which was housed in an unprepossessing basement room of the science building.[5] Led by Donald Greason ("I must remember to pronounce it Grayson"), a local painter who had recently started teaching art at Deerfield, the Art Club attracted about a dozen serious student artists.[6] As soon as John opened the door to the room, he discovered a scene that captivated him, though not entirely positively: "There were several boys over there, all extremely sophisticated, brilliant, and homosexual, including one disgusting looking boy with rouged (I think) cheeks who I had been trying to ignore and who is really an excellent painter." That "disgusting looking boy" was Bradford Wilson, an attentive and sensitive student who had earned the ironic nickname "Brute" by way of his epicene appearance. John felt both judgmental and enthralled as he surveyed an entire room of boys painting still lifes. Despite doubts, he stayed at the studio all afternoon and began a new painting "which (I think) fooled no one."[7]

The art studio quickly became his favorite place on campus and a haven from everything else that was going wrong. His four academic classes—French III, History, Chemistry, and English—startled him with their pace and difficulty.[8] On rotation as a waiter, "I dropped a tray of dirty dishes."[9] Even worse were daily sports practices and games, another Deerfield requirement for which he felt ill-suited.[10] A member of senior soccer, John was placed on a team of "soccer players as dumb as myself."[11] The requirement he hated most, however, was harvesting vegetables on nearby farms "due to the acute labor shortage which is threatening farmers throughout the country," as Boyden explained to students.[12] John had looked forward to escaping those very same chores by attending Deerfield, but the school's farm program had expanded, rather ironically, through Chet Ashbery's encouragement.[13] John used any flimsy excuse to get out of work: a cold, a nosebleed, no available old clothes.[14] Finally, he escaped to the art studio one afternoon and started a "still life of copper pitcher, blue bottom, black backdrop and a basket of yellow flowers" which "everybody likes." "Everybody" included the core members of the club: Schuyler Dodge, Gillett Griffin, James Wilder Green, Ed Douglas, Brute Wilson, and William (Bill) Haddock III. Greason chose John's new work as picture of the week.[15]

John started to feel more comfortable at Deerfield, but rumors "that

After John Ashbery's still life was named picture of the week in November 1943 by Donald Greason, Deerfield's art teacher and the head of the Art Club, John painted one he liked better, which his grandparents framed and hung above their living room fireplace in Pultneyville.

I am an h.o. [homosexual]" threatened his peace.[16] Classmates insulted him under their breath as he stood on line at the post office. John remained in the supportive company of his closest Art Club friends: Gillett, a squat, gentle boy from Greenwich, Connecticut, with a passion for antiques; Ed, a skinny, odd-looking student with a quirky sense of humor; Brute, the most mature member of the Art Club; and Bill Haddock, who was "interested in modern poetry as few Deerfield boys were."[17] Bill, a sophomore, was also a wealthy Philadelphian who boasted of "descending from among Hungarian nobility."[18] John was shocked to discover that Haddock had started the rumor about him. When he confronted his friend and asked why, Haddock apologized so profusely that John forgave him. They grew closer auditioning for the Drama Club's all-male production of *The Man Who Came to Dinner*. After second tryouts, John won the role of Nurse Preen; even better, word spread that he was really funny in it: "Fame and fortune will be mine," he wrote, voicing his social ambitions.[19] When downpours canceled all outdoor activities—"I love rain!"—he felt almost happy at Deerfield for the first time: "I love to wear my new raincoat thrown over my shoulder. I assume an affected walk and feel very theatrical." At the performance, "I got several ovations and countless laughs," he wrote, sorry afterward that the play was over, because "it has been such fun."[20]

Happier, he turned increasingly to music and poetry. He found a stack of classical records and players hidden in a room behind the gym, a sign of the small population they served. He completed a composition called "A Few Modern Poets," focusing on Auden, Spender, Thomas, Wylie, and Robinson, favorites in an anthology he had just been assigned in his English course.[21] During a November weekend, for the first time in months, he devoted an afternoon to reading poetry. He "loved" Edna St. Vincent Millay's "elegant, artistic" poems, especially "Eel-Grass" and "Second April."[22] The next day, he jotted down the end of one of her sonnets from memory: "I love Millay's sonnet ending 'Francesca with the loud surf at her ear / Lets drop [sic] the coloured book upon the floor.'" He misremembered "drop" (Millay wrote "fall"), but the exercise whetted his appetite.[23] He began a new practice of composing an epigrammatic statement in verse each day. He felt inspired by Brute's suggestion to write down two ideas a day, and he composed them instead in lines. Thinking about poetry reminded him of home, and he wrote letters to Miss Klumpp and his mother, who missed him so terribly (even visiting her son once) that she sent him a letter or package nearly every day through the end of final exams.[24]

From the moment John stepped onto the train bound for Rochester, he started to imagine new poems he might write during Christmas vacation. He jotted down a "token poem" during the ride, his first finished piece since summer. He viewed the slight verse as merely an exercise because he felt so out of shape. After nearly four months away, he reveled in his family's attention and the comparative freedom of home. His mother was demonstrably overjoyed to have him home again. He slept late, lolled about in his own room, ignored his noisy cousins, saw *Princess O'Rourke* and *Above Suspicion*, "a really super movie" with his grandmother, visited his grandparents in Pultneyville, and did exactly "as I pleased."[25] Then he went to see Miss Klumpp, who asked to read his new poems. He felt irritated at himself that after an entire semester away, he had no new work to show her.

He "made a beeline for the library" in Rochester and took notes on a new poem idea.[26] He started jotting lines about a man who "lives a life both cheerful and refined" and yet is so intensely afraid when alone that sometimes "words do not make sense and birds obscene / Dance on a plain of blue and emerald flame."[27] As his sixteen-line poem "Not Normal" took shape, John felt "pleased about its being Christmas, but even more pleased about my poem idea," which he finished over the next few days. The poem's sympathetic depiction of the man's rich interior life directly contradicted its seemingly judgmental title. "Abnormal" was the term that Philip Horton had used to describe Hart Crane's homosexuality.[28] John's poem used the term instead to describe a man with vision and quiet genius. Back at the library with Carol Rupert on the afternoon of New Year's Eve, John began another poem with the same theme. In "Inmates of the Palace," he contrasted the august architecture of the library and the seemingly lonely, austere women who worked there during the holidays: "Sweet vestals of the brassy drawer, / queens of the receding shelves."[29] The forms of his two new poems were different, but in both, his sympathy for the distinction between a person's exterior and interior experience of life was paramount.

At home after such a long absence, he was more aware than ever before of how he felt there. John and Carol visited Pultneyville together and "gazed on the familiar scenes of our childhood," sharply aware of their feelings of separation from it.[30] That night, for the first time, they planned to celebrate New Year's Eve at a fancy restaurant by themselves. Throughout, John kept thinking about improving his new poems. At the beginning of 1944, he purchased a plain brown spiral notebook

John and Carol on New Year's Eve 1943, out for a celebratory dinner at Lorenzo's

into which to recopy all his old poems.[31] He placed his newest two poems last, adding a note about the sonnet:

> Miss Klumpp: The preceding is a first draft and incomplete, of course. I intend to fill in the second stanza with a couple of lines about the heart's pointing to the brooch as proof that the woman is a woman, not a machine. I will send you the final version, after doing this and changing some words which I know must mystify you . . .

He walked to his old school with the notebook—a modest, first "volume" of work—leaving it for Miss Klumpp's critique.

On his last day of vacation, John once more "rushed . . . to the library's protecting walls."[32] He felt anxious about returning to Deerfield. He spent the night feeling agitated at the Wellses' house in Rochester before an early train. At the station, he bought a new diary and an astrology magazine, underlining traits he felt most reflected his personality:

CUSP OF CANCER
July 21–28
Super-sensitive, conservative and often over-confident.
Deep thinkers, lovers of books. Very domestic.

LEO
July 24–August 24
All are kind-hearted, generous, sympathetic, idealistic, executive and magnetic. More merciful than just. Prone to anger and to excess pride. Excitable and accessible to flattery. Generous with money and expect the same in return. Great optimist. Fairly domestic. Can't harbor a grudge. Likes danger and adventure. In matters of state, bold and sagacious. Happy in responsibility. Best companions—Aries and Sagittarius.[33]

This exercise in self-analysis was an attempt to ward off the depression and insecurity he had been overwhelmed by when he had first arrived at Deerfield. Still feeling "super-sensitive," he braced himself for his second semester.

He felt a "sadistic joy" to be back on campus, a phrase that encapsulated his excitement and anxiety.[34] The weather was extremely cold, and he listened as the layer of ice on top of the snow made noise—"snaps and crunches"—as he walked on it, piercing sounds that heightened his sense of alertness to danger. At the art studio, he started a self-portrait.[35] He received several immediate critiques: "I am painting a self-portrait which nobody likes."[36] He had invited criticism by boldly ignoring Greason's injunction to work on still lifes, but the critical comments also weakened his resolve, and he started to feel depressed. He worried he was "not wanted," even by people he thought were friends.[37] He noticed Brute Wilson and Bill Haddock growing closer, and though he and Haddock were allies again, he believed Brute was somehow betraying him. Feeling increasingly insecure, he recounted for Brute "the details of a purely fabricated romance which took place on a ditto visit to New York."[38] To make matters worse, Haddock spread a new rumor that he had caught John masturbating in the bathroom. Haddock apologized for lying in a "self-abusing" letter he handed to John, in which he said "he liked me terribly."[39] Even so, a few days later Haddock planned an expensive trip to New York City with mutual friends without inviting

William Haddock III in his Deerfield yearbook photo, 1945

Bradford Wilson, nicknamed "Brute," in his Deerfield graduation photo, 1944

John, who was so upset by the snub that he became ill.[40] When he recovered, he dismissed Haddock as "mediocre," a particularly damning
insult.

Four years later, Ashbery fictionalized his emotionally demoraliz-
ing social experiences at Deerfield in an unpublished short story, "The
Daunted," which connected his misery to his nascent sense of himself
as a writer. In one scene, Wilfred, who stands in for Ashbery, is repeatedly abused and ignored by classmates, including his friend, the
Haddock-like character Christopher Striker. Out of his feelings of pain,
however, Wilfred finds a way to strike out on his own:

> During the next week Striker and Rose became increasingly
> friendly, which according to the social laws of the school, ne-
> cessitated a corresponding coolness between Striker and Wil-
> fred. Wilfred was not really upset, since he counted on friends
> only to a degree, and had always secretly disliked Striker,
> whom he considered a born subordinate. Besides, he had sud-
> denly to explain a larger and more puzzling phenomenon: a
> sudden wave of open hostility toward himself. In class[,] boys
> kicked him under the desks; they shoved him out of line at the
> soda fountain. During athletic periods they took every oppor-
> tunity to pile on top of him and beat him. Even the masters
> seemed to share unconsciously the general hatred, which, it
> occurred to Wilfred, might possibly result from secret feelings
> of hate for themselves. At any rate, he found it exhilarating, for
> he realized for the first time that he was actually lonely, and it
> gave him a feeling of power. Calmly observing the boys around
> him, he reflected that he knew their names and where they
> came from, and had even seen some of them with their parents.
> While I, he thought, being nothing, must always remain a
> mystery.[41]

Wilfred's misery at realizing he is "nothing" at this unnamed
boarding school becomes his provocation to court a sense of "mystery."
In deciding to enjoy the experience of "being nothing," he upends the
school's system of determining value only by money and social connections, a choice that is "exhilarating," and gives him "a feeling of power."

The raw, emotional story, written so long after the events it depicts, reflects how angry and hurt Ashbery still felt. Yet this anger and pain were also the spur he needed to reach a clear-eyed decision about his future. On February 24, he declared, in the last diary entry he wrote:

I shall rent Brute's typewriter tomorrow. I will write better poems than I ever have and publish them. If I die in the attempt, I'll make them respect me yet.

Shortly after beginning his first diary in 1941, he had quietly declared that he would become an "(artist)."[42] Now he assertively avowed his commitment to an artist's life. He was no longer writing only for himself, but to "make them respect me," an unnamed mass encompassing Haddock and all others who made him feel, by virtue of his class and sexual orientation, that he was less than human—"nothing." His decision to devote himself to poetry accelerated his need to stop keeping a diary and finally relieved him of the burden of his original promise to himself to complete each empty diary page.

Almost immediately, Ashbery's poetic voice became more sophisticated and curious.[43] He composed a two-stanza self-portrait, a literary counterpart to the painting he had recently completed. In the poem, the process of observing a face in a mirror (the technique he had used to create his painting) precipitates thoughts about oneself. His emotional experiences at Deerfield and his efforts to retain a sense of self were in the background of the poem. The provocation for writing, however, was a letter from his mother with news that his grandmother Elizabeth Ashbery had suffered a major stroke, resulting in partial paralysis and loss of speech. "Poem," even in its title, suggests Ashbery's developing attitude toward poetry as a form in which to address unanswerable mysteries of private experience:

Always the left hand flickers, falls to right;
The eyes groping at mirrors
Strike the sought self, opaque and firm,
Safe in its frame. A sweet disorder
Arranges mirrors, and the tensile gaze
Turns inward, calls the turning love.

Let our dual sight
See not so clearly, and turning, take daylight.
And before mirrors long unvisited
Award the milk white and translucent face
That stays there, that we know not how to name.[44]

In 1974, Ashbery would write "Self-Portrait in a Convex Mirror," which similarly begins by studying the painter's hand as a way into his mind: "As Parmigianino did it, the right hand / Bigger than the head, thrust at the viewer."[45] In 1944, Narcissus, the mythical figure who wastes away for love of self, haunts the first stanza of Ashbery's poem. The process of observing the self is: "A sweet disorder / Arranges mirrors, and the tensile gaze / Turns inward, calls the turning love." He borrowed the phrase "a sweet disorder" from the opening of Robert Herrick's droll fourteen-line lyric "A sweet disorder in the dress / Kindles in clothes a wantonness."[46] In the second stanza, building on his allusion to Herrick's poem, Ashbery suggests that it may be best not to look in the mirror too closely, nor to be too demanding about precisely naming what one sees. This idea to observe oneself but in a detached, open way, and through this relaxation of effort see more deeply, was new. In its close attention to the complex contemporary experience of interiority, the poem represents a turning point.

Six months earlier, as John read twentieth-century poetry for the first time, he had worried that it was too difficult. After studying James Joyce's tale "The Ondt and the Gracehoper" in the *Imagist Anthology* (1930), he had confessed to his diary that he thought it was "good," but "I'm afraid I'm not modern enough as I don't know whether I understand it or not."[47] Intrigued by Marianne Moore's poetry, which he found "mysterious," and the few Auden poems he had so far encountered in anthologies, he still felt uncertain about what they might mean.[48] Perusing the shelves of the Deerfield library in late winter, however, he discovered Gertrude Stein's *Three Lives* (1909) and *Tender Buttons* (1914), and her writing thrilled him.[49] Inspired, he wrote a pastiche (now lost). Reading Stein's experimental work gave him creative confidence to try more of his own. In February he submitted a new poem to Frank Bogues, his English teacher: "I left all the punctuation out, which he considered unorthodox but he liked it anyway."[50] In March he handwrote a couplet and included his own critique of it:

So, musing, she fell asleep, still sorry about the bed
Glad of the flickering stars, now green, now red.

Whoever criticizes this poem adversely must admit that it is at
    least bizarre.

Fragmentary but complete, the poem represents Ashbery's attempt to create a new sound and style that could be both emotional and whimsical. This odd, unexpected voice wavered between remorse and joy, pain and pleasure, silliness and seriousness.

By early spring, John had written several new poems but had not yet applied to college. Although he had begun the year as a "senior boy," Boyden advised John's parents that he should return to Deerfield for a second year, and they agreed.[51] The entirety of the class of 1944 was entering service academies. John's friend Gillett's elder brother had been killed in action, news delivered to his distraught friend at school.[52] Headmaster Boyden's horrific weekly reports of recent alumni killed in combat terrified everyone, and Boyden encouraged students to develop safely in school as long as possible. Although more settled into his Deerfield routine, John still felt insecure. One spring weekend, John Anson's mother arrived from Sodus to take John Ashbery for the day; that evening, he had her drop him off far from the center of campus so his classmates would not see him emerge from her beat-up station wagon.[53] In May, Malcolm White visited campus on an errand for his job as a clothing salesman and waved to John, who walked away as though he had not seen him; they never spoke.[54]

Helen Ashbery arrived at Deerfield in June to drive her son home for the summer. John was immediately put to work babysitting his cousins, picking and sorting fruit, and doing other domestic tasks. Elizabeth Ashbery's stroke had left her incapacitated, and she needed constant care at home. Addie Lawrence had also just undergone the first of three major operations to remove cancerous tumors. In early spring, an electrical fire in the barn had killed several pigs and destroyed expensive pieces of farm equipment.[55] None of John's friends were around. Billy Graeper had joined the navy. Mary Wellington and Carol Rupert were both busy with school, boyfriends, and plans to marry soon.

When he could escape from chores, John shut the door to his room and wrote. Four distinct new poems emerged that vividly imagine the thoughts of human beings at moments of extreme crisis. "Railway Catastrophe" describes passengers on a train, drifting unconsciously through their lives until an impending derailment almost awakens them. In its fourth and final stanza, the poem captures the passengers' confusion just before the train crashes:

> Who are all these people and where did they come from,
> Think the smiling passengers. But the grin of disaster
> Freezes to their masks, rails cannot pierce their actual
>   darkness
> And the train on the rails is moving faster and faster.[56]

The passengers are "smiling," unhappy people, but the civilized "masks" they wear in their daily lives are suddenly shaken through the terror of death. The same week, he wrote "The Long Game," a poem in which "costumed children" discover they are in a parade that ends "treading among the dead" in the cemetery. In the final two quatrains, the speaker tries to explain his sense of misery as he blindly follows the children:

> We followed. Our blindfold gestures could not freeze
> A winter's logic, ambush tomorrow's smile.
> We gauged an era's insult with our thumbs
> As all the boundaries went down in drums.
>
> O were we wrong, child? On lawns of piety
> Throughout our land I see no suppers spread.
> And over the real grass of a fenceless cemetery
> Go the costumed children, treading among the dead.[57]

The poem wonders what has led to such a feeling of misery, suggesting that the "era" and "our land" are to blame. "We" share this modern distress, but only the speaker of the poem and the children ahead seem to be able to comprehend this unhappiness.

In early August, Ashbery wrote two new poems about an artist's muted power as a Cassandra-like visionary who can express our shared misery, but no one listens to or learns from him.[58] In his dark love lyric "Salvage from Love," the narrator describes a romantic entanglement through a series of disturbing images ("I dreamed of you last night: your breasts had eyes") and expressions of powerlessness ("Alone we find no right goal in an age of motive"). In the final stanza, a failed romantic union is all one can "salvage from love":

> Together nightmare love is the only end.
> Let it not interrupt the heart's clocked slumbers.
> O let no look but mine fail in your eyes.[59]

In "Dark River," the poet is completely alone, except for his words. He eventually drowns because even "his speech was no raft":

> The dark river passing overhead, or
> Passing of a dim keel, perceived by
> The sinking swimmer only. Thus the poet
> Approaches his casual zero.
>
> Suns, planets falling. As the poet went down
> Some tried not to drown
> Some begged the fallen features
> For a promise, for a tear.
> But his speech was no raft,
> Vowels lied to their paper.
>
> Swimmer, where are you now? And the slain
> Suicide fell forever
> From sun, water-lights, river.
> Officials now condemn that dangerous stream.
> But one who leaped its highest bridges
> Daily reshapes the vision of his fall
> In crumbling water: first stagger in surmise,

And blind smile canceling down the fatal vistas
To yawning tomorrow, the river of his name.[60]

In the final section, an objective speaker suggests that one who takes risks sees differently from others: "But one who leaped its highest bridges / Daily reshapes the vision of his fall." This "daily" work of the imagination brings "tomorrow." The poem expresses an artist's shifting vision as a crucial way of looking ahead, but the poet remains an isolated figure, a kind of unwanted prophet. In all four poems, Ashbery was investigating his chosen vocation with increasing attention, observing the parameters and possibilities for the poet writing in and about modern life.

Bill Haddock arrived in Pultneyville to spend the last week of August on vacation with the Ashbery family, and John asked for his opinion on his newest poems. All summer, the two had corresponded about poetry and painting. Haddock had also repeatedly apologized for his antics the previous school year and promised that they were over for good. They had even decided to room together at Deerfield in the fall. Haddock was so impressed with John's new poems that he asked if he could show them to his mother's friend Vicki Baum, a well-known writer whose novel had become Hollywood's *Grand Hotel* (1932). John was impressed by Haddock's family connection, which gave Bill an "even more glamorous air," and he was flattered by his praise. (Haddock later reported to John that Baum termed his poems "errant nonsense.")[61] A week later they moved together to an attractive, spacious room in Ball House. At first the arrangement promised to work well; they trusted each other. Haddock confided, as John had suspected, that he was attracted to men. During the day, they remained completely closeted, but late at night, lying in bed, they talked openly about art and sex, sweeping conversations in which both boys admitted intellectual ambitions and sexual fantasies, thoughts John had never shared with anyone before.[62]

Though they were initially close, tensions escalated between them. By the end of the first month together, his grandfather advised John to be "an agreeable roommate," to "keep . . . clothes and other possessions in order," and to "not let him outdo you in orderliness and good manners."[63] Soon, John described a worsening situation to Mary Wellington:

I room in what used to be the living room of a private house in Deerfield—along with another boy named Haddock. We get along rather well, seeing as we're roommates. We may be on good terms for a week, then on slowly increasing bad terms for about 5 days, and we generally end up in the note-writing stage for about 2 days. After that another week of harmony.[64]

"Harmony" ended when Haddock falsely accused John of smoking inside the room, a serious offense.[65] Then John discovered Haddock copying his schoolwork. His grandfather encouraged him to "just sit tight and keep good mannered and good tempered. After all it is only for a short period that you will have to endure imitation . . . life is full of situations that must be endured. It is usually more important to get through without engendering personal animosity."[66] The housemaster, Nathan West, got involved and recommended Haddock's expulsion because "I can't trust him."[67] Boyden refused, explaining that because Haddock's father pushed him mercilessly to get a competitive edge, he would mature more effectively at school.[68] John, meanwhile, joined the Drama Club's production of *Arsenic and Old Lace* as Martha Brewster, a spinster who cheerfully poisons (using wine laced with arsenic) elderly gentlemen

John Ashbery (standing) as the spinster Martha Brewster serving arsenic-laced wine to gentleman boarders, in *Arsenic and Old Lace*. In its December 9, 1944, issue, the *Deerfield Scroll* called the performance an "outstanding success."

boarders.[69] Haddock joined the play as well. Despite the tension, the play "was quite a hit," he told Mary Wellington.[70]

John requested a room change.[71] He also decided that he had waited long enough to see New York City. He planned his own "educational" trip at the beginning of Christmas vacation, taking the train to Grand Central, checking into the Hotel Roosevelt on East Forty-Fifth Street, and rushing to the storied Gotham Book Mart, at 51 West Forty-Seventh Street.[72] He found Marianne Moore's *Selected Poems* (1935). Rummaging in a bin, he discovered a small chapbook, *Poems*, by F. T. Prince, a poet of whom John had never heard, but whose verses he read in their entirety standing up. He bought both books with his limited funds.[73] For the next few days he traveled all over the city, visiting the Museum of Modern Art, the aquarium at Battery Park, and then meeting Gillett Griffin for dinner at a German restaurant and a trip to a print store. On consecutive nights, he and Gillett saw Broadway shows.[74] A week later, John gave Mary Wellington a blasé account of his adventure:

> We "did the town" in a modest way. We saw *Carmen Jones* and *The Late George Apley* and went to all the museums and art galleries (as we are both interested in art) besides seeing the usual sights.[75]

In fact, there were no "usual sights"; everything was thrillingly, breathlessly new. John liked the city so much, he posed in his letter as one who had already experienced it—the native city dweller he later admiringly declared "that rare bird, a born New Yorker."[76]

Sodus was comparatively melancholy. Elizabeth Ashbery's health continued to decline. After another operation, Addie Lawrence had to wear a colostomy bag, which she changed herself in a three-hour ritual every Sunday.[77] There was a huge blizzard at Christmas, and "the Graepers rented a horse and hitched him up to that old sleigh out in their barn," which was "lots of fun" and temporarily lifted everyone's spirits.[78] In January, John moved into a single in the large, social senior dorm for his final semester. A classmate noted the arrival in his diary:

> Ashbery has moved in Spicer's old room. He is really awfully nice. But one element in the corridor . . . don't like him at all.

Of course he is effeminate and there have been rumors as to his being a homo; but until I have more obvious [*obvious* crossed out] conclusive proof I'm not going to hold that against him.[79]

The diary keeper was Richard Alexander Gregg, known as "Sandy," the *Deerfield Scroll*'s literary editor. Sandy was a modest, bright fellow poet with blondish-red hair, widely spaced teeth, and a gangly gait. He loved learning languages, reading cartoons, and making up limericks on the spot. John impressed him a few days after his arrival by reciting every single student's home address: "John Ashbery I have discovered has a photographic memory."[80] Soon after, having closely read the entire student population's home addresses, John also changed his permanent address listing from Maple Avenue to Lake Road, the wealthier sounding of Ashbery Farm's intersecting roads.[81]

They applied to Harvard together. Sandy was a legacy student and expected to attend.[82] The previous summer, John had met a couple in Pultneyville from Cambridge, Massachusetts, who praised the school and the city.[83] He had always assumed he would go to the University of Rochester, because of family connections, but the idea of moving near a bigger city was much more appealing. He discussed his idea with Frank Boyden, who immediately mailed in a letter of recommendation:

Sandy Gregg in his Deerfield yearbook photo, 1945

John L. Ashbery is a boy of the highest character, quiet but pleasant personality, and excellent scholastic ability. He comes to us a year ago last fall from the Sodus, New York, High School with an extremely fine record, and we have been well satisfied with his academic work here and also with his adjustment to boarding school life. His first year here we found him quite shy and retiring, but this year he has developed very satisfactorily in his relationships with his classmates. He is strongly inclined along artistic lines and has done some very interesting work in our studio and is also very interested in writing and hopes eventually to make writing his life work. I am glad to recommend him strongly for admission to Harvard.[84]

A personal recommendation from Boyden to Harvard was almost enough on its own to guarantee admission, but John and Sandy waited nervously for their acceptances, which finally arrived.[85] To his own family, John downplayed his excitement. Henry Lawrence, though, was characteristically encouraging, reminding him that if he did not like Harvard, he could easily transfer to Cornell or Rochester, or "you may be much pleased in which case you will know that you have made no mistake."[86] His grandfather was more worried that Harvard "is beyond the capacity of the family purse."[87] When Claude Allen, Deerfield's long-serving registrar, stopped John one afternoon in the middle of campus to say that "we could probably get you a scholarship, if you needed one," John, mortified that anyone might overhear, declined on the spot.[88]

John read modern poetry with ferocious intensity all spring. He articulated his newest ideas in "Recent Tendencies in Poetry," an essay for senior English.[89] John argued that "poetry of today . . . has the smallest audience of almost any period since the Middle Ages, yet . . . is *good* poetry" because

it shows an awareness and an intellectual responsibility which one might say has been rarely equaled in any era. Its high caliber and its extreme complexity may both be accounted for by the fact that the poet, neglected by a society of which he is a member whether he wishes it or not, turns from the outside world as inspiration for his poetry, and feeds on the process and intricacies of his own mind. Poetry becomes then highly personal and highly original, but due to the unavoidable membership in society it frequently has social themes, which are, however, treated from a purely personal standpoint. Thus the poems are complex because they spring from a mind which has been made complex by its double existence—its social responsibility and its inward enigma.[90]

He contended that T. S. Eliot's poetry was responsible for a shift from the limited perfections of imagism to a new poetry of the mind that remained fascinated by, but apart and critical of, the world. While Eliot made poetry modern, Ashbery declared, it was actually the works of younger poets "like Eliot in their awareness, but who have styles completely their own," such as Auden, Spender, Warren, Tate, and Ransom, who were now moving poetry in more exciting directions. These are poets, he continued, whose works "point the way toward a fuller realization of the powers latent in the human mind." Ashbery placed his own burgeoning poetic interests directly into this dynamic poetic tradition.[91] He concluded that the next generation of poets—and implicitly, he would be a leader among them—will "go even further in the fascinating and vital occupation of self-expression and self-analysis," producing a "highly personal and highly original" art from "the intricacies of his own mind."

He took on this "vital occupation" in two new poems, "Lost Cove" and "Seasonal," written over his brief spring break at a friend's house.[92] George Tuttle, his sole companion from their lonely year in Delano House, invited him to stay at his family's nearby rundown farm, a place that reminded John of home. John already felt melancholy, for he had recently fallen in love with Phillips Van Dusen, a popular, handsome, and straight classmate who showed no interest. For several days, John spent dull hours with George (and two other classmates) watching movies, reading, and listening to the radio. On April 12 they heard the announcer describe FDR's death, and John lay on the floor all day listening to news programs recounting Roosevelt's twelve years in office. Ashbery's new poems emerged from these dreary, quiet days. In the six-stanza "Lost

Cove," the longest poem he had ever written, his lost childhood world
of trees and coves served as a backdrop for new ideas about intimacy
and loss:

> Where the sun delved in trees and darkly
> Faltered, we made our stopping place
> And that day swam off the naked beaches
> Or pried in the swamp for specimens
> Or simply tanned and talked on the rocks.
>
> But our words were not ours, our eyes had frozen
> Dark when we saw this place, our faces assumed
> The look of whatever we happened to see,
> And less alone in the marshy wood
> We grew apart, from tree to tree
>
> Further, but as from a single stem.
> I knew that your eyes had this in mind
> For when the trees cast their rings and spots
> Of light, it was your eyes that said:
> <u>We know the secret you walk with here</u>
>
> And weight of leaves around my head
> And far off the waves insisting
> Was death, was death. For fated to stand
> Apart till the final junction of hearts
> We cannot call the time or place fortunate
>
> That chances these intimacies of flesh.
> Forcing the last ounce of legal pain
> From the child's song, the field in nostalgia.
> We know how dangerous the task, flesh and stalk wither
> Together, once bound in ritual
>
> And each foreign shape is earth's
> Promised enemy of love's stature. Night fell,

Phil Van Dusen, a classmate at Deerfield

We hurried to leave our cove. The trees
Tore our hearts back with them from the canoe
And the boughs bled bright with our sacrifice.

The poem anticipated his future, more concise love lyric "Some Trees" (1948). As a young boy playing with friends in Pultneyville, trees had been their castles and kingdoms. His childhood love for trees was vulnerable to all sorts of dangers, including the chores and responsibilities of adulthood, which "tore" children from their imaginations. He could still remember very clearly what it had been like to feel another way about trees and about other hidden recesses that made parts of his childhood mysterious and enchanting. Growing up, "we hurried to leave our cove"; in this inevitable act of maturing, one "sacrifices" the self formed in one's childhood, and the poem mourned the loss. Only love, the poem suggested, could ever restore, even for a moment, "the canoe / And the boughs," a phrase that suggested the safe shelter he had felt in his finest summers in Pultneyville.

In "Lost Cove," the things one has loved always retain a measure of that enchantment; in the concise "Seasonal," love's passing is "a fact" and not an enchantment, but no less powerful:

Though we seek always the known absolute
Of all our days together, love will not occur
For us. Love is a fact
Beyond the witches' wood of facts that is
Our sorcery's domain. And though we may
Charm lion into squirrel, push back the sea,
Love is made outlaw, set beyond all art,
The ultimate error of our reasoning.

But when I see you walking, or catch your face
Edged with the season's most erratic leaves
Love grows superfluous, and I look at you
As I would look at flowers. Our only need
Is still the understanding of silences,
The sympathy of darkness for the seed.[93]

Here, love is "set beyond all art," and it does not make one see, hear, taste, and touch with greater sensitivity. Instead, "I look at you / As I would look at flowers," a phrase that describes an aesthetic, not a romantic, love of beauty. Yet there is still a "need" for a deeper connection, a desire for "the understanding of silences" and "sympathy," which the idea of love provokes. In these "highly personal and highly original" lyrics, which John hoped were as good as he felt they might be, he described love's powerful capacity to transform one's thinking.

Ashbery returned from his vacation to an unexpected literary opportunity. Boyden arranged for the best students in English V—Ashbery, Haddock, and just three other boys—to participate in an inaugural "special poetry class," to be held at the home of local poet and retired Amherst professor David Morton during the final six weeks of the semester.[94] Morton had convinced the reluctant headmaster to hire him as the school's first "Resident Writer."[95] Excited about this new opportunity, John read Morton's first book, *Ships in Harbour* (1921), concluding that he did not admire its bland, New England sensibility but looked forward anyway to studying poetry with someone who had been published in *Poetry* and other professional literary magazines.[96] Encouraged by Morton's invitation to read student work, John typed his best poems—the recent "Lost Cove," "Seasonal," and several earlier poems—and submitted them for feedback. Morton handed them back without saying a word. Although John felt his work always needed further revision, he was shocked that Morton had found them so terrible that they did not even merit a response.[97]

In fact, Morton loved the poems. He liked them so much that he immediately recommended their author, whom he believed to be Bill Haddock, to *Poetry* magazine as having a "mystical imagination," a poetic voice of "authentic eloquence" with "contours and texture and music." Early in the course, Haddock had secretly submitted handwritten copies of a handful of Ashbery's poems to Morton, who was so impressed that he sent a letter to Marion Strobel, an editor at *Poetry*, suggesting she publish them:

> Here are three poems by a quite young hitherto unpublished poet whose work interests me a good deal. I begged these three from him after making him work them over with a view to sending them on to you—in the thought that the individual quality of his somewhat mystical imagination might interest you, as well as a kind of authentic eloquence that sounds here and there.
>
> I'm trying to get him started in publication. It will not be easy, I think. The slick conventional will not be interested, of course. But it seems to me his work has its own peculiar contours and texture and music. . . . I believe in his work, and I hope you may find room in your liking for something, here. He needs to have the stimulus of publication about now.
>
> If you find it possible to take something, I think it would be fine if you communicated direct with him. If not, will you reply to me, instead?[98]

Marion Strobel responded directly to Haddock, accepting "Poem"— John had already changed its title to "Seasonal" in a later draft Haddock had not seen—and suggesting minor changes to "Lost Cove."[99] Haddock, thrilled but also probably frightened that his deception might be traceable in a national publication that he knew John read, took nearly a month to compose a typed reply:

> I hope you will pardon my tardiness in answering your very welcome letter of June fifth accepting POEM for publication.

It was very kind of Mr. Morton to submit some of my work for your consideration. However, the work which he chose to send you I did not feel was the best I could offer, with the possible exception of POEM. I will be very glad to work on the fifth stanza of LOST COVE and send you the result as soon as possible, but I would much prefer that you first consider the other poems which I will submit for the first time along with the rewritten LOST COVE.

Enclosed you will find a few short autobiographical notes. Please note particularly that I wish my work to appear under the name of JOEL MICHAEL SYMINGTON, which is the name I was christened. Since then I have been legally adapted by my step-father.[100]

Haddock's lies snowballed, for he was not "christened" Joel Michael Symington nor afterward adopted (or "adapted," as he had mistakenly typed). He wrote to *Poetry* again requesting more time.[101] The poems were already in page proofs (under Haddock's given name) for the August 1945 issue, but the magazine agreed to wait.[102] Haddock submitted five of his own poems, which the magazine rejected as "not quite sharp enough."[103] Then Haddock agreed to publish "Poem" ("Seasonal") and "Lost Cove," and they went to press as the work of "Joel Michael Symington"—for his pseudonym, he had borrowed the surname of Deerfield's senior class vice president (and future member of Congress)—in the November 1945 issue. Throughout these secret negotiations, Haddock remained very friendly to Ashbery, giving no indication of his deceitfulness.

John was distracted in any case by intensifying anxiety that he was going to be "expelled for homosexuality."[104] All spring, he had been keeping a journal that detailed his feelings for Phil Van Dusen, locking the book each night in a private cabinet assigned to him in the main building, "one of the very few spots on campus where I could actually lock something up." Just before graduation, Boyden appointed a small committee of students to clean up campus, including emptying lockers.[105] When the boys handed John his diary, which was the only item he had kept in there, he felt immediately afraid and asked if they had read it. They said no, "but in a way that convinced me they had." A few days earlier, John had sent a love letter to Van Dusen, who had replied with a handwritten note "warning of the dangers of homosexuality" and "imploring" John not to pursue "such a path." Ashbery later reflected that "I viewed his letter as kind, in its way," but he also feared that Van Dusen, a member of his venerable family, or Boyden's committee might use evidence against him to insist that John be expelled. John immediately destroyed the diary.[106] As his family arrived for graduation festivities, though, he awaited his fate.

Shortly before graduation, Chet wrote to Boyden: "Thanking you again for all that you and Mrs. Boyden have done for John. Our only regret is that we do not have more boys to send to Deerfield."[107] This unassuming lament for Richard was powerful, for it was Chet's sole written statement of his private grief.[108] For nearly twenty years, he sent Boyden a fresh turkey and a crate of apples each year at Thanksgiving.[109] Along with every gift was a letter, in which Chet boasted of John's accomplishments more openly and proudly than he did to anyone else, "because I know you have an interest in your boys."[110] The opportunity to communicate his pleasure in his son's achievements to someone who prized Chet's interests in farming and sports far above John's interests in art and literature, and yet who understood both, motivated Chet to stay in

John Ashbery in February 1945

touch with Boyden for the rest of his life. In response to Harvard College's request for information about his son, Chet highly praised the high school: "John has always been somewhat shy, which has made it hard for him to make friends. His two years at Deerfield have done a great deal to counteract that difficulty."[111] At John's graduation weekend, Chet's sense of loss was for both sons, for he would never learn as much about John's life from anyone else again.

Despite his weeks of fear, John collected the French Prize—which he clinched by delivering an oral presentation in which he analyzed each classmate's personality by the necktie he wore—and graduated without incident. At home, he immediately sent nostalgic letters to Deerfield friends: "two days out and already I feel as if I'd been away from it two years. I miss it a lot and all the kids in it."[112] His former Sodus classmates had plans to enter the army, to get married—or both. He knew his life looked odd to them, but he felt rather pleased by those differences:

> Incidentally, I've beaten everybody here that I've played tennis with, which has added a slight continental athletic torch to John

July 4, 1945, family picnic in Pultneyville. *From left to right*: Carolyn (Connie) Graeper (at head of table), Addie Lawrence, Debby Taft (child), Henry Lawrence and Helen Ashbery (standing), Ottilie "Teal" Rupert (in front of Henry), Olga Graeper (in front of Helen), Pede Rupert, John Ashbery, Larry Taft, Carol Rupert, unidentified person with back to camera, and Grandma Ashbery (Elizabeth Koehler Ashbery).

Ashbery that queer duck who left Sodus a couple years ago to go to some private school. Guess the high school wasn't good enough for him. They say he's goin' to Harvard. Well, that is a good place for him, lot of queers there. He always was pretty bright—too bright for his own good, some say. (The foregoing just about sums up local opinion of me.)

For two weeks he lounged in bed and read: Elizabeth Bowen's *The House in Paris*; Bacon's *Essays*; the *Sodus Record*; and Joyce's *Ulysses*, recommending to Sandy Gregg that he start the novel—"You ought to: It's *dirty*!"[113] Poised to leave for Harvard by the beginning of July, John wrote to Mary Wellington to share his news. He self-deprecatingly described what he now looked like: "seedy and gangling, with a limburger complexion and dandruff, good-looking only from certain angles in poorly-lit rooms." He requested a new picture of her because the "quite old" photograph he still kept of them together was from a photo booth in 1939. Although he had heard "what a hole" Harvard was and felt "petrified at the thought of entering that den of sin and corruption," he also precisely expressed the necessary survival skills he had attained at Deerfield. With modest self-confidence, he succinctly avowed, "I suppose I'll come out of it intact."[114]

6

"Undergraduate Reflections"

1945–1947

John set his sights on finding a poetry mentor at Harvard. He scoured the catalogue and chose the young poet and English professor Theodore Spencer as his adviser, explaining to Sandy Gregg:

> [H]e is a top-flight modern poet and I intend to get very palsy with him so he'll invite me over for a cup of Herba Maté, glance at the modestly proffered armful of poetry I shove in his face, and rush to phone Simon and Schuster screaming "God! Talent!" Just like our greasy chum Mr. Morton didn't.[1]

Courses started July 9. Many more freshmen than usual were enrolled in summer school in order to matriculate before turning eighteen. John's sense of "perplexity and anxiety about the draft" was shared by nearly every student he met.[2] The war had largely emptied Harvard of upperclassmen; dorms and clubs remained shuttered. John planned trips to Boston with Sandy instead: "I see we don't have anything after 3 o'clock the first Saturday—would you like to go out to Revere Beach (the amusement park)? I've got a map of Boston and I think I could get there." He had ideas for other trips, too: "I'm told Mrs. Jack Gardner's house is well worth seeing."[3] Classes were fine, but John found everything else even more appealing. Here was "a bigger world, literally and figuratively."[4]

He wrestled, however, with the "black cloud over my head" that he

had brought with him from Sodus.[5] A week before leaving, his mother
found a letter he had just written to Brute Wilson. In intimate and bawdy
detail, he described his attraction to his Deerfield classmate Phil Van
Dusen and his fears that Boyden knew about it and was going to expel
him. Out of practice being at home, he had thoughtlessly left the letter
unsealed on his bedside table before visiting his cousin Wallace in
Buffalo, realizing his error only on the bus ride. He was sure his mother
would see it, and he could only imagine the explosion that would occur
if she showed it to his father. Increasingly panicked, he talked at length
with Wallace, telling him for the first time that he was attracted to men.
Wallace casually responded that John should not worry because "the
full force of the sexual drive hasn't hit you yet."[6] (Was it possible that he
would simply outgrow his homosexuality? Since his cousin was five years
older, John briefly entertained the possibility that he might be right.)
Back home, he knew by the distressed look on his mother's face that she
had read every word. She waited until they were alone in the car and then
"begged" him to stay near home for college because Harvard "was in a
big city and would be too full of temptations."[7] The more she talked, the
more hysterical she became. John made her promise not to tell his father,
and after her outburst, she never mentioned the subject to him again.[8]

Three years later, in a draft of John's unpublished short story "The
Daunted," Wilfred expresses anger at his mother for her lack of understanding. Ashbery dramatizes the mother's narrow-mindedness and the
boy's hurt feelings:

> "Why do they dislike you here?" his mother asked him once,
> having sensed this a few minutes after arriving at his school . . .
> Wilfred goggled . . . his eyes at first seeming to turn inward and
> finally presenting her with a hard and inscrutable glare. "We
> keep to ourselves, that's all. We have our different interests."
> "It's not as if you played with dolls," his mother went on. Then,
> noticing how angry he had grown, she finished, "still, I suppose
> you're happy or you'd get out and mingle."[9]

In the summer of 1945, however, John did not feel "angry" at his
mother for her disappointment and hysteria, but responsible. His feelings of guilt overwhelmed him during his last few days with her before

college. When his parents drove him to nearby Newark station for the direct train to Boston, he left feeling lonely and miserable.[10]

He spent his eighteenth birthday alone. He heard that a B-25 bomber "battling heavy fog" had crashed into the north side of the Empire State Building in the morning, igniting a huge fire that killed fourteen people.[11] The frightening accident seemed like a bad omen and cast a pall over the day. Later that night, Sandy Gregg and some neighbors invited him over to their dorm room for poker and a pitcher of Cuba Libre made of "second-rate rum and Pepsi." By midnight, John was so drunk that he staggered back to his room, vomited, and passed out. For nearly a year afterward, he could not stand even the smell of alcohol. His dorm room in Winthrop House, Gore F-45, was a grand single with high ceilings, a fireplace, and two large windows overlooking the courtyard, but the stench from becoming so suddenly ill, despite his purchase of "multiple Airwick air fresheners," clung to the floors.[12]

On August 6, Harry Truman announced that the United States had dropped a bomb on Hiroshima and that Japan could expect a "rain of ruin" if it did not agree to end the war.[13] Nine days later, John, with Leslie Wallwork, the most outgoing of his new group of friends, walked from Cambridge to Boston to see crowds spilling onto the streets celebrating the war's end. Late in the afternoon, they bypassed throngs for a cool, dark theater, Judy Garland, and her new film, *Ziegfeld Follies*. Summer session ended, and everyone scattered, but John balked at going home. His notebook was full of drawings, sketches, and occasional notes on Spinoza, Hume, and Kant ("Kant stinks"), just enough to earn him a C in his summer classes on modern philosophy and French reading.[14] He enjoyed his composition course taught by graduate student Raymond Joel Dorius much more, and he stayed in touch with Dorius for a decade.[15] His A freed him from having to take another required English writing course, and he signed up for Theodore Spencer's fall semester lyric poetry class instead. Despite his initial goals for college, he had neither met Spencer yet nor written a single new poem.

He still thought about Phil Van Dusen constantly, though they had not talked since graduation. These fantasies helped distract him from more pressing anxieties. By October, when John arrived at his Selective Service examination at an army building in nearby Winthrop, his apprehension about the draft had intensified to the point that he felt physically ill. Another young man sat in the waiting room. "You go to Harvard?" the man queried. "Yes," John answered. "Do you sleep there?" the man asked. John wondered if the man was trying to pick him up, and the strange conversation gave the proceedings a surreal air. After more than three hours of physical and mental examinations, he was taken into a room by the head psychiatrist, who seemed like "a nice man." He asked if John sometimes felt so nervous that he had uncontrollable diarrhea. After rendering a diagnosis of "anxiety neuroses," the doctor immediately assigned him 4-F status (a classification for mental or physical deficiencies).[16]

John wrote the thirteen-line "Prayer" shortly after. A sympathetic observer describes a fragile world:

> Some rode forth to fight and were killed immediately,
> Some remained on the hills to tend the beasts and fires.
> The aged offered prayers to a God
> Who had stopped believing in himself. There was
> Little to do. The trees flamed and fell,
> The sky broke like an egg.
> 				Only remember
> That men fought gallantly, though their defeat
> Have been ungraceful, and that the proud lovers
> Ate out each other's hearts, and that the rejected
> Wrote of the loved in journals. From the cube's rim
> Crawl to the colder center of your luck, and there O send up
> The phoenix from the ashes of a poem.[17]

In this mythic modern landscape, people are engaged in crises so massive that God has lost faith in his own powers. "Trees" fall. Even the "sky" falls. The second part of the poem includes a memory of an earlier, "gallant" period. Even then, people hurt one another. In pain, "the rejected / Wrote of the loved in journals," and hoped to reach, at least, "the colder center of your luck." Both these phrases referred to recent emotional crises, including Ashbery's destroyed Deerfield journal and his Selective Service examination. (Sandy, who was two weeks younger than John, had been less lucky. Drafted for at least eighteen months, he was about to leave college to serve in the army.) Although the poem describes a world of intense pain and loss, it ends with an uplifting image of a phoenix rising "from the ashes of a poem." This final line, with its pun on Ashbery's own name (he often signed letters "ashes," a favorite nickname) highlights his ambition even in the face of a serious personal struggle.[18]

John shared only excitement about his new college life with his family. His grandfather felt "much relieved and pleased" that John seemed happy: "You have made a good start acquiring friends. . . . Harvard is no mistake. Its only fault is largeness with correspondingly large competition. But it has correspondingly larger opportunities. . . . Go to it."[19] His cousin Wallace and Wallace's mother, Norma, drove from Buffalo to Harvard to visit, the first members of his family to do so. They toured Cambridge and Boston together, saw a comedy on Park Street, talked about Wallace's study of symbolic logic at the University of Buffalo, and spent time with John's new friends. Besides Leslie Wallwork and Sandy Gregg, John had become especially close to three others: Bubsy Zimmerman (later known as Barbara Epstein, one of the founders of *The New York Review of Books*), an independent seventeen-year-old Radcliffe student from Boston with a distinctive laugh, bohemian taste in clothing, a love of poetry, and a withered arm, which she kept hidden by angling her body, something John immediately observed about her

"The four amigos," as Sandy Gregg called them: Sandy Gregg, Les Brown, Bob Hunter, and John Ashbery at Harvard University in 1945

but never mentioned; Les Brown, a dour, well-read son of an English professor who spent his childhood listening in as Robert Penn Warren, John Berryman, and others held forth at his parents' art "salon," in their house near the University of Minnesota; and Bob Hunter, a gentle, wry, whip-smart writer from South Dakota who had graduated from the Blake School in Minneapolis with Les Brown and Leslie Wallwork.[20] They started to meet daily for afternoon tea at the Window Shop.

Shortly after Thanksgiving with Sandy Gregg's family, John picked up the current issue of *Poetry* and, in confusion, read his own poems, "Lost Cove" and "Poem" ("Seasonal"), published by "Joel Michael Symington." Astonished by this theft, John knew immediately who was responsible. He had been surprised to see Bill Haddock at Harvard over the summer, as Bill had originally accepted a spot at Princeton the previous spring. As John hunted for him across campus in the November chill, he felt sick. The memory of David Morton's cold response to his poems, and the curt note—"sorry"—received from the *Poetry* magazine editor when he had submitted those same poems over the summer suddenly made sense.[21] He realized now that both Morton and the *Poetry* editor had assumed that *he* was the plagiarist. He believed "my career as a poet had ended before it began."[22] When John found Haddock in the middle of campus, he screamed at him. Haddock admitted everything,

Wallace Ashbery Jr. at his graduation from the University of Buffalo, where he studied philosophy

was abjectly apologetic, and promised to write *Poetry* magazine immediately to tell them what he had done. The next day, he showed John the
letter he claimed to have already sent to *Poetry*.[23]

Two weeks later, John opened a letter from his mother informing
him that his cousin Wallace was dead. There had been a bizarre accident at his University of Buffalo dorm, she said. Wallace fell on a stair-
well in the early morning and hit his head on concrete steps, and no one
had found him in time.[24] Just a month before, he and John had parted
casually, with plans to see each other soon. Such a sudden, unexpected
death of a young man (he was only twenty-two years old) felt more like a
disappearance. There was no funeral. An expensive call to his parents
to express his shock and sorrow was out of the question. John wrote
"Local Anesthesia":

> The diseased nurse and the sterile patient know
> How love may contract in death, and the delicate sickness
> Cherished in the bone, expand to corruptible tissue
> In the end for which time has made no allowances.
>
> Unhappy often, by friends lured away
> From what is splendid or difficult, which forever seems
> The terrible cat that pretends to ignore its prey
> We live: from the burnt out, wishful autumns
>
> Pass on to the winter's maze, hung with lights and smoke
> And move without pain and without direction
> As under the implements of sanity—the crutch, the spoon
> The dying patient smiles at the enormous joke
>
> Recalling the phrases of love that last, frightful summer,
> That yield to no meaning now. The chill bacterial smell
> Unnoticed at first, grows, and the evil scalpel
> Dredges from the flesh its secret, innocent tumor.[25]

Death is especially horrifying because it is the common, shared
experience "we live with." We feel terror watching "friends lured
away," helplessly "prey" to the "terrible cat" that looks for any oppor-

tunity to pounce. In the final stanza, a memory of "that last, fright-
ful summer" is a reminder that "phrases of love" mean nothing after
death. Recollections of the shock and horror John experienced when
Richard died, and again after Wallace's sudden death, lead to a description of a terrible sight: a tumor being pulled from flesh (an operation
recently performed on Addie Lawrence to remove several new cancerous tumors), the intimation of another death. The poem offers no
comfort or sentimentality about death, but only the realization that it
is random—an "enormous joke."

When Haddock, in a further effort to make amends, invited John
to fly home with him to Pennsylvania before the start of spring semester, John accepted. Why not? He increasingly believed that life was a
game of chance from which he should occasionally benefit, and he had
never flown in an airplane before. (The visit was brief and pleasant.
Haddock's parents were "very nice," especially his mother.)[26] When
he returned to Harvard, John moved into a clean, newly painted single
in Dunster House. The farthest house from campus, situated right on the
river, Dunster sported a lit tower that served as a beacon for students
at night.

The buzz on campus grew as GIs returned and more dorms reopened.
On March 5, 1946, John and Bob Hunter watched Bubsy Zimmerman
march by the Widener Library steps, chanting in a large protest rally
after Winston Churchill delivered his "Iron Curtain" speech in Fulton,
Missouri.[27] Eight days later, an even bigger crowd assembled to hear
thirty-nine-year-old W. H. Auden read his poems.[28] As nearly nine
hundred students crammed into the assigned room, Professor Harry
Levin announced that the event would have to move to the much larger
New Lecture Hall.[29] Infuriated that he had to stand at the back of the
first space, John raced with his copy of Auden's Collected Poems (1945),
just purchased from the Personal Book Shop in Boston, to a seat in the
front row of the new one. At the end of the reading, he asked Auden to
autograph his book.[30] A year later, when they met again and Auden, of
course, had no recollection of their previous encounter, John felt disappointed: "[O]ne is just out of the running these days if one can't count
Auden as a personal friend, I've decided."[31]

Hearing Auden galvanized him to read and write more, but he felt
frustrated and stuck.[32] Ashbery jotted "Pastoral" in the back of an old

notebook.[33] In the final two verse paragraphs, he retold the Orpheus myth as a cyclical, unending drama of love and death:

How do I die
How often, thrusting
Your unwanted body
Among the grass-spears, have I wept
To call it back

and slept where coupling field-mice
obscene birds of the night
Bathed my sleep in terror
The village, its quaint poplars
Have sunk behind the mill
Long your face burned in the sky
But my death is mine

In an essay for Frederick Deknatel's "Modern Art" course he was writing at the same time, Ashbery criticized the work of recent surrealists as too logical and limited:

Dalí . . . is unwittingly killing the movement by bringing the idea of surrealism to a logical conclusion. Take for instance *The Persistence of Memory*; though Surrealist paintings are supposed to have no meaning, this one obviously does . . . Dalí breaks down the frail barriers between the "subconscious" paintings and allegory—showing that nothing can exist without an objective meaning. Which is why surrealism, interesting as it is, is not *the* escape. If art is to flee the external world, it cannot do it with the aid of the surrealists.[34]

He wanted art to move beyond the limitations of "objective meaning," but he was unsure how to engineer his own "escape" from these same limitations.

John dreaded spending an entire summer in Sodus. His transition home was bumpy: "since retiring to this fortress of tranquility I have done little else but read, eat, and sleep, usually to a constant obligato of 'John, <u>will</u> you mow that lawn!' "[35] Bob Hunter promised to write from South Dakota, and John deluged him with letters because of the quality of his replies: "a new experience, unequalled even by Henry James in his more virtuoso moments."[36] Bob worked at his family's stone quarry, lived at home, and read in his spare time; John did the same but complained bitterly about interruptions from daily chores "until the 'churry season' (local pronunciation) reaches its long awaited close."[37] He drew a droll picture of his home life for Bob: "your <u>quatrain</u> . . . was very clever—in fact I read it to my parents, who registered amusement."[38] His mother seemed to have forgotten her anger at John from the previous summer, but his father was so gruff and cold to him that he wondered if she had shared his letter. (Helen told him shortly after John left for college. Extremely upset, Chet drove alone to see Philip Rupert in Rochester, and they spoke for over an hour standing in the Ruperts' kitchen.)[39]

John announced to surprised friends that "I have gotten religious all of a sudden."[40] He blamed his new passion on his recent reading, which included T. S. Eliot, the Bible, and "Hindu philosophy . . . *A Passage to India, The Waves* (Virginia Woolf—it stinks) . . . *The Bostonians* by James." He admired Forster's *A Passage to India* as "one of the best books I've ever read—in fact parts of it made me ecstatic—especially the big religious shindig at the end."[41] He continued to send ribald poems ("Virtue / Won't hirtue / But vice / Is nice") and notes ("P.S. Don't forget to send for our <u>free</u> booklet, 'Sex <u>Can</u> Be fun'") to Bob, and he also promised that his religious exploration "will pass."[42] Over a month later, however, he reported that "I still feel quite religious, and probably will when I get back to Cambridge, so watch out. I mean, there must be a <u>reason</u> for everything, even for evolution."[43]

In the throes of this religious feeling, he composed a new, lyrical poem, "A Sermon: Amos 8:11–14," which he liked but that still did not exhaust his curiosity about the consequences of desire.[44] He vigorously defended his religious interests to his increasingly impatient friends:

> I never mentioned Christianity—in fact I perhaps had no special religion in mind, though Christianity may perhaps prove the best. . . . [T]he idea of a personal God with whom everyone "has a chance"—no matter how weak, depraved, selfish, cold,

preyed upon and preying on he is (I think I am all of these) intrigues me.[45]

Bob suspected that John's flirtation with religion was primarily a desire to resolve "the vast contradictions that existed within his soul."[46] John argued that it was even more self-interested; at the very least, he said, it would "be a pity to be caught on the losing team on the Day of Atonement."[47] Beneath his jokes, however, was a serious fear that "in the long run I may not achieve the goal of a creative artist I have set myself, or even succeed in becoming a genuine person."[48] He was eager to resolve a conflict he felt between his life and art. He complained that "people talk about the lost generation and corrupt modern civilization—things are this way because people are always trying to be sincere and finding it is physically impossible, don't you agree?"[49] He was asking himself how to live freely in the world and still find ways to write about it.

The "strange melancholy" he felt all summer made him especially eager to "plunge . . . back into the Harvard routine."[50] "Fiddling" with the Harvard catalogue, he contemplated courses in Slavic or "Greek . . . so that I will be able to write poems with little Greek quotations at the top like T. S. Eliot."[51] As the start of John's sophomore year drew closer, he had an "apocalyptic flash . . . that I am badly read."[52] He searched for a course on Pope, Swift, Dryden, or Spenser. (As a senior, he finally took a year-long Spenser tutorial.) On the one hand, he wished to "go into retirement in a delightful inner world," and do nothing but read and write, but he felt "always dependent on my friends for ideas, entertainment, and affection."[53] He arrived at his Dunster House dorm room (G-46) to discover no chance for either. A stranger, an upper-crust returning GI from Boston, who introduced himself as Abbot Montague Geer, lay on a newly installed bunk bed in John's former single. They were immediately uneasy roommates: "I continue to lead a monastic existence, hardly disturbed by the presence of Geer, who makes no demands on one's mental or conversational powers."[54]

In fact, John kept his distance. In October, he and Dick George, a classmate in Dunster House, began a brief romance, his first sexual relationship at Harvard. Shortly after, John and Norman Steed, Dick's handsome roommate, started a more serious relationship. Norman referred to himself as "gay," a term that John had heard used in that way for the first time only recently, during an anonymous sexual encounter in Harvard Square. Norman was from nearby Newton, knew Boston's nightlife well, and introduced John to several gay bars in the area, including the Chess Room in the Hotel Touraine, John's favorite, which had an appealing old genteel décor. As he spent more time with Norman and other new gay friends, John pulled himself away from his former group.[55] He hid his identity as a gay man from his straight friends, writing to Sandy Gregg, who was still away in the army, that

> I got a note . . . last week inviting me to eat dinner in Kirkland, so I went over there when what to my wondering eyes should appear but a gathering of fairies from far and near, all drinking cocktails and worshipping some ballet dancers who had appeared on the scene. Eeek! There wasn't a single heterosexual there; I foolishly asked, "Aren't there any women?" and someone retorted "Women's place is in the house." I hastily made my adieux.[56]

To maintain two separate identities, however, was difficult in the small Harvard literary world. John felt the strain, but he could not tell the truth about what was happening to him. He included his new poem draft, "Point of Departure," in the letter:

> The planes of light and dark
> Lock on a hurrying man
> And the seasons run together
> Like the fingers of a hand
> Framing his little street: the leaves
> Hiss, It is time to go, and the pale
> Snow descends like a benison
> Upon the placid town.

A few weeks later, he changed the end of this first stanza to "the consoling / Snow descends like a benison / On the afflicted town." *Afflicted* was the word John had always used to describe what felt to him like the burden of his homosexuality. In the poem, "seasons" change, and though dangers still "hiss" nearby, "snow descends," bringing with it a sense of peace. To a sensitive reader such as Sandy, this revised version of the poem would have offered a quietly momentous confirmation that John was gay. Bob Hunter, who had been observing John's struggles all semester with compassion, sent him a note to say that he could date anyone he wanted, and he hoped they would remain friends. When he accompanied John home to Sodus for Thanksgiving, he felt shocked by Chet's "angry" behavior toward his son. As soon as they left the farm for New York City, Bob verbally reiterated his unconditional support for his friend, and John cried.[57]

He moved out of Geer's room. Leslie Wallwork (G-14) invited him to stay. Although Leslie's noisy, messy, flamboyantly gay style became "very trying" at times, it was preferable to Geer's insulting silence.[58] Leslie was also supportive of John's emotional dramas that spring. He and Norman Steed broke up after John discovered he was having an affair with Bill Haddock. Shortly after, John began a new relationship, with Dick Shevlin, a handsome local sailor whom he met at the Silver Dollar bar in Boston. Homosexuality was grounds for expulsion at Harvard, and no overnight guests of any kind were allowed in dorms. John's room was on the first floor, directly across from the building manager's room, so Dick snuck out John's window late each night.[59] He began to get a reputation: "I don't give a healthy damn. . . . I have been living rather dangerously of late . . . feel saturated with vice." He felt ill and

Bob Hunter, John, and Helen Ashbery at Niagara Falls, Thanksgiving 1946. Photograph taken by Chet Ashbery.

"depressed."[60] Helen Ashbery wrote with more bad news. John's grand-mother Elizabeth Ashbery, very ill since her stroke three years earlier, had passed away.[61]

John found solace in reading poetry. The previous summer, he had written to Sandy Gregg, mentioning in a postscript that "you should investigate the poetry of Wallace Stephens (or Stevens, maybe) Unter-meyer's selections of it are poor!"[62] Between his uncertain spelling in the summer of 1946 and the spring of 1947, his appreciation for Stevens's work rapidly grew. This shift began when he discovered "The Emperor of Ice-Cream," a poem from Stevens's first book, *Harmonium*, which Untermeyer had not included in his *Anthology*.[63] The poem's subject is a dead woman lying on a bed "cold" and "dumb," but this fact is revealed primarily through other descriptive details. That a poem about the ordinary things we live with could be so powerfully about the strange experience of witnessing death was astounding to John; he felt as though he had finally discovered an extremely good version of what he had been long trying to express about the experience of death. When Wallace Stevens made a very rare public appearance at Harvard, on February 11, 1947, to read his poems, John was in the front row—a good thing, because "nobody could hear him beyond the fifth row."[64] He was sur-prised that Stevens "stood like a statue and wore an overcoat and scarf the entire time." Despite the nearly inaudible, stiff reading, John loved his poems even more after hearing them.[65]

Stevens's poetry was an exception; Ashbery often felt repelled by contemporary writers. The previous summer, Aldous Huxley's *Point Counter Point* (1928) had angered him as "somehow vulgar. It ain't art."[66] He increasingly looked to earlier models.[67] In his otherwise "dull" fall course, "English Literature: 1630 to Restoration," Kenneth Murdock remarked that "Donne is trying to discover a poetry that will fit the needs of men of his age."[68] In the class "English Literature Since 1890," Theodore Spencer argued that "Hardy, James, and Con-rad" tried "to investigate all of life." In John's favorite fall class, "The Epic," classicist John Finley emphasized "what in [literature] transcends history and is valid for all time."[69] In an essay on the *Inferno* that Finley judged "intelligent and well-written," Ashbery concluded that Dante's depiction of the relationship between contemporary experience and eternal truth was crucial for modern writers to understand:

Dante's value for us lies, then, not in his conception of the universe, for it is one in which we can no longer share, but beneath it. It is rather the fact that Dante was able to create an idea of the universe applicable to his own time that is important. For just such an idea is what we desperately need. . . . Dante is a constant incitement to the creative minds of our century, for whether or not we believe in any religion, we cannot gainsay his assurances that eternal truth, harmony, and proportion continue to exist in spite of man.[70]

He argued that "what we desperately need" is "an idea of the universal applicable" to our own time. He read Dante's "assurances that eternal truth, harmony, and proportion continue to exist in spite of man" as an "incitement" for his own poems. He had always worried that if he used recognizable details from his current life in his poetry, he would cheapen the moral emotional universe his poems described. Dante's *Inferno*, however, includes specific details of moral failings in early fourteenth-century Florence in service to the story of a flawed man's journey toward enlightenment, a poem still so powerful that Ashbery viewed it as an ideal poetic model.

He skipped classes and read modern poetry with increasingly critical fervor. He regularly updated his assessment of modern poets in letters to Sandy Gregg: "Did I tell you about the new additions to Ashbery's Definitive list of major modern poets (which Frost would give his right tit to be on)—John Berryman, Byron Vazakas, Wallace Stevens."[71] John's brief enthusiasm for Vazakas, an American of Auden's generation who had recently moved to Cambridge, was primarily a rejection of Robert Lowell, whose poetry John disliked. (Lowell won the 1947 Pulitzer Prize for *Lord Weary's Castle*, for which Vazakas's first book of poems had also been nominated.) Ashbery complained that Lowell "commits the common fault of stringing together a lot of images so overweighed with meaning that they cancel each other out and mean nothing."[72] He composed a parodic stanza—"Mudgulping trawler, Truro in the ooze / Past Peach's Point, with tray of copper spoons / For Salem's Mayer Caldecott to suck, / For his doll's calico corpse, red-needled in the book"—to prove that "anybody can write like" Lowell.[73] Although he praised several modern poets—"Robert Frost is good. So is Patrick Anderson

(Canadian), William Empson (English) and John Berryman. Auden really is the best of all forever and ever. I just read Caliban's long prose speech in *Sea & Mirror* for the first time. Brilliant and exhausting. I cried a little"—he soon after revised his list.[74] Eliminating several favorites since he was a teenager, he concluded:

> My opinion of [Frederic] Prokosch as a poet is not high. At the age of 16 I cherished one of his poems—"The Birdwatcher." . . . Perhaps Berryman isn't as wonderful as I'd thought. . . . As long as I'm on the subject of writers I hate, I may as well go on with the complete list: George Barker (ugh!), John Malcolm Brinnin, Henry Treece, Nicholas Moore (when is someone going to puncture his balloon), Howard Moss, William Abrahams, Oscar Williams, Edith Sitwell. Why not be brave and throw in T. S. Eliot too . . . a coldly intellectual juggling of symbols apparently not contrived to move the reader, but written with some other mysterious end in view.[75]

He reserved his deepest and most consistent praise for just four writers: "The only modern poets within whose portals I occasionally stand awed are Marianne Moore, Auden, F. T. Prince, and occasionally Stevens."[76]

The Harvard Advocate, "a literary mag which is currently being exhumed from a well-earned grave," accepted Ashbery's "A Sermon: Amos 8:11–14" for its first postwar issue.[77] Despite the undergraduate magazine's illustrious literary history, which had published student work by T. S. Eliot and Wallace Stevens, it had been suspended for several years ostensibly due to soaring costs. Its April 1947 cover celebrates the magazine's rebirth dramatically in a drawing of a phoenix rising out of the fire. A *Harvard Crimson* reviewer criticized the magazine's first new issue as "thrown together haphazardly," but praised Ashbery, the only undergraduate among three exceptional writers, including "Richard P. Wilbur . . . and Ruth Stone."[78] To friends, John downplayed his excitement about the *Advocate*'s reappearance, but his first contributor's note—". . . he had two poems in the November, 1945 issue of *Poetry* under the pseudonym Joel Michael Symington"—proudly repossessed his stolen poems. He began spending more time at the *Advocate* offices,

Kenneth Koch (without shirt, on right) in the army, stationed in the Philippines in the mid-1940s. John met Koch at Harvard in the spring of 1947.

on the second floor of 40 Bow Street, especially if Kenneth Koch was around. Three of Koch's poems were published in the same November 1945 *Poetry* issue as Ashbery's stolen poems, and John had read and admired them.

Their new friendship furthered a conversation about poetry that each had already been having alone. As John said to Kenneth much later, "[W]e seem to have been working along parallel lines as usual."[79] Two and a half years older, a veteran of the army who had served as a rifleman in the 96th Infantry Division, and an ambitious, confident junior, Kenneth had irrepressible intellectual energy.[80] He already held a position on the *Advocate* staff and encouraged John to enter into competition to become literary editor. John, however, had heard that no homosexuals were allowed on the literary board. Assuming that Kenneth did not realize he was gay, John said he could not apply. Kenneth was aware that neither blacks, Jews, nor homosexuals were welcome on the board and had already ignored these rumors for his own sake. In fact, *Advocate* administrative records show that in the year leading up to the reopening of the magazine, all these scenarios for exclusion were discussed but never officially enforced.[81] John was not chosen, even after completing "funny stuff like my having to paint the office door (I actually did that)."[82] The rejection stung: "No goddamn you, I did not make the *Advocate* as I am in the habit of acidly replying to numerous inquirers."[83] A few months later, he took a different tack: "The A is really quite a stylish little Mag; I was assured by a reliable source that only sheer graft kept me from getting on the lit board, and that if I try again in the fall it'll be a pipe."[84] He published "three more specimens" in the *Advocate*'s final issue of the year, "which came out the day after everybody left for home."[85]

John returned to Sodus determined to write better poems. He felt no closer to his goal of becoming a "creative artist" than he had a year earlier, and he declared to his friends that he was planning a new approach to summer vacation:

> I have decided that the reason I never write is because I'm always reading something, so I'm going to read practically nothing this summer, except stuff which I find to be of an inspirational character (James, Kafka). Times when I'm neither reading nor writing I will just sit still, opening and shutting my eyes.[86]

He broke his own rule immediately by reading a long novel by Trollope, Shakespeare's *The Tempest*, Virgil's *Georgics*, and "my favorite 17th c. poets . . . Herbert, Milton, Marvell and Donne—in that order."[87] Returning to Henry James, he concluded that *The Golden Bowl* was "his longest and least comprehensible work," and that "the burden of the style makes one swoon; I expect to feel purified when it's all over."[88] Ashbery liked James even more when "[b]etween innings I quaff the cooling draughts of Gertrude Stein's *Three Lives*."[89] Since "home life is dismal," John ignored it.[90] Still, it intruded. Letters had to be cut short because "I have to cut the grass now."[91] He complained that "I have to get a job."[92] He was afraid to receive mail at home from boyfriends, but had no time for a trip to Rochester "to invest in a P.O. box for my very own little self."[93] Eventually he secured a box "for erotica."[94] Despite interruptions, he wrote eight new poems by the end of the summer, including "The Dolors of Columbine," which Bob Hunter declared his friend's "breakthrough" and was one of his first poems accepted in a professional literary journal, *Poetry New York*.[95]

Shortly after writing the poem, John had a dream: "I was in Harvard changing my major from English to Comparative Religions . . . great confusion in getting petition signed, etc."[96] His confusion and curiosity about modern man's relationship to God, which had preoccupied him for a year, animates "The Dolors of Columbine." All year, Ashbery had attempted but failed to access an interior yet prophetic voice in earlier poems. In March, he wrote "A Fable," a brief lyric in which an oracle takes on the persona of "an uncle, aunt or brother." Early in June, he composed a serious poem about the relationship between feeling love and sensing God's presence. Its title, "Undergraduate Reflections," highlighted Ashbery's awareness of the banality of self-conscious collegiate musings.[97] John had already apologized to Bob Hunter for his private ramblings on religion, professing that "I must be intolerable at more times than I had previously supposed."[98]

In "The Dolors of Columbine," Ashbery expresses a desire for communion imaginatively rather than directly. The title suggests some very personal associations. *Dolor* is a Latinate term, recalling his earlier passion for that language. *Dolor* is also a crucial term in the *Aeneid*, which John had just read in Finley's course. The word invokes, through its forty appearances in the poem, a shattering sense of grief. An even more specific use of the term, to describe a parent mourning the death of a son, still clings to it.[99] From its first verse paragraph, Ashbery's poem resonates emotionally with this literary history. The poem accesses this feeling through dwelling in another's body and voice. The speaker is a young woman, Columbine, and in this first-person account of her experience, Ashbery creates a greater sense of intimacy than in any poem he composed before. While Columbine is sensitive and uncertain about herself, the world, and her place in it, her name also invokes an Everywoman, a stock character in sixteenth-century commedia dell'arte, the Italian Renaissance popular theater.

She lies thinking in bed, as we all do. She is a deeply melancholy person, yet one too divided from herself to know why. She slowly gains knowledge about her own interior life. By consciously lying "apart" from herself, she examines who she is and how she feels:

I.

In intervals of night's destruction, sometimes
When the silence arrests its hammers over
Daytime's indestructible corpse, I lie apart
From being Columbine. When love jackknifes
The roaring bed, I can feel her

Pleasure and pain, yet am not harmed.
Nor fired with her enjoyment. And this is good,
Like knowing the real Columbine, myself,
At a great distance, living, a brilliant puppet.
But the night's machinery, forever pressing
Its senseless question of identity, wakens
Me, stranger in a stranger's arms, and I cry
Seeing the real Columbine, at a too great distance
Outwit the guiding wires, escape her name.

In these lost interludes, many-colored dolors
Appear like toys lighting a child's night.
Though space seem empty, they are real
As a child's imagined playmates, to fear and disobey.
And doubt is never a fixed state
But a dancing mimic, teasing the actual
Premises of arms and legs and terrible
Hungering eyes, into tearful denials;
On branches in the dark droop paper wings
No longer lovely, shreds of a forgotten dress.
There, uncertain delights put on the solid
Reluctance of the living. Night's cruelest magic
Renders its metaphors possible, vanishing actions.

II.

Here, in the daytime, everything's in a mess.
I sit in the flat, I scrub, I save, I vacuum.
Nobody minds if I lean at the window
Watching for a new face at the opposite houses
Whose panes may catch my face or the falling sun
But never what's unexpected. But often
The wind, or a huge unseen audience
Catches its breath, and I step forth
All glitter, and trailing colored patches,
And I dance forth, modest and assured
That I love, am loved, that I am
Columbine for myself and the applauding world.

Or, in winter, in the snow's hushed languors—
Or summer, in the close-leafed twilight—
In the car cheek to cheek, rain at the windshield—
Death hums its destructive lullaby offstage, and love
Is almost real, in the traffic, though half seen,
Is the shape of a giant moth or swaying flower.
These are my moments of sharpest knowing:
When, faintly dolorous though still advancing
I join him in a marvel of well-wishing. When sleep
Like a firm hand at base of skull, at last
Comes. And I lie most surely, my thoughts folded,
Myself the implement of his delight, of the delight
Of audiences, and read in their gaze my name.[100]

The second section takes place in more modern public rooms, with windows and neighbors. Columbine is suddenly vacuuming a mid-twentieth-century apartment, as though she went to sleep in the 1500s and woke up in the present. As a child, John saw at Rochester's Memorial Art Gallery a reproduction of Picasso's portrait of the clown Pierrot trying to catch a dancing Columbine. In the poem, the painting is described as though from Columbine's perspective inside it: "I step forth / All glitter, and trailing colored patches, / And I dance forth" in front of "the applauding world." Columbine loves this public world. She explains that through the "gaze" of the appreciative audience, she can finally see herself clearly. Still "dolorous" but at least "advancing," she achieves her goal of self-knowledge onstage. She communicates this understanding in the beautiful, climactic line of the poem: "These are the moments of my sharpest knowing."

As soon as he finished writing, John sent the poem to Bob and welcomed Sandy Gregg for "a lively" reunion in Sodus after nearly two years apart. Just released from the army, he arrived still wearing his uniform. They had a "good time" together and caught up on gossip.[101] Norman Steed and Bill Haddock had moved in together, to an apartment on Beacon Hill, and John heard it was "all like something nightmarish by Gogol. I am putting my own expressive words in his mouth, but I guess they really are drawing beads on each other."[102] He was feeling particularly venomous because of his recent discovery that

"Haddock published another of my poems."[103] Haddock had probably stolen Ashbery's "Dark River" during his visit to Pultneyville in the summer of 1944; he had just published it in a "not too chic mag called *Voices*." Ashbery was irritated, but also flattered since "[i]t was a little thing I wrote at 16, and which Bill has evidently been cherishing ever since."[104] "Dark River" had won Haddock ten dollars and an "Honorable Mention" in a special "Young Poets Issue." Haddock had also provided a "Contributor's Note," claiming that his poems had earlier appeared in *Poetry*, despite his admission that he had stolen those poems, too. John asked him to recant, and "he wrote the editor explaining—he sent the editor's letter to me—and they are going to publish a correction."[105]

Despite his enduring anger at Haddock, the experience helped John. He viewed himself at twenty as a much better artist than the sixteen-year-old who had written that poem. Then, he had been proud enough to show the poem to Haddock; three years later, he did not feel the same attachment to it. Still, for Haddock to save it such a long time meant it must have had something worthwhile in it. Haddock had not changed a single word in the poem, not knowing what to improve, or how. In the meantime, Ashbery had written dozens of new poems. In

John with Sandy Gregg at the Sodus farm in the summer of 1947. As soon as Sandy was released from the army, he came to visit, arriving still in his uniform. Photograph taken by Chet Ashbery.

the next issue of *Voices*, Haddock's promised confession appeared in the magazine:

ERRATUM

The poem "Dark River" which appeared in the Summer issue of *Voices*, was written by Mr. John Ashburg of Sedus, New York, and not by Mr. William C. Haddock.[106]

There was no admission of guilt. The "Erratum" was written as though it were explaining an editor's error. Nonetheless, it was better than nothing. "Mr. John Ashburg of Sedus" planned to keep his poetry far away from Haddock in the future. In fact, the episode made him feel more anxious about sharing his work in general. Only half joking, he even asked Bob Hunter, who had written to tell him that his new girlfriend admired "The Dolors of Columbine," to promise she would not steal any poems.

After Sandy left, the Ashbery and Rupert families took their first trip together since the summer of 1940. During the drive to a lake cabin in Canada, John caught "an evil virus" and developed a very high fever. Immediately, his parents cut the trip short and hurried him home to bed. He rested in his childhood bedroom for nearly two uninterrupted weeks. When he finally recovered, he stayed in bed officially to avoid "a relapse coming on," but actually to preserve his delicious solitude.[107] Dozing on and off, reading and writing a little bit, he rested, and in the private, enclosed space of his room, he started to dream up new works to write.

He imagined two journeys. In a "poetic play entitled 'Everyman,'" an ordinary modern American man gets lost but eventually finds his way home through the aid of his beloved Columbine.[108] His verse drama, which borrowed its title from a fifteenth-century morality play and modeled its plot on the spiritual relationship between Dante and Beatrice in the *Divine Comedy*, was, he joked to Bob Hunter, "guaranteed to be unintelligible to anyone under the age of 900."[109] Still recuperating, he also started to draft "Embarkation for Cythera," a brief lyric based on Watteau's famous painting, which depicts passengers from a crowded ship arriving on Venus's island.[110] In Ashbery's lush, sexual verse, the boat's "slow lunge into shimmering prospects" offers a "breathless vision" of the sensual, liberating landscape ahead.[111] Both works described pilgrimages, but toward utterly distinct harbors. He had found no Virgil, no Beatrice to guide him on a single path during his first two years in college. Midway through Harvard, Ashbery's ambitious plans to "rip modern poetry wide open!" and his private desires to achieve "a genuine" sense of himself had led him creatively in rich and divergent directions.[112] Savoring dwindling summer days, he stayed in bed, dreaming.

7

"Some Trees"

1947–1949

John and Bob Hunter were assigned Norman Mailer's old rooms (Dunster B-43).[1] They placed their desks back-to-back in the spacious top-floor suite, with a Victrola and a large stack of classical music records between them. Ashbery began writing "Fête Galante," a short story inspired by Watteau's painting (and style) of the same name. Ashbery's bubbly, mischievous piece, which he published in the *Advocate*, describes a party:

> There is so much noise! Two sylph-like young men, one with an accordion, the other with a guitar, hurl themselves at the groups of guests, breaking up conversation, making bad music. . . . Then all the lights go out, all the noise and the music stops. . . . Something makes Lucy's fingers explore, explore, along the balcony rail to where Frank's hand last lay. Very plump and appealing in the moonlight, it seemed. Now she has found it, now they are holding hands. What a lovely sensation.[2]

The *Harvard Crimson* raved that "John Ashbery . . . has turned his ever-competent hand to prose. . . . [T]he result is a dream-like story of innuendo. . . . [N]one of the machinery shows through the delicate and expertly woven surface."[3] Soon after, Ashbery earned a "literary associate" position, finally appearing on the *Advocate* masthead in the

Christmas issue. The Signet Society, an exclusive undergraduate art and literary society with its own yellow building at 46 Dunster Street, also invited him to join. He and Kenneth Koch, who was already a member, "played" and "invented" games over their lunches, finding anagrams, assigning feelings to objects, or debating "Auden's sexuality and his religious professions."[4] At the end of December, John wrote and performed a Henry James parody, "Return of the Screw," the story of "a Harvard student's nearly erotic encounter with a Dean Flotcher," at his Signet Society initiation ritual.[5]

He was also invited to read at the Widener Library Poetry Room by its director, John Sweeney.[6] Since 1945, John had been a constant presence in the Poetry Room, listening to its vast collection of poets reading their own work. Sweeney convinced both Harvard poetry professor John Ciardi and local established poet Richard Eberhart to attend.[7] Sandy Gregg, Bob Hunter, Bubsy Zimmerman, and Antonio Giarraputo, a Harvard undergraduate poet whom John had never seen before and never met again, completed the small audience. After reading for thirty minutes, John ended with "For a European Child," a dark poem of four stark quatrains he had written the previous summer, which asked whether love could survive in such a violent modern world. The poem attacked those "lovers / [who] Lay on the newsprint," blindly frolicking over a photograph of some new horror.[8] Bob Hunter was impressed by its line "a famine knowing no appetite," which he interpreted as an indictment of modern man suffering "from a deficit of true love and self-respect."[9] At the end of the reading, Giarraputo asked Ashbery why the subject of the poems was "only love or death." He answered that these were "very important subjects," a response that Bob Hunter found flippant because John declined to elaborate.[10]

Ashbery had too much to say about both subjects. Not long after the semester began, he spotted a new classmate at the *Advocate* offices, Fred Amory, "who looked just like the Arrow Collar shirt man." He felt immediately attracted to this extremely tall, "clean-cut" returning GI with an open, intelligent, handsome face. Very soon, he discovered he also "liked his mind."[11] They quickly became friends, often meeting for dinner and talking late into the night about art, literature, and themselves. They had similar interests in poetry and "paradoxes and oxymorons."[12] Their developing relationship seemed so completely romantic to John that he pushed for more, but Fred said no. When John mentioned that he had heard rumors about Fred's involvement with an older boy during his high school years at Groton, Fred angrily denied them and stopped speaking to John. Despite the breach, John asked him for comments on his new poem, "My Friends," and they started talking again a few weeks later. Fred liked the short poem but objected to its descriptive lines "Lucky Alphonse, the shy homosexual / Draws on his gloves in a room full of ferns," Ashbery's first direct allusion to homosexuality in a poem. Fred felt that the reference to a three-some, a "lucky Pierre," was unnecessary.[13] He added, "homosexuals are already discriminated against so you shouldn't make a class of them. You shouldn't do that," a comment John found touching but confusing.[14] He wanted to believe that Fred's defense of homosexuals meant that he was gay, but their relationship remained intense but platonic.

All spring, John remained preoccupied with thoughts of Fred. Every time the already intimate relationship seemed on the verge of turning physical, Fred withdrew. John would not see him for several days, and then they would run into each other at the *Advocate* offices or at a campus concert and start talking, and the cycle would repeat. As his emotions churned, he wrote "Why We Forget Dreams." He had begun the new poem in Bubsy Zimmerman's company as they walked together along

Frederick Amory in his Harvard yearbook photo, 1949

Commonwealth Avenue on a late winter's night. She looked up at him (he was six feet tall and she was five foot two), and sighed deeply, saying, "It is the spring semester." She loved him, which he knew, though she had never explicitly told him, and they would never be together, which she knew, though he had never explicitly told her. They remained respectfully silent with each other about their feelings and their secrets, neither ever mentioning his homosexuality or her withered arm. In her warm, melancholy voice, she communicated to John a sense of time passing and all the promise and loss that their platonic friendship made her feel.[15] Her commonplace words conveyed a question he felt, too, and he posed it in this new poem: "Who can make his sorrow or his happiness last, / Or make of their changing a beautiful thing?"[16]

John began to keep a new diary after seeing Fred for the first time in "a while." They talked and then "got something to eat and he came back here," spending a wonderful evening that reignited all John's former feelings.[17] He wrote cautiously about his desires in a plain spiral notebook, substituting the symbol "<>" for Fred's name in case anyone found it. Although he tried to take his mind off Fred by dating Walter Scott, an older man from New York City whom he had met in a Boston bar, he could not make himself fall in love with someone else. One afternoon in May, John and Bubsy accompanied Kenneth and his girlfriend on an outing to Revere Beach and its amusement park.[18] The day reinforced his fondness for Bubsy—"How I like her!"—and his sense of loneliness, for "it was like in E. M. Forster when everyone starts out on a gay picnic and it all turns out wrong."[19] A thick fog encased the sun by the time they reached the beach. All the rides except "dodgems" (bumper cars) were closed. The food was expensive and inedible, and the only affordable attraction was to make a record, but "you can hear nothing except [Bubsy's] giggle, which I am glad to have perpetuated on wax." The hardest part was to be on a double date, when "Ken. and Nan. were in love, and Bubsy and I aren't."

John listened to classical music intensively. He spent hours alphabetizing his record collection and creating an index card catalogue.[20] He felt increasingly anxious about final exams and a lack of summer plans: "Wish I knew what I was going to do."[21] He was certain only that he did not want to go home to Sodus and that "I don't want to be in Boston this summer!" He studied for his Metaphysical Poetry exam, his favorite course all year, reading Herbert and Donne while listening to Beethoven's *Ninth Symphony*.[22] He searched for new records and sold some old clothes to buy Stravinsky's *L'Histoire du soldat* and Octet for Winds and Ravel's Piano Concerto in G Major "in a wonderful new recording by Bernstein."[23] He wanted to find "Walton's Sinfonia Concertante (piano and orch.)—this is an impressive piece of music, rather grim, I feel."[24] He went alone to hear the Boston Symphony Orchestra. Finally, he concocted a plan to accompany Sandy Gregg home to Scarsdale, then to New York City to visit Walter Scott, find a job, and secure an apartment for the summer.

Relieved, he reread his play *Everyman* for the first time since September. The *Advocate* published "Song from a Play"—three stanzas pulled from *Everyman*—in its commencement issue, a poem that was awarded "honorable mention" in an annual competition. (Kenneth Koch's poems won top prize.)[25] Encouraged, John added new material to the play for the first time in a year, pleased that Kenneth liked it. He had recently started reading a translation of André Gide's first novel, *The Counterfeiters* (1925), a story about a gay artist in Paris; its depiction of contemporary men irked him and motivated him to improve his own new work. After finally ending the long, aimless, and anxious period of exams, he arrived in New York City. He was very excited to be there, but ran out of money before finding either an apartment or a job.[26] When he asked his parents to wire him some more money, they sent only enough for a train ticket home. Stretching out his last few hours before rushing to the station, he and Sandy visited "the Museum of Modern Art . . . an exhibit of Bonnard which left me rather lukewarm."[27]

As soon as he arrived in Sodus, he felt irritable and bored. His diary entries grew shorter: "I did nothing today." He slept late, dodged chores, and listened repeatedly to Berg's haunting Violin Concerto and Poulenc's Sonata for Horn, Trumpet, and Trombone, though his father complained that the latter recording "sound[ed] like the Pultneyville fireman's band rehearsing."[28] John visited Carol Rupert, who was engaged to be married and energetically planning a busy, bright domestic future in Rochester, and he left her as soon as possible to wander slowly around the city. Home again, he started reading C. K. Scott Moncrieff's translation of Marcel Proust's *Remembrance of Things Past*.[29] He had begun reading Proust once before, but had not gotten far. This time, though, he found that the work's contemplative and winding rhythms fit his meandering thoughts. Every day, he listened to Berg and read a little more Proust: "I savor him, reading very slowly. It is all so beautiful—but I don't remember hearing anyone say that—people just say he is morbid."[30]

His former schoolmate, John Anson, invited him for dinner. For the first time in five years, he saw Miss Klumpp, who had just become engaged to John Anson's older brother Frank. Hearing that her former student would be at the Ansons' home, she brought him the handwritten spiral notebook of poems he had submitted for her feedback in 1944. In the intervening years, John had completely forgotten the notebook existed. At home later that night, he read through his old poems and was shocked by how poor they were: "My old poems are quite embarrassing."[31] The spiral notebook was filled with the kind of concise imagist poems he was writing in the spring of 1943, just when he started to dedicate himself to poetry. They demonstrated to him the poetic strides he had made in the years since then, but they also highlighted how far he still probably was from writing the kinds of poems he imagined. His month of diary entries only exacerbated this feeling, for all he saw was "a lot of junk I have recorded!"[32] He had always felt frustrated by the kinds of ordinary, unimportant details that he put into a diary. He wanted to write about what he thought each day, not only what he did, but he could not capture those fleeting, crucial impressions.

He had been thinking about this subject while reading poetry all year. In his final essay for Douglas Bush's course "Metaphysical Poets: from Donne to Marvell," for which he earned his first A since 1945, he analyzed Marvell's "The Mower to the Glow-Worms," finding in the poem a description of great poetry:

> The poem owes its impact . . . to the insignificant glow-worms, who remain with us after we have forgotten the point of it all, only remembering that it has left us in that magical, suggestive land where all great poems take place . . . in all great poets, we are released from the things of the world to find a new significance in the world of the imagination, though the separation from "things" is never complete, and the higher meaning of the poem will invariably have its roots in them.[33]

The things we use and do in our daily life always have meaning, yet poetry ultimately emerges from the way a poet imagines a separation from these things. At the same time, the fact that these things of the world (objects, relationships, activities) are understood by the poet adds to the intimacy of his experience of leaving them behind. Great poetry necessarily includes a residue of things but exists in the world of imagination. In writing the essay, Ashbery started to think about how to make his poems' subject less central. This idea was the beginning of a deeper response to the question (or criticism) his classmate had posed about the subject of Ashbery's poems at the end of his first reading.

Just as studying Marvell helped him to see "new significance in the world of the imagination," reading Proust enabled him to view his ordinary experience through a wider lens. He reread his diary, trying to learn how to enact the creative jump he understood Proust making: "Perhaps I should try to copy down my thoughts, if I could make something beautiful of them, as Proust does."[34] He was also learning about poetry by listening to Berg's Violin Concerto:

> Berg's Violin Concerto—this is on the phonograph now. . . . It was written as a requiem for Manon Gropius, a young girl. First she dances, then death steps in and chases her around. Near the end a Bach chorale (unfamiliar to me) is presented (atonally—a strange effect but very beautiful). During the rest of the piece the violin elaborates on this in a slow tempo—this part is stunning! It is really a heavenly piece—in feeling as well as subject like "Sonnets to Orpheus."[35]

He heard Berg's inclusion of a quotation from Bach's seventeenth-century church music as the musical equivalent of what he was trying to do poetically. The piece reminded him, "in feeling" and "subject," of Rilke's rendering of the story of Orpheus, the poet-singer who twice loses his great love, Eurydice, and sings of the loss from the deepest grief. Ashbery's later poem "Syringa" matter-of-factly describes Orpheus as someone who "liked the glad personal quality / Of the things beneath the sky." The moment Eurydice vanishes, Orpheus begins to understand these "things" differently, as imbued with feeling he had not realized they had. Yet the speaker explains that Eurydice was always going to disappear: "She would have even if he hadn't turned around," because Eurydice is the past, which always disappears. Berg's brief invocation of Bach is a version of Orpheus grasping and losing Eurydice, for the memory of that phrase resonates through and illuminates what remains.

John spent two days in bed with a summer flu. He had very little energy: "I don't feel well—my joints ache, and I'm very tired."[36] He slept on and off with odd, fitful dreams that left him feeling strangely dreamlike even while awake, though this produced "rather a pleasant sensation."[37] Afterward, he read more of Rilke's *Sonnets to Orpheus* and listened, "vastly impressed," to T. S. Eliot's *Murder in the Cathedral* on the radio. The next day, still dizzy, he lingered in bed. Late in the afternoon he took up a sheet of loose leaf and started writing. That night, he considered what he had done: "I wrote a poem (in sestina form) which I'm quite pleased with. Title—The Painter" (June 17). The sestina, a thirty-nine-line Italian form made up of six six-line stanzas and one three-line conclusion, called an envoi, used an elaborate system of end-word repetition. Ashbery had never tried to write his own sestina before, but he admired sestinas by Dante and Petrarch and especially loved two twentieth-century examples that he knew well, Auden's "Paysage Moralisé," and Elizabeth Bishop's "A Miracle for Breakfast." In his first longhand draft of his new poem, he kept a running list of numbers between one and six down the side of the page to work out accurately the pattern of end words as he composed each new stanza.

Within its formal, repetitive structure, "The Painter" powerfully reimagines Ashbery's recent thoughts. He narrates his own artistic frustrations as a version of the Orpheus myth. A young artist chases after an idea and fails to capture it. This idea, like Eurydice, is always disappearing before one can grasp it. For many years, Ashbery had tried but failed to capture the essence of experience in a poem. "The Painter" was his first poem to elevate the artist's inability to capture "subject" and "feeling" *as* his most important experience. The poem succeeded in communicating this essential, even haunting failure in the relationship between his life and art that he had never been able to say before:

> Sitting between the sea and the buildings
> He enjoyed painting the sea's portrait.

But just as children imagine a prayer
Is merely silence, he expected his subject
To rush up the sand, and, seizing a brush,
Plaster its own portrait on the canvas.

So there was never any paint on his canvas
Until the people who lived in the buildings
Put him to work: "Try using the brush
As a means to an end. Select, for a portrait,
Something less angry and large, and more subject
To a painter's moods, or, perhaps, to a prayer."

How could he explain to them his prayer
That nature, not art, might usurp the canvas?
He chose his wife for a new subject,
Making her vast, like ruined buildings,
As if, forgetting itself, the portrait
Had expressed itself without a brush.

Slightly encouraged, he dipped his brush
In the sea, murmuring a heartfelt prayer:
"My soul, when I paint this next portrait
Let it be you who wrecks the canvas."
The news spread like wildfire through the buildings:
He had gone back to the sea for his subject.

Imagine a painter crucified by his subject!
Too exhausted even to lift his brush,
He provoked some artists leaning from the buildings
To malicious mirth: "We haven't a prayer
Now, of putting ourselves on canvas,
Or getting the sea to sit for a portrait!"

Others declared it a self-portrait.
Finally all indications of a subject
Began to fade, leaving the canvas
Perfectly white. He put down the brush.

At once a howl, that was also a prayer,
Arose from the overcrowded buildings.

They tossed him, the portrait, from the tallest of the buildings;
And the sea devoured the canvas and the brush
As though his subject had decided to remain a prayer.[38]

"The Painter" describes the difficulty of creating something beautiful from the things that surrounded him as a child, for it originated in his familiar and beloved view of Lake Ontario. Ashbery wrote the earliest kernel of the poem in an entry in his 1943 diary: "It was windy and the lake was bright blue flecked with white. It was a scene that came to me almost the same thing a few weeks ago. I shall paint it some time."[39] This poem was the earliest he wrote that he included in his first volume, *Some Trees* (Yale University Press, 1956).

Over John's strong objections, his parents arranged for him to attend secretarial school in Rochester, and his writing slowed "to a mere trickle."[40] They installed him in the home of elderly friends in Rochester, who woke him up each morning by seven thirty so he would arrive on time at Monroe High, "a gloomy building" full of students who had flunked a course in high school. From "8:30 to 12:30 I take typing and shorthand; in the afternoons I sort of wander around, trying to cultivate a sunstroke."[41] If his summer activities had a soundtrack, Schoenberg's *Pierrot-Lunaire* would have been playing as he scrambled to keep separate his various identities—responsible college boy, poet, and gay man: "I am at present leading a triple life which threatens to split at the seams any day." He ate dinner with his hosts, and then, "as soon as night falls, I don an enigmatic, eternal expression and issue forth into languorous, perfumed dusk. Rochester is mad."[42] Because of his late nights cruising for men at bars and clubs, early mornings were increasingly difficult to manage, but "the general effect of all this is complete unreality; I barely perceive at all."[43]

He resolved to recover in time for his senior year, but as soon as he arrived at Harvard, he ran into Fred Amory and immediately felt overpowered by his attraction once again. He spent evenings in the company of Bob Hunter, Sandy Gregg, Les Brown, and Bubsy Zimmerman for beers at Cronin's, one of the "chief pleasures" of college, but he thought about Fred even there.[44] To distract himself, he and Bob began making collages in their dorm room. Fascinated by Max Ernst's spatially disorienting images, which he had studied in Deknatel's Modern Art course, John especially liked *Garden Airplane Trap* (1935) and works from *Les malheurs des immortels* (1922) by Ernst and Paul Éluard, which he borrowed from Widener.[45] Two years earlier, he had made a miniature collage of a kitten in a nightie and a cap as a joke for Bob Hunter.[46] In September, John created two bigger and more sophisticated pieces, including *Seaport*, from images he cut out of a recent issue of *Vogue*, and *Late for School*, which told a disturbing story of a schoolboy attacked and replaced by a vulture, from illustrations in a German schoolbook he picked up at the Cambridge foreign-language bookstore Schoenhof's. Since John and Bob were also taking Harry Levin's popular lecture class on Proust, Joyce, and Mann together, they began a semester-long ritual of reading Proust at the same time, usually in adjoining chairs in the Dunster House library.[47] For the second time in six months, John carefully read all two thousand pages of Proust's novel.[48]

John asked Fred, who had recently become a literary associate for the *Advocate*, to collaborate on a new collage for the November 1948 cover. Over several weeks of late-night work, they created an image of a Greek figure spouting vases (shaped like penises) from her toga, watching them fall into a copy of Hans Holbein's *Anne Cresacre*, the painting John had once produced from a copy hanging in his parents' living room.[49] One late evening, while working on the piece and talking about himself, Fred said to John, "I guess I haven't let the bear out yet," which John interpreted as an overture to intimacy.[50] When Fred fell silent again, John asked him what he meant, but Fred would not say more. When John pushed, Fred grew angry. During this period of close collaboration with the object of his desire, John wrote several new poem drafts. Each illuminated feelings of longing and frustration. "Three A.M." begins with a command: "Don't say it," and suggests later that the speaker is "fully aware / Why you are being punished."[51] "Poem About Autumn" compares a quickening feeling that accompanies a change of seasons to a similar sensation in love, since "in change is a kind of happiness / That is not created by us."[52] At the end of the previous summer, after thinking about what kinds of information belonged in a

Two of John Ashbery's earliest collages, *Seaport* and *Late for School*, which he made in his Dunster House dorm room

Harvard Advocate cover, November 1948, a collage that John Ashbery and Fred Amory created together

poem versus a diary entry, Ashbery wrote a poem, "From a Diary," in which the speaker complains that "Poets found out long ago / Love is a rose, a hatband, or a flute." Poets employ "love's own borrowed voice" as poorly as diarists fill up their pages with superfluous facts.[53] Ashbery searched for a more original language to express precisely his experience of loving Fred.

In the middle of October, John found an unexpected model for a new kind of love poetry. He had first read Marianne Moore's poetry at the age of fifteen, in Untermeyer's anthology (1942), which printed five poems ("A Talisman," "That Harp You Play So Well," "To a Steam Roller," "England," and "The Fish"). In 1944, after John purchased Moore's *Selected Poems* (1935) at the Gotham Book Mart, despite his very limited funds, he brought it back to Deerfield to read, but found its poems "mysterious" and too "difficult."[54] At Harvard's Poetry Room, Ashbery listened repeatedly to the school's one recording of Moore (from her visit in 1941), but again the poems "intrigued" but escaped him.[55] In the fall, Harry Levin announced that Moore would visit Harvard to give the prestigious Morris Gray Reading on December 9, 1948. Ashbery's sense of anticipation was even greater than for any other reading he had attended. He had just discovered a new Moore poem, "Efforts of Affection," in *The Nation*, and copied it onto a small sheet of blue paper.[56] Three days later, he composed "The Statues."[57] While the title recalls John Berryman's "The Statue," which Ashbery had admired recently after reading Berryman's *Poems* (1942), John's new poem was much more directly influenced by Moore, especially in its opening question:

> What shall we do? Sincerity
> Demands constant attention
> But is threatened by an intervention

He sent a copy to Kenneth Koch, admitting "a certain resemblance to Marianne Moore," and then he announced seriously that "I have discovered Miss Moore." It had taken him "a long time to like [her poems] . . . to fall in love with them."[58]

His revelatory feeling emerged after reading the most recent issue of the *Quarterly Review of Literature*, which was devoted entirely to a discussion of Moore's work. John especially liked Wallace Stevens's essay on the "potency" of her poetry.[59] Stevens praised Moore for her imagination, which had enabled her to create "a reality adequate to the profound necessities of life today" without "speak[ing] directly of the subject of the poem by name." Her poems rejected "unsubstantial . . . facts of the world about us" and created "some communion with the objects which are apprehended by thought and not by sense."[60] For Ashbery, these comments provided him very nearly with a blueprint for how to read a Moore poem more astutely. They also explained to him how he might shift the weight between subject and emotion in his own poems. He copied her new poem, "By Disposition of Angels," printed for the first time in the *Quarterly Review*, into his letter to Kenneth:

> Messengers much like ourselves? Explain it.
> Steadfastness the darkness makes explicit?
> Something heard most clearly when not near it?
>   Above particularities,
> these unparticularities praise cannot violate.

One has seen, in such steadiness never deflected,
how by darkness a star is perfected.

Star that does not ask me if I see it?
Fir that would not wish me to uproot it?
Speech that does not ask me if I hear it?
    Mysteries expound mysteries.
Steadier than steady, star dazzling me, live and elate,
    no need to say, how like some we have known; too like her,
    too like him, and a-quiver forever.

Ashbery loved how Moore's poem gracefully enacts a relationship between the "particular" and "unparticular." Stars are things beyond human comprehension, yet they reflect back to humans a reminder of time, light, silence, and speech. Through that humbling experience of remembering a sense of the mystery of things, one becomes connected again to one's own humanity.

Three weeks later, during the brisk, dark evening of November 16, 1948, John sat at his dorm room desk and composed "Some Trees," his concise love lyric. Bob Hunter could hear him writing steadily in pencil at his desk for an hour. There was silence and then the scraping of a chair. John handed Bob a single sheet of paper: "I just finished a poem. Do you want to read it?"[61]

These are amazing: each
Joining a neighbor, as if speech
Were a still performance.
Arranging quite by chance

To meet as far, this morning,
From the world as agreeing
With it, you and I
Are suddenly what the trees try

To tell us we are;
That their merely being here

Means something, a sign
That we may touch, can love, explain.

What joy not to have invented
This comeliness! It is what we wanted:
Silence about to be filled with noises,
Canvas on which emerges

A gathering of smiles, a winter morning.
Season of puzzling light and fading
Your days put on such reticence,
Our errors seem their own defense.[62]

Filled with intimacy and mystery, the brief and beautiful lyric illuminated how the scale of one's experience of the world becomes exaggerated through love.[63] Everything means something. Signs fill one with joy, puzzlingly so. Everything (light, dark, trees, smiles, explanations) becomes imbued with a delicate and trembling sense of special meaning. Trees had weight as both symbol and image for John from childhood; the word *tree* conjured his summers in Pultneyville, castles, climbing willow branches, Robin Hood, his boyish and fragile brother, playful Mary, loyal Carol, the awkwardness of crushes, and the relief of old friends. The poem manages to access these resonances by making the lovers seem like things, so small and grounded, and the trees seem like ideas, so "amazing" and tall. It is one kind of intimacy in the face of another, older and greater one, and the oddly distorted mirror image of lovers gives both pairs additional dignity.[64]

Ashbery had expressed his current experience of love without including any specific details about his life. He had achieved this milestone, in part, by studying Moore's approach and adapting it:

Speech that does not ask me if I hear it? (Moore)
as if speech / Were a still performance. (Ashbery)

Something heard most clearly when not near it? (Moore)
Silence about to be filled with noises (Ashbery)

One has seen, in such steadiness never deflected, (Moore)
That their merely being here / Means something, (Ashbery)

By putting his own sense of rhythm and line length directly in dialogue with Moore's language, as though they shared a secret, he had created something new. The melancholy poem finally expressed the combination of experience and transcendence he had been attempting to communicate for many years.

Shortly after *The Advocate* published "Some Trees," the poet Richard Wilbur stopped John on Bow Street to compliment him on it.[65] Fred, however, stayed silent; if he knew the poem was about him, he did not acknowledge it. Just after they submitted their collage, he disappeared, even avoiding the *Advocate* offices. John's parents arrived for their first visit to Harvard, which provided a pleasant distraction. They brought news from Deerfield, having stopped by to visit Frank Boyden on their way.[66] Chet, who had been studying the New England photographs of Samuel Chamberlain, was eager to see Concord. His parents took John, Sandy, Bob, and Bubsy, whom they were meeting for the first time, out for lunch at the famous Wayside Inn.[67] John was relieved that his father seemed less hostile, even cheerful, toward him on this visit.

Barbara "Bubsy" Zimmerman (later Epstein), John, Bob Hunter, and Sandy Gregg walk in Concord, Massachusetts, 1948. Photograph taken by Chet Ashbery.

Bob Hunter, John, and Sandy Gregg outside Dunster House, fall 1948. Photograph taken by Chet Ashbery.

After they left, there was still no word from Fred. A week later, John and Bob Hunter attended Moore's reading together. Unlike other readings, which were held in huge auditoriums, for this one Moore was introduced by F. O. Matthiessen in Sever Hall, a regular classroom, and the audience was small. Moore loomed so large poetically that John was shocked to see a tiny, sixty-one-year-old woman in "a frumpy old suit and white collar."[68] She spoke of her admiration for the boxer Joe Louis, read for less than twenty minutes, and then sat down again.[69] John had hoped to see Fred in the audience, but he did not appear.

By early February, John felt so depressed he could not concentrate. James Munn, his Old Testament course professor, was "compassionate" when John "nearly flunked my Old Testament final exam. I was supposed to write an essay and couldn't." Munn asked him, "Are you by any chance in love? You have not done very well but just do the best you can."[70] On February 7, the first day of spring classes, John saw Fred by chance while standing in line for tickets to an all-Stravinsky concert at Sanders Theatre. They decided to go together.[71] This incident brightened John's mood for the next few days. The concert with Stravinsky conducting the Boston Symphony Orchestra was "wonderful," as were their conversations afterward—until Fred suddenly became furious. He snapped at John for being too "importunate" and declared that he did not want to see him again.[72]

John's depression worsened. He moved to a nearby single (H-41) because Bob Hunter was graduating early and moving off campus. John's evenings felt strange and lonely without Bob, who was busy with a job in the newly opened Lamont Library and excited about arranging plans to teach overseas and travel. John stayed in his dorm room alone and hardly got out of bed. He ignored his classes and read Keats's "great poem, 'Isabella, or The Pot of Basil'" in his room.[73] Forcing himself at least to attend his Twentieth-Century American Poetry course, taught by F. O. Matthiessen, he appreciated the professor's "very conscientious and insightful" teaching.[74] Still, the course did not change his opinions: "(Something there is that doesn't love Robert Frost)," he noted to himself one afternoon during Matthiessen's enthusiastic lecture.[75] He wrote papers on three of his four favorite modernists, analyzing Stevens's wordless sounds in "Chocorua to Its Neighbor" and creating an imagined anthology of Auden's and Moore's poetry.[76] Matthiessen liked John's Stevens essay but felt his student was "more squarely on the mark in dealing with Miss Moore" than with Auden.[77] This criticism was disheartening because, after recently changing topics from a study of Henry James's novels, John was struggling to write his senior thesis on Auden's poetry.

Because of his depression, he had already procrastinated too long. His thesis was due on March 15, but by the end of February he had written nothing except a new poem, "The Egoist," which described "the artist" alone, still, thinking as he "[s]tands in his wintry studio."[78] John stayed in bed or sat at his desk staring out his dorm window and onto the frozen Charles River. He was stuck, staring at his utterly bleak "wintry" view. He heard that Bubsy had already turned in her eighty-page thesis, "Edward Taylor and the Puritan Mind," to her adviser, Perry Miller.[79] John had been reading and listening to Auden's works with increasing intensity for six years, yet he still could not start writing. He had spent the past year debating Auden's poetry and plays in detail with Kenneth and others at the *Advocate*, but he did not want to write the paper. He had even become friendly with Auden. At an *Advocate* event the previous April, they had chatted awhile, and then Auden had invited John to walk with him back to his hotel suite. After accompanying him as far as his room, however, John demurred. Despite his boundless admiration for the man as a poet, he "could not go to bed with him" and returned to his dorm room, where he described the almost-sexual encounter to Bob.[80]

Now the deadline loomed. He lay in bed, skipping class and reading nothing but Keats's "The Eve of St. Agnes."[81] He finally emerged from his room only to inform Professor B. J. Whiting, the chair of the senior thesis committee and the "strange little man" who had taught the year-long Chaucer course John took as a junior, that he had decided not to write a thesis.[82]

Professor Whiting talked John into beginning the essay. Because Whiting treated the issue as an entirely administrative problem—how to get his student to complete a commitment—he helped to free John from the unconscious psychological dilemma that plagued him. Instead of having difficulty writing about a gay artist (and near love interest), John summed up Auden's career trajectory, dwelling on just a few poems. Once he started, he did not stop writing for four feverish days. When he forgot he was writing a thesis and just described what he liked most about Auden's poetry as a fellow poet, he even enjoyed himself a little. He still loved Auden's *The Sea and the Mirror* most, because of its "beauty which we prize more highly than his ideas, worthy as they are." "Beauty," John explained, arose from "mystery, the unconscious quality that is an element of all great poetry."[83] He saw in Auden's work something he had admired in Dante's: "the artist seeking truth . . . [which] by its very lucidity and penetration achieves the unconscious which we find in the greatest poetry—our view of the poet himself, the unsatisfied voyager."[84] On the evening of the fourth day, John traveled to a remote part of South Boston to have his essay quickly typed. Since all the good typists had been already secured by more organized students, he booked a second-rate, slow, error-prone typist, but he managed to submit the paper on time.[85]

Unburdened, he began to leave his room. A few weeks later, he went alone to the Mandrake Book Store to see the opening of an exhibition of watercolors. The artist, Edward Gorey, the tall, idiosyncratic writer and artist whom everyone called Ted, was an acquaintance from the *Advocate*.[86] In the crowded room, John "heard someone with a voice that sounded like his own." That flat, nasal voice "expressed a preference for Poulenc over Wagner, for *Sécheresses* over *Tristan*," brash statements given a Harvard music faculty who considered such ideas foolish. John heard "what

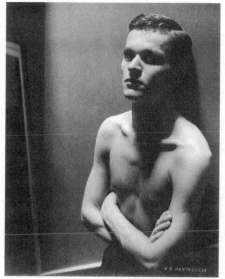

John Ashbery in the spring of 1949.
Photograph taken by George Montgomery,
a fellow Harvard student, at an
entrance to Dunster House.

John Ashbery and Sandy Gregg in spring 1949, painted by Tony
Haas, a friend and the valedictorian of the class of 1949

seemed like" his own voice speaking his own thought. Even more powerfully, he heard someone sharing his particular penchant for saying
exactly the opposite of prevailing opinion, regardless of the precise
truth of the comment. He turned around and was surprised to discover
Frank O'Hara, whom he already knew as a talented *Advocate* writer
and Ted Gorey's roommate. Since enthusiastically championing O'Hara's

short play *O the Danger of Daily Living*, the first *Advocate* submission by "Francis O'Hara (class of 1950)," which was published in the March 1948 issue, John had avoided contact with the writer. He thought O'Hara, who had a bent nose and a "pugnacious" expression while walking, looked rather tough and mean.[87] At the party, however, they began to talk.[88]

Several weeks after meeting Frank, John wrote to Bob Hunter about this life-changing new friendship:

> I made many good friends as the term began to end, the greatest of these being Frank O'Hara . . . O'Hara I suspect of being my identical twin; I saw much of him the last few weeks, spending most of my time in Eliot visiting with him and attendant spirits.[89]

Frank was twenty-three and John twenty-one, but because Frank had served in the navy, John was a senior and Frank still a junior. Although Frank had grown up in Grafton, near Boston, they shared a voice, an accent, and many interests. Frank, trained as a pianist, played Debussy and Poulenc for John, and then his own composition, "a three-second sonata." Impressed, John wrote a piano work as a present for Frank, titled "Op. 1, No. 1."[90] Unlike John's romantic crushes, which heightened his senses and made the real world seem stranger and more mysterious, this new friendship clarified and sharpened a world he already knew. (Shortly after meeting Frank, and locked out of his dorm room late one night, John knocked on Fred Amory's door. It was the first time they had seen each other in a long time, but Fred was very kind and let him sleep in an empty bed.)[91]

Almost every afternoon for the final three weeks of Harvard, John and Frank "lay on the grass" in the sun by the banks of the Charles River.[92] In Frank, John had found a brother more like him in sensibility and sound than the one he had lost. Frank, though, was also freer and more candid than John, in both his life and his art. Bubsy had remarked during sophomore year that John's poetry was sometimes too serious; she even suggested that his phrase "I sense the fatal chill," a line she had read in his poem "The Perfect Orange," published in *The Advocate*, was melodramatic.[93] Although he admired her "refreshing views of music and literature," he had not taken her advice to change it.[94] After spending time with Frank, though, he understood her comment much better.

Because he had been elected class poet (after running unopposed), John had to deliver the class poem at graduation. Throughout May, he tried but failed to write a new work for the occasion. Finally, he gave up and chose one of his old poems, "A Sermon: Amos 8:11–14," which he had written in Sodus the summer between his freshman and sophomore years, when he was thinking about the relationship between religion and modern life. He felt the poem was "possibly the only one" he had ever written that felt prophetic and that had a sense of a grand, public occasion. It contained added symbolic value because it was his first poem published in the *Advocate*.

Henry Lawrence, who became ill, was very sorry to miss seeing his grandson deliver the class poem: "When I recall the little poem you wrote when you were eight years old I must say I was pleased then, but did not foresee that it would lead to the present distinction."[95] Addie, Chet, Helen, and Aunt Janet were in the audience as he spoke:

In this land travel light
And lightly: keep rude hands from sight
Nor with speech design fidelities.
Break vows as fagots: ignore
Promises, prayers, lusting before the door,
Nor press the sinning Tartar to his knees.

Move as water: soon gone,
Lightly girdling the dry stone.
Touch nothing long: involve
Nothing ever. Your fate and history
Meet in geometry
And in radiant law dissolve.

I explain: imagine
A young man or fair virgin
At dark, at sea's edge wading.
And now drawn in a strange light

Into the sea. Nearing night
Locks tongue, ties eye. Fading

From shore line the swimmer
Forms with his ocean brother
A complex unity: sea immolates
Matter in distance, and he or she
Buries desire in motion. And does not see
Where, at far left, oars raised, a small boat waits.

My people, what is intended
Let the cool martyr, whose distant head
Now seems a swimming dog's, explore,
Sustained in a vast disinterest.
But learn that distances are kindest,
Not the correct sun striking the shore.

The poem had the rhythm of a public prayer, offering wisdom to graduates, advice it never seemed to have contained so directly before. The end of the poem encourages the reader to travel widely and to explore without worrying about being correct. He had written the poem at an

John Ashbery's graduation from Harvard, June 1949

Frank O'Hara's graduation present to John: a hardcover edition of *Georgian Stories* (1922), purchased from a bookseller in his hometown of Grafton, Massachusetts. The book included a story by Mary Butts, a writer Frank introduced to John, who quickly developed a passion for her prose. The inscription reads:

John: A Meditation on Aesthetics and
    Thomas Hardy:
Be it arse-backwards or arse-forwards that
    wins the day?
Frank O'Hara

earlier time in his life, when he was trying to find the right path for himself as a man and a poet, but it felt prophetic in a new way as he graduated, left Cambridge, and embarked on a new odyssey.

In a lighthearted mood, he drove home with his parents. His friendship with Frank O'Hara and the coterie of young artists who fluttered around him—"attendant spirits," as he called them, alluding to Titania and her attendant spirits in *A Midsummer Night's Dream*—harkened back to his childhood experience with Shakespeare and poetry. Then, his first poem came to him instinctively, not burdened by any expectations about what it meant for poetry to be modern or good. He felt a similar sort of giddy mood about poetry when he talked about it with Frank. Anything was possible. Everything was possible. Even the "green world" of Ashbery Farm in late June did not oppress him this time, because he was going to leave it before "churry" season started.[96] He began writing "The Calendar" with these thoughts of the past and future:

Spring tempts me back to green areas
From which I had strayed, and I allow my mind

Again the luxury of attempting too little, of hearing
My words go uncared for in the rejoicing wind.[97]

The poem has a dreamlike summer fancy. After celebrating the
July 4 holiday at home, he took this buoyant feeling with him to New York
City, despite his family's objections. His father was "anti-New York,"
and particularly unenthusiastic about his son's potentially expensive
plan to move there, but John was determined to live in the city as he had
long wished and finally to begin his life as an artist.[98]

8

"Darkness Falls Like a Wet Sponge"

1949–1951

Very quickly, John secured an apartment, a job, and a new friend. The apartment, in a narrow four-story tenement house at 170 Third Avenue, was being rented by Kenneth Koch, who was visiting his parents in Cincinnati for three weeks. The friend was Kenneth's upstairs neighbor, a dark-haired, twenty-four-year-old painter named Jane Freilicher, from whom he retrieved the key. She told him about the job prospect, which she had just applied for, over tea in her apartment. Within a week, he informed his surprised family of his full-time appointment at the Brooklyn Public Library; they confessed to "having been skeptical about your venture."[1] His grandfather, who knew from experience how tenuous one's "first encounter with the world" after college could be, congratulated John, reminding him "to stick and make good," and "never throw up a job until you are sure of something better."[2] He guessed that John already wished to quit his new position in the Foreign Language and Literature Division. Even in the heat wave of July 1949, the city beyond the library beckoned as an "open place" worth "walking into."[3]

In the evenings, after going downtown for an inexpensive dinner with Jane, John headed to gay bars on Eighth Street to pick up men—"if I was lucky."[4] He could barely drag himself to work in the morning. Once there, he often fell asleep at his desk. Although he claimed the library "profession" was "a fairly painless one" and had promised to attend library school as a condition of accepting his position, he knew almost immediately after starting the job that he did not want to keep it.[5] Best about the library was meeting his coworker Richard Elliott, a "tall, lanky" man of about forty "with a long, washed out, bland face and a toothy grin." Elliott, a well-read writer, had close friendships with many contemporary artists, including Jane and Paul Bowles.[6] At Elliott's recommendation, John's summer reading included Jane Bowles's *Two Serious Ladies* (1943), Raymond Queneau's poetry, and "In Bayswater" and other stories by Mary Butts, whom he grew to admire greatly as "a very good writer . . . very weird; rather like Djuna [Barnes], but tight-lipped and suppressed hysterical."[7] In fact, John appreciated that "every writer you ever recommended to me (with the exception of Jean Rhys, whom I did not like) I have loved."[8] Despite his enthusiasm for Elliott, John's time card, which clocked a later arrival each day, registered only apathy for library work.

"Anxious to see" Frank O'Hara, who was about to begin his senior year in college, John reapplied to the Harvard English Department to begin graduate school in the fall.[9] He had already been rejected once, in May, but Richard Ellmann, a young professor, encouraged him to send in stronger recommendations. John wrote F. O. Matthiessen to request a letter, explaining that his "personal vocation of poet is perfectly clear in my mind," and he now knew "definitely" that he also wished "to become a teacher." He blamed his "average grades" at Harvard on his former "uncertainty about my professional career after college."[10] Matthiessen offered to meet during his vacation in Long Island, and John took a few days off from the library to talk with him.[11] Despite Matthiessen's willingness to write a letter of support, John heard from the department soon after that he had been rejected again. Desperate to leave his job, he took Kenneth's advice and applied to Columbia University's English literature graduate program, which quickly accepted him.[12] He immediately resigned from the library. Feeling almost giddy with relief, he threw a "grand party" over Labor Day weekend to welcome Frank O'Hara for his first visit to the city, before traveling home to Sodus.

As soon as he arrived in Sodus, John shut his bedroom door and went to sleep. He had "left New York in a state of near collapse," so exhausted that he "spent almost all of my stay here in bed, deaf to the groans of my parents."[13] In bed, he finished *The Great Gatsby*, discovered Boris Pasternak's poems, and read more Mary Butts stories. At the recommendation of both Richard Elliott and Frank O'Hara, he began the slender early-twentieth-century novels of Englishman Ronald Firbank, whose works he had previously dismissed as "too silly and campy." He suddenly recognized that "every single line is funny and beautiful."[14] Before long, he was encouraging these same friends to hurry up and read more of Firbank's "sublimities": "HAVE YOU READ *VALMOUTH* YET?" He praised the novel as "the greatest . . . of the century next to *Remembrance of Things Past*, and it may be greater since Rinaldo says just what Marcel said, only in 120 pages."[15]

Just before leaving Sodus, he wrote his first prose poem, "A Dream," which evocatively imagines Paris in winter.[16] "Gusts of snow creep down the little street in Paris," as Sibelius's "Valse Triste" plays in the background (citing the piece he correctly identified to become the Rochester Quiz Kid in 1941). Sibelius fades, replaced by strains of Rachmaninoff, a composer John always felt was "too silly" but whose compositions Frank had encouraged him to hear again with a more open mind.[17] A man is haunted by flickering sounds and sights, which seem some "strange dream" of his past. He feels a "swollen, tortured melody" buried inside, which might one day burst forth and "would no doubt be successful in battering apart my childhood on the eternal stones of this hard-hearted city."[18] Like Frank, John had begun to "look to France" for its "encouraging sentiment" of freedom.[19] Among his new artistic friends, several of whom, such as Jane Freilicher, had grown up in Brooklyn, "the dream was to live in Paris," and John already felt a similar tug to go abroad.[20] He had spent his childhood wishing for an artist's life in New York. A few months into his new city adventure, he was already hoping to leave for France because Paris "is magical" and New York "isn't."[21]

For the time being, though, he found a fourth-floor apartment at 60 West Twelfth Street, with a garden view. Despite the "splendors" of the place, the steep hundred-dollar-per-month rent required his finding roommates. In October, Les Brown, his old Harvard friend, moved in for a few months, surprised to see "a different man at breakfast with John every morning."[22] Although Columbia was "[u]ptown" where "giant canyons or apartments" offered cheap rents and the chance to "live a clean, contemplative life," John preferred downtown, where "one could call on friends in the Village."[23] Less social, just as academic, and even more conservative than Harvard, Columbia left John cold. Susanne Nobbe's Nineteenth-Century Prose course included an "absolutely impossible reading list . . . all two-thousand pages of Proust in three weeks . . . *Magic Mountain* in a week," a pace that turned even reading into a chore.[24] John's adviser, William York Tindall, a specialist in twentieth-century British literature, was "a stuffed shirt" and aggressively anti-gay.[25] In the midst of privately reading all Ronald Firbank's novels in a state of "rapture," John asked to write his master's thesis on the British writer. Tindall, who described Firbank as a "corrupt dandy," refused.[26] In December, when Auden favorably reviewed New Directions' five-volume set of Firbank's novels for *The New York Times Book Review*, John asked if Tindall had changed his mind. He replied that Auden's piece was merely an example of "homosexual calling to homosexual over the abyss."[27]

Irritated, John spent more time at "this wonderful bookshop, 'The Periscope,'" on East Fifty-Fourth Street, with Jane, who was an insatiable reader. Run by Bob Vanderbilt, an Anglophile, the bookstore imported contemporary English books, favoring dry, witty novels by Henry Green and Ivy Compton-Burnett. John skipped classes and immersed himself instead in vivid and strange prose about family gatherings and boarding school life, books that were concise and sharply written. John referred to "ICB" as "one of our leading poets."[28]

He felt happiest among "the friends I've made."[29] Jane was a "connoisseur of horrible types," and he could talk to her about the "loathsome," "worthless," or "downright depraved."[30] Her boyfriend, Larry Rivers, a jazz musician turned painter whom she had met during her brief marriage to Jack Freilicher, was taking classes with Jane at Hans Hofmann's painting school on Eighth Street. Tall, "very skinny," and "very loud," Larry seemed "kind of dumb in a lot of ways," but also "totally unorthodox," which John admired. At every opportunity, Rivers made "a willful effort . . . to thumb his nose at the establishment."[31] He lived with a roommate, Arnold Weinstein, a poet and playwright, in a loft on Second Avenue just off St. Mark's, where other painters their age, including Albert Kresch, Alfred Leslie, and Grace Hartigan, congregated. John also accompanied Jane to West Twenty-First Street to visit her closest friend and confidante, the painter Nell Blaine, whom he found "funny and amusing" and kept "having dreams about."[32] To Nell, who was slightly older, John seemed more "wistful" than Jane's other friends.[33] She invited him to her Halloween party, and he brought Bubsy, who was working in the city for a publishing house. For Thanksgiving, he stayed in New York and cooked Thanksgiving dinner with Jane, who was no more domestically inclined than he was. John's grandfather chastised him for avoiding his family: "Why do you not write your mother? You should write each week."[34] Spending almost all his free time with painters, he finally borrowed an easel, canvas, and paints, set them up by his kitchen window, and began to paint his view.[35]

Despite his wish to see Paris, he could not wait to share more of New York City with Frank. He made plans to meet at his apartment after a quick trip to see his family for Christmas. Feeling lonely and depressed in Sodus, he wrote two serious poems: "Beguine," a dialogue between a man and a woman (which he composed just after seeing Carol Rupert—now Carol Doty—in her new home on her first wedding anniversary), and "The Party," a gothic tale about a hostess who disintegrates in front of her anxious guests. In both, the speaker evocatively describes

Barbara "Bubsy" Zimmerman (Epstein) in New York City in the early 1950s

a hostile, confusing world from which he feels disconnected, but John did not like the heavy feeling in either poem. To keep his spirits up, he listened to a new recording of Darius Milhaud's esoteric Symphony No. 1, "full of giddy reminders and heartrending blasts." He also made new collages, which he sent to Frank: "I am enclosing some pretties, which may delight you. I have also made a little picture book of them which I will show you. It's too c-mpy for words!"[36] He begged Frank for news even though they were going to see each other in a matter of days: "full of post holiday blues . . . write soon and give me a lift."[37] John suggested they attend a "g-y party" at Katherine Anne Porter's apartment for New Year's Eve.[38] As he explained, "[I]t seems so important what we do because you know this is the middle of the century." He arrived in the city just in time to usher in 1950 with Frank, and they traversed the city in high spirits for several days. "How sweet you were to me," Frank wrote gratefully later.[39]

Alone again, John began to write with new "vitality."[40] "[A] poem a month is about my speed," he concluded by September, looking back with satisfaction on his productive first eight months of 1950.[41] By the end of January, he had already written an insouciant one-act comedy, *The Heroes*. He found inspiration in his new course, Classical Drama and Its Influence, taught by a young professor, Moses Hadas.[42] John declared Greek plays so weird and intense that they must have been written by men, "all obviously mad."[43] On his own, he also read André Gide's *Theseus* in its recent New Directions publication. He thought Gide's Theseus was an even more nimble, original, and modern character than the imaginative examples he already knew well from childhood: Shakespeare's *A Midsummer Night's Dream* (in which Theseus appears as the Duke of Athens, and only Titania and Oberon seem aware of his semi-immortal provenance) and Charles Kingsley's *Heroes*, which recounts the exploits of a very heroic Theseus.[44] All these retellings, as well as stories of the Trojan War and its aftermath that he knew well from Homer's *Iliad* and *Odyssey* and Virgil's *Aeneid*, were in his mind as he started to write his new play. As it begins, Theseus, Ulysses, and Circe arrive for a weekend at a beach house where Achilles and Patroclus have settled together following the Trojan War. They fall into awkward, intimate, and very funny conversations about themselves and the past.

Theseus mistakes Circe for Medea, awkwardly insulting her; Achilles tries to get Ulysses to go home to Penelope before Circe "decide[s] to change us all into pigs for no reason at all."[45] Theseus complains that no one wants to talk with him about anything but killing the Minotaur. In the climax of the play, Patroclus, annoyed by Achilles's antisocial habits, dances with Theseus, with whom he is falling in love. Thrilled by his funny romp, Ashbery began to wonder if two men dancing together onstage was "too gay."[46] He put his play into a drawer. After finishing two more poems ("Antistrophe" and "A Taste for Mozart"), neither of which he liked, he traveled home to Sodus, where he remained so idle that he joked his parents complained he could easily be "mistaken for part of the furniture" and was costing them "a fortune in worn-out antimacassars."[47]

Rested, he wrote "Meditations of a Parrot" in a single afternoon as soon as he returned to the city. While its fragmented style and "strange juxtapositions" were new, the tiny poem had deep roots.[48] The iron parrot Ashbery rescued in 1941 just before his grandparents sold their Dartmouth Street house was still affixed to his bedroom door in Pultneyville. Just recently, he had discovered Joseph Cornell's aviary boxes (including a parrot) exhibited at the Charles Egan Gallery in New York City, which he had wanted to see ever since studying photographs of Cornell's boxes more than a decade earlier, in Julien Levy's *Surrealism*. Using the singsong quality of nursery rhymes and simple vocabulary (one- and two-syllable nouns), he created an effect in which fragments of childhood memories flicker through the poem: bright bits of color in a cereal bowl; a view of the sea; shouts of "Robin Hood"; and "dazzling canopies" of leaves, trees, and music. In "A Dream," he writes that, one day, a "swollen, tortured melody" would escape and "be successful in battering apart my childhood." This new poem delivers on this promise by including specific details and images from childhood and eliminating their original contexts to create, through their reassembly, an entirely new sound:

Oh the rocks and the thimble
The oasis and the paraphrase[49]
Oh the jacket and the roses.

All sweetly stood up the sea to me
Like blue cornflakes in a white bowl.
The girl said, "Watch this."

I come from Spain, I said.
I was purchased at a fair.
She said, "None of us know.

"There was a house once
Of dazzling canopies
And halls like a keyboard.

"These the waves tore in pieces."
(His old wound—
And all day: Robin Hood! Robin Hood!)[50]

Two weeks later, Ashbery wrote "The Picture of Little J.A. in a Prospect of Flowers," a poem that emerged even more directly from the "swollen, tortured melody" of "childhood." As an epigraph, he quoted the final sentence of Pasternak's lyrical and poetic autobiography, *Safe Conduct*, which he had recently finished reading: "He was spoilt from childhood by the future, which he mastered rather early and apparently without great difficulty." The experience of the loss of childhood was a feature of everyone's autobiography, but he suddenly understood anew this idea, which had been percolating in his mind for some time.

On April 1, John was shocked to read in the newspaper that his Harvard professor F. O. Matthiessen, whom he had last seen during their friendly talk on the beach in Water Mill the previous summer, had committed suicide by jumping from the window of a Boston hotel.[51] Ashbery's poem opens with a six-word description of the onslaught of depression: "Darkness falls like a wet sponge," and echoes of this overwhelming feeling of melancholy at different points in a life rapidly follow:

Darkness falls like a wet sponge
And Dick gives Genevieve a swift punch
In the pajamas. "Aroint thee, witch."

Her tongue from previous ecstasy
Releases thoughts like little hats.

An image of children playing rough shifts to adults acting in a drama ("Aroint thee, witch," from *Macbeth*, which Ashbery saw in a performance with Maurice Evans on March 5, 1942). In the third (and final) section of the poem, the speaker narrates an origin of these unsettling feelings as though it were a scene in a play he watches:

Yet I cannot escape the picture
Of my small self in that bank of flowers:
My head among the blazing phlox
Seemed a pale and gigantic fungus.
I had a hard stare, accepting
Everything, taking nothing,
As though the rolled-up future might stink
As loud as stood the sick moment
The shutter clicked.[52]

This imaginative description had autobiographical roots in a particular series of photographs Ashbery remembered seeing. The pictures were ones his father had taken in Sodus one afternoon in early August 1940, as he finished the roll of film started during the family's trip to Blue Mountain just after Richard's death. The images reveal John and Helen as unwilling subjects, standing awkwardly as they watch their dog running around the yard. Their pained expressions are harshly illuminated by the sun. Chet and his camera are visible, too, in the long shadow pooling at their feet. John's body is framed against the "blazing phlox," a word that describes both the blooming flowers in their summer garden and (through the pun on "flocks") his family. While the raw, disorienting image intimates how "the rolled-up future might stink / As loud as stood the sick moment / The shutter clicked," the poem continues. In the final two sentences, the narrator explains how "feelings / Must soon find words," but then other words will "yes, / Displace" those words, too. The poem enacts this process. The "darkness" that opens the poem becomes brighter by the end; the tragic, "sick moment" that the photograph captures becomes a comic one when the speaker decides that "I am not wrong / In calling this comic version of myself / The true one." An image becomes what words say it is, because of the enormous power language contains to shape and reshape a life.

John confided only to Frank when Delmore Schwartz at *Partisan Review*, the esteemed literary journal in which he most wanted his poetry to appear, accepted "Little J.A." for publication six months later. He did not elaborate on "my own very silly but firmly grounded reason for not wanting you to tell this to <u>anybody</u>." By then he was feeling such extreme anxieties about nearly every aspect of his life and work that he had ceased to write.[53] Initially, though, writing "Little J.A." felt exciting. In the prolific spring that followed, Ashbery composed an even longer poem, "The Mythological Poet," submitted a seventy-page thesis on three of Henry Green's novels, and successfully completed all his coursework at Columbia. He also costarred with Jane Freilicher, Ann Aikman, and Larry Rivers as a baseball player turned modern artist in Rudy Burckhardt's twenty-minute film, *Mounting Tension*, which delighted the audience during its June premiere, especially Kenneth, who "thought we were all wonderful."[54] This frenetic schedule, however, left John ill. His exhaustion was compounded by daily newspaper articles speculating on the likelihood that the Soviet Union would drop an atomic bomb on New York City. A recent letter from his draft board stating that his 4-F status had been updated to 1-A, which meant he was newly eligible for the draft, compounded his anxieties.[55]

His newest poem, "The Cool Head," reflected in its ironic title his palpable fears about the Cold War.[56] John wanted to leave the city as soon as possible. Kenneth had recently been awarded a Fulbright to study in France beginning in the fall. Larry Rivers and Nell Blaine were also about to visit Europe. On Sunday morning, June 25, 1950, as John, Jane, and Kenneth lay on Jones Beach listening to the radio, they heard that North Korea had invaded South Korea and declared war. Kenneth said quietly, "It's very serious."[57] John, who had been uncertain about his summer plans until then, quickly decided to return to Sodus. He postponed final exams at Columbia, which he felt unprepared to pass anyway, secretly hoping that he could devise a strategy never to return to take them. He hastily packed up his apartment, went out for a drink, and returned with a man who surveyed the scene the next morning and concluded, "I guess I'm closing out the season."[58] The man's remark reminded John of the sexual freedoms he was voluntarily giving up by returning home.

Almost as soon as he arrived in Sodus, John left again for "a delightful week in Frank's company" in Boston.[59] He "just adored the atmosphere" at Frank's sublet on Beacon Hill, where he read Williams's *Paterson* (and loved the prose passages) and Cocteau's aphorisms, and where, in "a room full of people," he wrote "Mencius in Milk Street," an "ornate" poem that "sounded like the poet F. T. Prince."[60] Although the concerns of the poem—"the sweet boredom of childhood"; the relationship between "old obsessions" and "today"; and what "poetry will not let happen"—were familiar, its mood encompassed in the last line, "And all shall be well," was notably upbeat.[61]

Officially, he was in Cambridge to request new letters of recommendation. He planned to reapply to Harvard graduate school and told Jane he was also interested in Kenyon's writing program. Frank's poetry teacher John Ciardi recommended the graduate writing program at the University of Michigan, and Frank also encouraged him to apply, hoping that they could land someplace together. Jane had just returned to the city from a visit with Frank, and they all began corresponding. Her darkly witty letters, with their penchant for gossip and brilliant asides about poetry and painting, rapidly became "required reading."[62] John explained to her that he did not want to return to Columbia because, among other irritations, he was incensed that Tindall had called James Joyce's *A Portrait of the Artist as a Young Man* "the greatest novel of adolescence ever written." (In that category, Ashbery vastly preferred "*Swann's Way, David Copperfield* and *Faust*.")[63] Frank read aloud his newest poems, "Today" and "Memorial Day, 1950," works that excited John so much he typed up copies to send to Kenneth.[64] On the train ride home, catching up on *The New York Times*, he read a review of Sydney Freedberg's new book, *Parmigianino*, which was accompanied by a reproduction of Parmigianino's 1524 painting, *Self-Portrait in a Convex Mirror*.[65] John felt a rush of pleasure at seeing the painting for the first time and began referring to the painter in letters to friends as the "truly divine Parmigianino."[66] Not only had the trip to see Frank rejuvenated John creatively, but returning home on his twenty-third birthday, he received his "nicest present," which was "a notice saying I'm 4-F." He assured Jane that "I'll be of far more use to this nation on the home front bolstering the morale of three nervous aesthetes."[67]

Relieved, he wrote three new poems soon after returning to Sodus. "Le livre est sur la table," "The Hero," and "Illustration." He sent Jane an early (now lost) draft of what was then called "Two Promenades" (with "Le livre est sur la table" included as an epigraph), but he immediately sent her a revision because he was "so mortified by the version of my poem I sent." He felt that the mechanics of his first draft were too transparent, and "I have a natural horror of letting people see how my mind works."[68] (He worried about revealing himself even to Jane, his "dear Marcel," with whom he had grown so close that "our Proustian relationship seems to have caused us to switch sexes, which I however have felt for some time was imminent anyway.")[69] The revised title recalled phrases from his high school French exercises—"fill in the blank est sur la table"—as did the line in the poem "the table supports the book," which was a witty rendering of a clumsy translation.[70] The French title (his first) also boldly announced his increasing attentiveness to French language and culture. He put his general opinion simply: "isn't everything good when it's written in French?"[71] The opening tercet reinforces an idea about language and ingenuity: "All beauty, resonance, integrity, / Exist by deprivation or logic / Of strange position." Phrases in "strange" order followed, alongside lines such as "The young man places a bird-house / Against the blue sea" and "the shadow of the sea," which resonate with the mood and feeling of his childhood landscape, ordinary things, but displaced and decontextualized to highlight their new "beauty" in the poem.[72]

He wrote "The Hero" quickly. In reading Frank's new poetry in Boston a month before, John had become particularly exhilarated by what he viewed as a "freedom of expression" and a way of "amusing himself" in writing to a degree that he had never witnessed in any poet's work before, except maybe Rimbaud, and which inspired him to find material for poems everywhere and in everything.[73] Ashbery's new poem was provoked by one especially moving scene from an otherwise mediocre film about a woman climbing the Swiss Alps. He told Jane that "for some reason, this *sospiro* found its inspiration in a befuddled movie called *The White Tower*," which he watched one dull afternoon in Sodus with his mother.[74] In the film, Carla (played by Alida Valli) climbs the forbidding snowy mountain, despite a previous attempt with her father, one of the greatest climbers of all time, that ended in his disappearance. John's initial two-part poem, which he called "Doctor Gradus ad Parnassum," after Claude Debussy's *Children's Corner*, a suite of six piano pieces, did not satisfy him. He changed the title to "Harold in Italy," after Berlioz's tone poem, but that did not seem quite right, either. Then he lopped off the entire second section, saving it for his next new poem, "Illustration," and renamed the new spare lyric "The Hero." He wanted to translate a sense of failed effort into music, using words as sounds. He sent drafts to Sandy Gregg and Jane, explaining that the poem's "atonal" sound arose from its "Webernian brevity," a condensed and intense romantic expression:

> Whose face is this,
> So stiff against the blue trees,
>
> Lifted to the future
> Because there is no end?
>
> But that has faded,
> Like flowers, like the first days
>
> Of good conduct. Visit
> The strong man. Pinch him—
>
> There is no end to his
> Dislike, the accurate one.

Each of the poem's short lines link to the next through an emotional, not an intellectual, connection. The original second section of "The Hero" became the second section of "Illustration," a poem he wrote a week later that describes a suicide, how "naked / As a roc's egg, she drifted slowly downward." The second section begins "Much that is beautiful must be discarded," an unsentimental approach to loss. John, Kenneth, and Frank freely praised one another's new poems as "beautiful," a term that John was also examining critically through these poems.

By the time he finished "Illustration," he knew that Frank had been accepted to the University of Michigan and he had not. The rejection stung, which he confided only to Jane: "What I find stranger than the fact that I didn't get in is that Frank *did*, as he applied late and his grades are far inferior to mine (he flunked Chaucer at Harvard, which ranks as a deadly sin)."[75] To Frank, John shared only that he felt "just miserable at your being so far away."[76] John weighed two unpleasant options: to return to New York City or stay in Sodus indefinitely. He had just "read a whole issue of Colliers . . . devoted to an account of a hypothetical bombing of New York . . . [with] the gruesomest [*sic*] details," but staying in Sodus meant, he felt, the end of the possibility for love and sex.[77] He quickly arranged to take courses at Columbia for a second year before taking his master's exams (an unusual plan for a one-year program). Even though it seemed the better choice, the idea of returning to "that detestable school" depressed him.[78] He alleviated his gloom by reading Ronald Firbank's *Inclinations*, which "I'd been saving . . . for the dark night of the soul."[79]

Despite a hectic fall, John felt a terrible sense of "sterility."[80] He confided to Kenneth that "everything repeats last year, without the vitality of the poetry I read and wrote."[81] Although he had a brief creative burst in October, this energy quickly faded.[82] He wrote four untraditional sonnets and applied for a Fulbright to France, telling Frank to apply also so that they could go together. Soon after, he tried jotting down lines for two new poems, "Platitudes" and "Exequy," but felt displeased with every word and phrase he added. Frustrated, he ceased writing at all. In his depression, he repeatedly went to see Jean Cocteau's elegiac new film, *Orpheus*, at the 55th Street Playhouse. He also accompanied Jane to the first show at the Tibor de Nagy Gallery, a new space co-owned by John Bernard Myers, who was an excitable aesthete as interested in poetry as painting. He also looked forward to Frank O'Hara's visit from Michigan for a party at his apartment in honor of Bunny Lang, "a voluptuous and simply de-vine poetess" and one of the founders of the Poets' Theatre in Cambridge, with whom John had shared a memorable slow dance and kiss before he graduated.[83] Within minutes of meeting Larry Rivers, Frank had disappeared behind a curtain with him, an instantaneous attraction that surprised John and especially Jane, who had only recently ended her relationship with Larry.[84]

Nineteen fifty-one began with still no new poems and none of the feelings of renewal that the New Year usually ushered in. John appealed to Kenneth, wishing for "your presence" and "a good literary gab."[85] Even in February, when John traveled to Cambridge to see the inaugural event of the Poets' Theatre, including a performance of his verse drama, *Everyman*, he felt listless all evening.[86] Frank, who could not attend, had written a haunting piano-and-flute duet in "sympathy" with John's play, "wonderful . . . music" he appreciated much more than his own work, which he no longer liked.[87] Despite his depression, he performed "magnificently" as "John" in Frank O'Hara's Noh play, *Try! Try!* According to Freddy English, a college friend in the audience, Ashbery "was absolutely marvelous . . . as he finished one page he would throw it away onstage with such aplomb."[88] John felt less charitable about his performance and sat backstage brooding afterward, so he missed the commotion when playwright Thornton Wilder stood up after Frank's play to deliver an impassioned and impromptu speech on the state of verse drama in America.[89]

John fought his deepening depression with humor. Seeing Jane's "very funny letter" to Frank, to whom she had grown very close, "reminded me of the standard I should aspire to." With O'Hara's *Try! Try!* on his mind, he composed an "exciting forgery." His O'Hara imitation, "Incunabula," was "bound to perplex graduate students of the future":

If I were mme de scudéry
we'd have long drawn out adventures
heroes as base as giraffes would chase us
over mountains not desolate of a sound track

but the Chinese wouldn't know about us
or the Ethiopians or bears or lapps
I'd wear a twisted smile
sitting at my writing desk

here everything is battered
but what really intrigues me
is the way your hair stands on end
whenever I think of you[90]

Four months after writing the "parody," John continued to find it "so amusing that it causes me to laugh outright several times a day."[91] He had rewritten his own poetic concerns (including "heroes," "sitting at my writing desk" but not writing, and "everything is battered"), but in Frank's tone of insouciant amusement, which completely diffused their seriousness. John declared to Frank that "my speech and person" are being "made over in your image."[92] He recorded a recent conversation with a mutual acquaintance:

John: "I love trashy things as long as they're French."
Acquaintance: "That's a Frank O'Hara (!)"

While John sorely missed his friend, he was also mocking himself and his seriousness, which lightened up in Frank's presence.

He was worried that he could no longer write. In the past, falling in love had sometimes worked as a provocation for a new poem, but after briefly dating a kind young poet, Howard Wamsley, long enough to call it "an affair . . . the first thing I've had which deserves the dignity of this title," the promising relationship fizzled.[93] He doodled a poetic fragment in his Columbia University notebook, "Letters to the Sleeper," which was actually a revision of "Epilogue to Experience," written during his senior year at Deerfield.[94] As its new title suggested, this shortened version addressed an unresponsive self, one for whom "all exertion wanes, emotions tend / To a dry decline." The speaker explains that earlier in his life, "I looked up from my journal to the sea / And thought its gray insipid depths a map / Wherein all written was apparent to me." In his present "dry" period, however, the same "map" had become unreadable.[95] He forced himself to revise "Exequy," his long poem from the fall, glad to write "a fragment" of something new, "the first poetical activity in six months," but even that work stopped when he had to move. After six months at 51 West Twelfth Street, he was moving to a sublet around the corner, at 125 West Eleventh Street.[96] Finally passing his long-delayed exams at Columbia, he graduated and skipped commencement. By the end of the spring, when "Little J.A." did not appear in the May issue of *Partisan Review* as the magazine had promised, and he received a letter that he had not gotten the Fulbright, he succumbed to his dark mood completely, lamenting, "Oh Frank, I'm so depressed and this is going to be such a dull letter."[97]

Having made no other plans, he returned once again to Sodus for the summer. He worried that his poem was never going to appear in *Partisan Review*, and if it did, no one would read it during the summer anyway. In July he had a sudden premonition that he might finally see "Little J.A." in print, and he forced himself to write something new, a first draft of "A Long Novel."[98] The next morning, the magazine arrived with his poem in it. He explained to Jane that "last night I actually wrote a poem . . . it's funny—I've felt it vitally necessary that I write something before seeing my thing in *Partisan*."[99] Freed from months of nervous excitement about seeing his poem in print, he finally relaxed, even joking that "Louis Simpson in the same issue gives little J.A. rather a run for his money—something will have to be done about that one."[100] John listened to Scriabin, read more Pasternak, and began Saltykov-Shchedrin's "immensely readable" *The Golovyov Family*, but he suddenly wanted to reread Philip Horton's biography of Hart Crane for the first time since 1943, "nostalgia shoot[ing] out in all directions."[101] At fifteen, he had furtively read the book looking for answers to questions about his own sexuality and the new experience of being in love; at twenty-four, he felt protective of Hart Crane and all nervous gay artists. He told Jane that if he had only known Crane, "I'd hold his hand! on the days I wasn't holding Proust's or Firbank's."[102]

He had recently heard some good news that scared him. *The Heroes* had been accepted by James Laughlin for the prestigious New Directions Annual. Initially thrilled that Laughlin found the play so "amusing" and had declared "what a mad young thing I am," Ashbery soon started to worry because Laughlin's first question to him about the play was "Is it 'camp' or what?" He replied with a "carefully worded note" pretending that he had needed to ask his friends "what camp meant." He explained his anxiety to Jane: "I suppose this is a piece of luck, but I'm rather unhappy about it for fear it may blight my poetic career. It *is* awfully gay, and I hate to have people I don't know think of me as one of *those* young writers."[103] He was afraid that if people disapproved of his life, they would be unable (and he would, too) to believe in his art: "My poems are usually in the form of solemn precepts for spiritual conduct (I didn't mean that to sound so pompous)" so "once the people . . . start thinking that I'm below them these precepts will fall flat, as will my desire to write the poems."[104]

Two days later he withdrew the play and "immediately regretted it."[105] His official reason was "parts of the play which I feel are not as good," a misleading admission that left him feeling "very blue."[106] He desperately wanted to talk to Jane or Frank, but Jane was in Ann Arbor visiting Frank, who had just finished his writing program (winning a Hopwood Prize for poetry), and they were absorbed with traveling together to see the Art Institute of Chicago. She was also busy painting a portrait of Frank and did not respond to John as quickly as she usually did. He felt abandoned and all alone in making decisions. His parents were insisting he secure a teaching position, and he half-heartedly applied to an opening at a high school in Bethlehem, Pennsylvania (a place interesting to him only as H.D.'s hometown); he was relieved not to get an interview. Especially miserable at home, he felt trapped between his mother, who "tends to take the worst view of a thing," and his father, who "keeps me in delightful suspense" whether or not "I finished [farm] work today."[107] When Jane finally called John to check on him (a gesture that cost her a small fortune), he said almost nothing, and apologized only later, in writing, for "sound[ing] strange" because his family's phone was on a party line and he was too worried about "all the people listening."[108]

A few days later, Frank O'Hara surprised John by arriving in Sodus on his way home from Michigan. John's "very blue mood" began to lift, especially after Frank informed him of his plans to move immediately to New York. Jane—"dear me what a clever girl you are"—had convinced him to choose New York over Boston.[109] Elated, John showed Frank where he grew up. They sat in his bedroom in the farmhouse and talked, walked among the trees in the orchards, and lay on the Pultneyville beach. After dinner the first night, Helen Ashbery mistook Frank's voice for her son's.[110] On their last evening together, they hiked up Chimney Bluffs at sunset to see its splendid view of Lake Ontario. It was already turning dark and cold at the end of August, and the lake was full of rough and wild waves. Frank suddenly "stripped off his clothes" and "jumped into the cold water."[111] John peered into the distance and could just barely trace the outline of Frank's naked body splashing in the surf. Just a week earlier, he had written to Jane that "I still feel a wreck," but as he waited on shore for his friend to rejoin him, he began "crisping my veils for 'Autumn in New York.'"[112]

9

"*Greetings, Friends!*"

1951–1953

"I am constantly plotting how to spend most of my life amid my friends," John wrote to Jane Freilicher in 1950.[1] By September 1951, his scheme was taking shape. For two years he had been encouraging Frank to move to the city, where O'Hara had become "a symbol for kindness, virtue, and excellence in all the arts."[2] Frank responded to the compliment exuberantly by writing "A Party Full of Friends," a poem in which "Violet leaped"; "Jane, her eyeballs like the / crystal of a seer . . . advanced slowly"; "Larry paced"; "John yawked / onto the ottoman"; and O'Hara exclaimed, "What / confusion! and to think / I sat down and caused it / all! No!"[3] John admired Frank's "radiant magnetism," which drew people together.[4] Even more, his attitude that "being an artist" was "the most natural thing in the world" had an "explosive effect" on everyone around him.[5] For John, finally being together in New York City meant that "we could begin to be ourselves."[6]

John had always joked that landing a job was "a blow" from which a writer "might never recover," but necessity finally demanded that he find one.[7] In early October he took a typing test at the Oxford University Press offices in the beautiful art deco building at 114 Fifth Avenue. Invited for an interview soon after, he was offered a job in the publicity department, in large part because Fon Boardman, the scholarly head of the department, was impressed that Ashbery had just published a poem in *Partisan Review*. On October 8, while game four of the Giants-Yankees

World Series played uptown in unseasonably hot weather, he began work as a publicity assistant, typing address labels for review copies.

He immediately looked for a nicer place to live. Initially, he had stayed in a room at John Myers's place, on Ninth Street. Although grateful for the cheap rent, he disliked the noise and chaos of Myers's life as he prepared to launch Larry Rivers's first exhibition at Tibor de Nagy. After only two weeks, John moved to the only single he could (barely) afford, a bleak furnished room at 10 Charles Street. When Gerrit Lansing, a poet from college with whom he occasionally had lunch, mentioned that he was about to leave his rental at 44 Morton Street, John thought the small, minimally furnished studio with a fireplace would be ideal.[8] Morton, a curvy, tree-lined street, was one of the prettiest in Greenwich Village. Its street lamps and town houses evoked a feeling of nineteenth-century New York City. The apartment seemed a particularly auspicious find when he discovered that, in 1925, poet Laura Riding had lived at number 43.

With a regular but low salary (forty dollars a week), he could almost afford the place. His parents and grandparents were still sending him a small monthly allowance, but his mother informed him that the farm was in "financial straits," and that he needed to pay his own rent.[9] (In an attempt to consolidate farmwork and increase profits, Chet Ashbery was about to stop raising turkeys, a decision he explained only to Frank Boyden at Deerfield.)[10] John responded that he would "try to manage," despite the "expense" of living in the city. To help him, his mother still washed, folded, and mailed back his laundry every few weeks. She also sent him jam and bought pots and pans for his new place—though, after she sent them, John complained: "[Y]ou must think I have the appetite of a midget. The frying pan will hold 2 pieces of bacon (if they are cut in half) and nothing else. I'm only kidding; they are fine for me alone but I will have to get other things for when I have people over to meals. I have already invited Frank and Hal to Sunday breakfast."[11] Frank was sharing an apartment on East Forty-Ninth Street with his Harvard friend Hal Fondren and had just found a job working at the information desk at the Museum of Modern Art.

John had long been anxious about his "uncertain future, not writing, and the world situation," but he knew, at least, that "if I could write I wouldn't mind the other two so much."[12] By December, when he had still written only one new poem draft in over a year, he felt tremendously frustrated: "I remember writing poems during what I consider my dry period and I couldn't write anything I liked." He tried revising "A Long Novel" from the previous summer, but he could not make it better.[13] At Oxford University Press he found a damaged copy of Iona and Peter Opie's new *Oxford Dictionary of Nursery Rhymes*, which he was allowed to take home. He "devoured" the book, which reminded him of stories that his grandfather read to him as a young child at 69 Dartmouth Street, but when he tried to use these thoughts to compose something new, he produced only uninteresting fragments.[14]

For inspiration, he went to see the Living Theatre's "direct and engaging" production of Gertrude Stein's *Doctor Faustus Lights the Lights*. This activist avant-garde group had been recently founded by Judith Malina and Julian Beck, a young married couple.[15] A few weeks later, on January 1, 1952, John and Frank went together to David Tudor's piano recital, sponsored by the Living Theatre, which included the premiere of John Cage's *Music of Changes* on the second half of the program. Wiry and energetic, thirty-nine-year-old Cage spent the day in the box office selling out the concert (even seats onstage). If there had been program notes that night, John would have read that the piece was inspired by the I Ching, a philosophy of accident and luck that Cage used to guide its aleatory composition. As John listened to Tudor play Cage's piece for more than forty-five minutes with no apparent break between any of the four movements, he heard sounds change slowly, strangely, deeply: "there were banging chords, followed by long periods of silence."[16] He was hearing a musical equivalent to the world of his childhood: the vast expanse of the lake, hours on the farm with nothing to do, days that were silent, melancholy, and conducive to simmering creativity. He had hated that dull world and wished to flee its many pains and constraints, but he also knew best its slow rhythms and wandering moods.

Immediately, he wrote two acidic poems about childhood, "A Boy" and "The Pied Piper." In December, John and Frank had seen *The Red Badge of Courage*, a mediocre film starring Audie Murphy in its second run at the Fifth Avenue Playhouse, but one that tapped John's ongoing thoughts about war and America. He felt very anxious about Joseph McCarthy's attacks against groups the senator deemed threats to national security, an intensifying barrage that he read about regularly in *The New York Times*, and one that increasingly targeted homosexuals.[17] It was only after Cage's concert that he knew how to control the surface mood of his poems so that he could write something as angry and intimate as "A Boy." The new poem used simple words, but ones that contained within them the emotional weight of his experiences, including: *Dad, livid, rain, mess, thunder, my child, why, boy, cabbage, roses, Maple* (Avenue), *syntax, mincing, unendurable.*[18] Alluding to his father's rage ("The boy seemed to have fallen / From shelf to shelf of someone's rage") and an afternoon at Deerfield when he became ill under the bleachers after Bill Haddock socially annihilated him ("they're throwing up behind the lines"), the poem expresses anger at McCarthyism and at America: "the observer, the mincing flag" producing "an unendurable age." "The Pied Piper" offers an even darker and more frightening version of the end of childhood: "his hand / Falls like an axe on her curls." The poem is the darkest kind of fairy tale, depicting mistreated children and predatory adults beneath a meditative veneer.

Writing again was a relief despite the poems' bleak subject matter, and once he started, he did not stop. He briefly resumed his dormant affair with Howard Wamsley and wrote "Errors" one winter afternoon as they sat together at his Morton Street place in front of the fireplace, details he subtly worked into the poem ("In the street we found boxes / Littered with snow, to burn at home").[19] He also knew from his study of Latin that the original meaning of *error* was closer to *wandering* (and the exploratory feeling of Cage's piece) than the modern association with *mistakes*, and he drew on this older definition, which suited his thoughts and mood.

When Judith Malina asked if John might be interested in submitting something for the Living Theatre, he sent her *The Heroes*, which she thought was marvelous and immediately wanted to direct.[20] In the meantime, she offered John and Frank the part of two dogs in her next production, Pablo Picasso's *Desire Caught by the Tail*.[21] Judith was a year older than John and two months younger than Frank, but they seemed *young* to her (and she assumed they were a couple), though Frank, she thought, was "more sophisticated."[22] Although the role required only one spoken word—"bow-wow"—the actors were onstage behaving like dogs for almost all of the play.[23] She thought that, "as the Bow-Wows," John and Frank were "unbelievable." They "romped" and kept the "character of dogginess: scratching and sniffing . . . real puppy-dogs." At one performance, during a "wonderful episode" where "Onion dies and they put her in a coffin-like prop with handles and carry her off," John's costume fell down. He was revealed to be "butt-naked, but he held onto the coffin." She loved that "they weren't serious" and that during rehearsals they "behaved like kids." They were only serious "about poetry."[24] For four performances, each made $47.12.[25]

John started to think of himself as not only a poet but also a playwright and an actor. On April 3, 1952, the poet John Malcolm Brinnin introduced him to an audience at the 92nd Street Y as the first of three winners (the other awards went to Gray Burr and Harvey Shapiro) of its annual Poetry Center Introductions contest. He had been chosen by the three poet judges, Brinnin, Kimon Friar, and Richard Wilbur, with "meticulous consideration" from more than one hundred entries. In his remarks, Brinnin emphasized Ashbery's "theatrical" life and his

> Association . . . with the off-Broadway theatrical group known as the Living Theatre, and here he is an actor and as a playwright he will be represented very soon by a play the Living Theatre will produce that he wrote called *The Heroes*.[26]

The sixteen poems Ashbery chose that night for his first poetry reading since his days at Harvard included ten he wrote in the three years after college.[27] Kenneth Koch wrote to Jane: "First DO shower my congratulations on the unlucky head of that Ashbery with heart-shaped windows who won, tells me one of my traveling representations, a prize of the YMHA! . . . I am burning with pride and jealousy for him, and if I ever knew his address I would let him know."[28] Kenneth was in California teaching for the year and eagerly planning, after two years away, to move back to New York City and shape his future career as a teacher and writer. Even his phrase "the unlucky head of that Ashbery" was affectionate. He was quoting from one of his friend's college poems, "The Year's Midnight," which begins, "At twenty one having no one, / Wife or mistress to quarrel / For my unlucky head."[29]

Ashbery read a new poem, "Jane," that evening at the Y. It was an obscure piece (despite the straightforward title), prompted by Jane Freilicher's upcoming debut solo exhibition at Tibor de Nagy.[30] Freilicher was increasingly nervous as the May 6 opening approached. Her support crew included a new friend, James Schuyler, a poet whom John Myers had first introduced to Frank and John at Larry Rivers's exhibition the previous October. Since then, Schuyler had been dealing with a mental health crisis, but by March he was back in the city, pleased that his poem "Salute" and O'Hara's "Poem" ("The eager note on my door . . .") had just appeared in the same first issue of *New World Writing*.[31] Schuyler was "eager" to reconnect with O'Hara, who was helping Jane hang paintings for her show. Schuyler's new role gave him a perfect vantage point from which to view some of her old and new friendships, even as they were quickly becoming his, too. The painter Fairfield Porter, about forty-five years old and the new art critic at *ARTnews*, gave Freilicher's show a thoughtful and positive mini review, calling her paintings "traditional and radical" and "broad and bright, considered without being fussy."[32] After viewing her paintings in her studio in advance of the show, he had invited Jane and her young poet friends, whom his wife, Anne, referred to "as the de Nagy children, because they are all under thirty," to visit their home in Southampton.[33]

Jimmy Schuyler developed his own opinions about Frank, John, and Jane.[34] He articulated some thoughts in a poetic play, *Presenting Jane Freilicher*, which took its title and what little plot it had from Jane's nervous excitement leading up to her show. His opening dialogue perfectly captures each personality:

> JANE: Critics promulg. I am filled with fear like a taxi.
> JOHN: She is drinking the hottest cup of coffee in the world.
> FRANK: I rinse lilacs to praise her brushwork that makes lakes look sick.
> JANE: O dear. I'm not bitchy enough to go far. O dear. Perhaps Marie Laurencin presided at my birth. O dear. I long for an affair with Piero della Francesca; together, we would make big things. O dear. He's dead.
> JOHN: In Sodus land a saying goes, all a woman wants of life is life.[35]

Schuyler affectionately parodies Jane's darkly funny brooding anxieties about her painting career, Frank's attentiveness to painting and painters, and John's obsession with Sodus as a mythic land of strange and deeply ordinary wisdom and pain.

Among New York City artists, there was developing interest in this small group of friends. Frank devoted time to the Club, an artists' group founded by, among others, the sculptor Philip Pavia. Its original members, primarily abstract expressionist painters, held lectures, panel discussions, and informal meals and meetings once or twice a week, usually at 39 East Eighth Street. John rarely attended, but Frank asked him to participate in a panel he was putting together moderated by Larry Rivers (whose artistic success was very quickly surpassing that of his friends). He also asked poets Barbara Guest (whom Ashbery had recently befriended after reading her poems in *Partisan Review*) and Jimmy Schuyler.[36] Ashbery wrote a new painterly poem, "Two Scenes," to read for the occasion.[37] Shortly after, O'Hara and Ashbery were also invited to read their poems at the penthouse apartment of thirty-seven-year-old Broadway lyricist John Latouche, John Myers's new friend. Latouche lived with Kenward Elmslie, a wealthy young poet (Joseph Pulitzer's grandson), who was a Harvard graduate (class of 1950) from Dunster House, though he and John Ashbery had only a passing acquaintance there. O'Hara read "Easter," which impressed the crowd. Ashbery read "The Young Son" and "He." In his newest poem, a parodic manifesto of masculinity, every line began with *He* (a sample line: "'He is now over-proud of his Etruscan appearance"). Elmslie "liked" the "witty list," but he could not pinpoint its tone, particularly because of Ashbery's droll delivery.[38]

Latouche suggested they all make a short film together with his new independent film company. Schuyler's play, now more modestly called *Presenting Jane* (at Freilicher's wry suggestion) was offered. Latouche asked his friend the avant-garde filmmaker Maya Deren to shoot the film, but she declined and recommended her boyfriend, Harrison Starr, a highly intelligent but hotheaded young cameraman who had just finished shooting her short film *The Very Eye of Night*, which rendered movement and dance in a "very avant-garde, surrealist style." He met with John, Jimmy, and Frank, whom he especially liked, in a hotel lobby one afternoon and agreed to make the film. Privately, though, he thought Schuyler's script "terrible."[39] Another friend of Latouche's, Lenore Pettit, offered to lend her East Hampton home on Georgica Pond for filming.[40]

By early July, a large group began assembling at the house. Latouche picked up his star, Jane Freilicher, in his convertible at two in the morning, which she found "exotic" and a little "crazy," and he drove her out.[41] John, Frank, John Myers, Jimmy, Kenward, Harrison, and his assistant, Harry Martin, had arrived at the house, which was already messy and overrun by too many wildly divergent personalities at close quarters.[42] Larry Rivers was living next door, having recently been hired by Leo Castelli to make a sculpture for his home. He stopped by to see everyone, which irritated Harrison Starr. Larry got louder and stayed longer. As Harrison's temper flared—he was aggravated by unusually rainy and unstable summer weather, a tiny budget, and the insouciant attitude of almost everyone involved in the film—he and Larry nearly got into a fistfight. Another potential problem was the film's lack of story, but Harrison and Jimmy worked out a scenario in which Schuyler would portray a silent observer, watching two writers, played by John and Frank, and an artist with godlike powers, played by Jane.[43] For the final shot of the film, Harrison wanted Jane to rise from the water and then walk on it, Christlike. He and his assistant spent hours hiding wooden planks underneath the surface of the pond. He planned to shoot her falling backward into the water and then reverse the image so it would seem, in the final cut, as though she were rising out of it.[44]

As the small crew meticulously plotted each shot by the pond, the poets wrote inside. Jane observed her friends, who were "tireless workers" and capable of concentrating amid chaos. They would "spill out these poems . . . they were so spontaneous." John seemed to find ideas everywhere, "as though his mind were combing the universe" and "grabbing whatever it needed."[45] Jimmy, four years older than John, remained slightly distant from the rest, "original and very independent."[46] During the weekend, Kenneth Koch arrived, having been away two years. Kenneth and Frank, who had crossed paths only rarely, began to collaborate on a sestina, as a way of becoming friendly. For Kenneth, it was "the first time" he wrote a poem "with somebody else and also the first time I had been able to write a good sestina," an engrossing and intensely fun project that made others envious.[47] Kenneth also played tennis with Leo Castelli's daughter, Nina, provoking Larry to brand him an unlikable social climber.[48] Kenneth, Frank, and John had a way of talking that made Jimmy, the only poet not from Harvard, feel excluded.[49] Meanwhile, they felt envious of him: Jimmy's new poem, "At the Beach," had appeared that week in *The New Yorker*, and they made snide asides about the kinds of poems the magazine accepted.[50] John felt snubbed by Frank, who paid more attention to everyone else. He became so angry one night at feeling socially excluded that he "dropped" a few plates on the floor while doing the dishes.[51]

A still of Jane Freilicher, Frank O'Hara, and John Ashbery from the beginning of the short film *Presenting Jane*

James Schuyler in the final shot of *Presenting Jane*

When the film shoot ended, Harrison drove John and Jimmy back to New York City in his 1941 black Chevy Coupe. With Harrison occupied by his father, Jimmy suggested that he and John while away the hours in the car by collaborating on a novel. (They were both still envious of Kenneth's and Frank's ecstatic sestina collaboration.) They began *A Nest of Ninnies*, eventually published in 1969, in the car's comfortable backseat, setting the story in Long Island and New York City simply because those were the places they passed on their way home.[52] They had no plot, plan, or model for a book in mind, only the desire to make it funny. If anything, the idea of collaborating on a novel emerged simply because it seemed amusing. Beginning the project, however, meant that for the next seventeen years, they shared a repository for jokes, puns, reminiscences, and witty overheard dialogue.[53] Jimmy's childhood had been spent primarily in East Aurora, a suburb of Buffalo, a place not dissimilar to Sodus. In *Presenting Jane*, Jimmy gave John a line he could have spoken himself: "Reading my diary I recaptured our old depression."[54] Their deep sympathy came from an intuitive understanding that "we had escaped from the tyrannies of our family." They quickly discovered that "I can joke about it because things are different now," and

February 25, 1953, program for the premiere of *Presenting Jane*, before the film disappeared for the next sixty years these "camp reminiscences" had "a deeper resonance because of having escaped." Frank, Kenneth, and especially Jane, who John believed was "the same person she has been since the age of three, which is refreshing" ("so am I"), also shared this language. For all of them, "an allusion to a radio soap opera would be purgative."[55]

Back in the city, Ashbery spent every evening for the rest of July at the Cherry Lane Theatre, where *The Heroes* was scheduled to open in early August.[56] Judith Malina was directing and "crazy about the play," and she asked John to be "deeply involved in staging."[57] He sat next to her in the theater and requested "more clarity," wanting "each moment to clarify the play as a whole . . . like a jigsaw puzzle."[58] When she first read the play, she had interpreted it as "a poetic dissection of the foibles of the figures of the Greek myths," though "dipped in surrealism."[59] Sitting with John at rehearsals, she understood that "*The Heroes* was about relationships. Although it was a comedy, it was serious about problems of human relationships." She suddenly understood that "he had written a love story."[60]

The Heroes opened in a double bill with Alfred Jarry's *Ubu the King* at the Cherry Lane Theatre on August 5, 1952. The next day, Vernon Rice at the *New York Post* raved that *The Heroes* was a "gem of a comedy."[61] On August 8, by mandate of the Fire Department, however, it closed. Malina and Beck felt that "the closing of the theater was a political gesture because of the anti-establishment candor of the plays. The first word in *Ubu the King* is 'shit!' And 'shit' appears many, many times in the play." Ashbery's play had two men dancing together, which "you just didn't do onstage."[62] The emotionally draining days that followed felt "like a wake . . . each actor took away his things."[63] It was not until May 1953 that *The Heroes* received another performance (alongside James Merrill's *The Bait* and Barbara Guest's *The Lady's Choice*) under the auspices of John Myers's Artists' Theatre, with Herbert Machiz directing. Although Ashbery loved Nell Blaine's sets, he preferred Malina's sensibility. Still, after watching a dress rehearsal, Grace Hartigan confided to her journal that John's play was "a little masterpiece."[64] Although James Laughlin had intimated that *The Heroes* would launch Ashbery's career and Ashbery had worried the play would end it, neither happened.

Restless, John began a "mini-affair."[65] The dance critic Edwin

Arthur Gold and Robert Fizdale, dual
pianists, in a publicity photo, 1950s

Denby, with whom Jimmy Schuyler was having an affair, introduced
John and Jimmy to his friends Arthur Gold and Robert (Bobby) Fizdale,
a Juilliard-trained piano duo whose international careers were peaking
in the 1950s. Gold and Fizdale lived and traveled together and were
socially and professionally ambitious.[66] When in town, they entertained
at a stunning rented house in Snedens Landing once owned by Aaron
Copland. (It was known as the Ding Dong House because of the school
bell outside.) The home commanded dramatic views of the Hudson
River, which Frank O'Hara evoked later in the title of a play, *The Houses
at Falling Hanging*. The pianists were impressive hosts, and after his
first visit, John thanked Bobby and Arthur for a "wonderful time."[67]
Jimmy began an affair with Arthur; soon after, John and Bobby became
involved with each other.

Many Friday evenings, John and Jimmy took the bus to Snedens
Landing together. Because of these trips, they were conspicuously absent from a sketching group that convened with Larry Rivers, Jane Freilicher, Fairfield Porter, Grace Hartigan, Nell Blaine, Al Kresch, Frank
O'Hara, and Kenneth Koch.[68] Instead, they spent Saturdays writing and
gazing outside as Gold and Fizdale practiced on double grand pianos
in the living room. John was enamored by the duo's musical connections. They had close friendships with modern French composers, including Poulenc, who wrote a duo piano concerto for them, and they

received regular visits from Samuel Barber and Virgil Thomson. John enjoyed writing to Bobby about music. That fall, he especially loved Alban Berg's opera *Lulu*, which he found "very exciting . . . it thrills me to hear people converse for three hours in horrible shrieks, especially when they are saying things like 'May I have another cup of tea, please?'" He also wrote about hearing a performance of Virgil Thomson's *Five Songs from William Blake*, which "sounded like plantation melodies," and attending a performance of John Cage's concerto for prepared piano and chamber orchestra, "whose main feature was a gong struck while submerged in a pail of water to produce a very discouraging sound . . . very beautiful."[69] John was attracted to Gold and Fizdale's rarefied social world, full of not only musicians but also dancers—Jerome Robbins and George Balanchine were frequent guests—and painters.

John and Jimmy's friendship deepened as they spent more time together, but also because they both felt ignored by Frank. They "had various complaints about Frank which we could air to each other. . . . We sometimes referred to him as 'the little dear.'"[70] Jane also looked on with a mixture of amusement, resentment, and annoyance as Frank replaced her as his confidant with Grace Hartigan. As Frank became closer to Grace, Jane initially befriended her, since they already had a cordial, if distant, relationship. Jane discovered, however, as John and Jimmy had also, that Frank "used friends against other friends."[71] As Jane explained, "Frank was very nice to me when he wasn't horrible."[72] They all attended Fairfield Porter's first solo show together, which opened October 7 at Tibor de Nagy, but Jimmy became upset and wrote a story afterward, "Frank at Night," that included such phrases as "[h]e is picking his nose at the typewriter" and "Frank's morals: those of a boy scout with the only stapler in camp."[73]

John and Jimmy decided to collaborate. After attending "a marvelous Kurt Schwitters exhibition," they felt inspired to create a collage poem.[74] To assemble the page-long piece, they carefully found each line in a newspaper or magazine article, cut it out, and glued it on to the page. They sent the finished poem, "controls," to Arthur and Bobby. The odd conglomeration of phrases together became a new kind of love song. Of the lines they discovered, John liked two especially. The first, "Here is everything for everyone," he used again, with only a slight tweak, "Here's everything for everybody," as the first line in a new play,

Egbert: A Play for Dolls, a four-page romp he wrote a week later in which dolls talk. The second, "luminous lovelies that help to lighten the load," was so wonderful that he could not believe they had found it intact in a magazine.[75] As much fun as it was to create the poem for Arthur and Bobby, John was aware that he was not in love. He "did like Bobby," who was a decade older, though he was "not that attracted to him." Friends of the pianists, including Fizdale's longtime partner, the interior designer Arthur Weinstein, were even less enthusiastic and tried to shorten the affair.[76] One afternoon, Bobby brought John to the Chelsea Hotel to see Virgil Thomson, who played them a new piece. When John commented that the piece "reminded him of Berg," Thomson replied, "I really don't care what you think."[77]

When Bobby and Arthur left for a tour, John fulfilled a promise to visit Fairfield Porter and "his charming family."[78] Since their meeting casually several times at Tibor de Nagy and once over the summer when John accompanied Jane to the Porter's "very dilapidated" Southampton house, Fairfield had warmly encouraged the young poet to visit on his own.[79] He already admired Ashbery's poetry, which he had first read and liked in *Partisan Review*. As Eisenhower basked in the glow of a landslide victory—John's Republican grandparents were finally able to enthusiastically endorse a candidate for the first time in nearly twenty years (though their grandson voted for Stevenson)—John arrived in Southampton. Fairfield wanted to paint him, and John sat for a portrait on the broad brown couch, wearing a suit and a pair of argyle socks his mother had recently knitted for him. Although he had not expected to sit for a painting, he did not mind, as he often posed for his friends. As Fairfield painted, they talked about poetry. John felt flattered by the man's intense interest in him, especially since Fairfield was one of the few people he had met who seemed to prefer his company to Frank's. Porter saw in Ashbery a young, highly intelligent, ambitious, genteel, and restless spirit, all aspects of a personality that were extremely attractive to him. John did not like the raw and revealing painting, though. Later he wrote to Fairfield, hoping that "my picture is mellowing with time."[80] It stayed at Fairfield's home for a decade.

A week later John went to visit Fairfield at his painting studio on Avenue A, and they talked more about painting and poetry. Fairfield had sent him some poems he had recently written, and John had re-

Fairfield Porter's portrait of John Ashbery,
painted in the fall of 1952. John was wearing
new argyle socks his mother had just knitted
and mailed to him.

sponded quite critically in a letter: "Is it mean? I guess and am afraid
so."[81] When the conversation turned more intimate, John hesitated but
stayed. Fairfield told him about his attractions to men. Although he had
slept with only women, there had been a recent, unsuccessful attempt
to sleep with Rudy Burckhardt. John thought these "gay crushes" suggested that Fairfield "didn't know what he wanted," but Fairfield said
he did. A few nights later, they went to bed in the studio. John immediately felt he had made a terrible mistake. A year earlier, he had slept
with Larry Rivers when he had not really wanted to and was angry with
himself afterward. This situation seemed much more serious. Fairfield
had a "fixation." He wanted more, and when John said no, he became
"antagonistic."[82] Fairfield told Jane Freilicher that he wanted to leave his
wife, Anne, for John.[83] John refused to see him. Miserable at being cut off,
Fairfield punched John when he saw him unexpectedly a few weeks later
at the San Remo Cafe, a bar on MacDougal Street. The episode sparked
a great deal of gossip, especially between Larry and Frank, who partially
guessed what had happened. It took six months before John and Fairfield
could slowly begin to repair their friendship after the fumbled intimacy.[84]

As the drama unfolded, John wrote two new poems. "Pantoum" was
written in a form he had seen once in Claire McAllister's "Pantoum for
Morning," which an acquaintance at Harvard had shown him in 1945,
and he suddenly remembered liking it. The poem advanced by weaving

the second and fourth lines of one quatrain into the first and third lines of the next, repetitions that produced a wistful feeling, as though one faintly remembered hearing a fragment of a melody that suddenly disappeared before fully recalling it. Ashbery's poem begins with serious and melancholy lines that already suggest something lost or irrecoverable: "Eyes shining without mystery, / Footprints eager for the past."[85] John understood the pain of unrequited love, and he sympathized with Fairfield even if he could not return his feelings. He showed the poem to Frank, who immediately wrote to Larry Rivers that

> John has written the most beautiful poem of his career, an epic entitled "Pantoum", which uses and reuses the same lines repetitively and the lines are so astoundingly perfect that this has the effect of a steam press on one's sensibility. The poem is so serious, it's like a bulb going out.[86]

The pantoum's repetitive, slowly shifting form enabled the very mysteriousness at the heart of lines such as "the vague snow of many clay pipes" (an allusion to soap bubbles made by "clay pipes" found in, among other places, Joseph Cornell's *Soap Bubble Set*) to seem slightly, and disturbingly, familiar each time they reappeared.

At the same time he wrote "Pantoum," he composed a comic poem for Oxford University Press. He had recently been promoted to copy editor. Instead of typing addresses, he wrote blurbs for new books, including one for Conrad Aiken, who had been one of the first poets John liked. Ashbery praised the "musical" quality of Aiken's *Collected Poems* (1953), but the august and "crusty" poet did not like the description and sent the press a letter of complaint.[87] John was also made coeditor of OUP's eleven-issue-a-year newsletter, *One-fourteen*. For the Christmas issue of the company newsletter, Ashbery published "Greetings, Friends!" Written as a send-up of *The New Yorker*'s annual Christmas poem, it wittily celebrated the annual achievements of the staff (through rhyming his coworkers' names). Its title also ironically underscored the unraveling state of his friendships outside the office.[88]

His poetry was becoming darker and funnier. "The Thinnest Shadow," his first poem of 1953, reflects, in its spare lines and extreme comparisons, an exaggerated sense of a person's loneliness:

He is sherrier
And sherriest.
A tall thermometer
Reflects him best.

Children in the street
Watch him go by.
"Is that the thinnest shadow?"
They to one another cry.

A face looks from the mirror
As if to say,
"Be supple, young man,
Since you can't be gay."

All his friends have gone
From his street corner cold.
His heart is full of lies
And his eyes are full of mold.[89]

A comic image of a tall man in the first stanza is transformed into a rather horrid image of a forgotten corpse in the last. The use of the word *gay* in the penultimate stanza is as clear a pun as John had ever used. The tall man, a shadow of a self, is unhappy. The man, unloved and alone, dies.

John was rarely alone, but he felt lonely. In the spring, he and Bobby Fizdale saw each other on and off. Jimmy helped perpetuate the relationship, writing to Gold that John felt "gushy" about Bobby and "just called up and read me a sestina he just wrote. It's about a show-boat, very witty and beautiful."[90] Jimmy perhaps did not realize that "A Pastoral" also describes the cycle of a relationship ending. It includes such lines as "Tomorrow, finding him less handsome" and "lately worms have pestered the animals"; the "glittering showboat" becomes the "miserable showboat" and, finally, by the end of the poem, the "disappearing showboat." By this point, John thought that "Arthur Gold was a manipulative kind of not nice character and Bobby seemed nicer," though he was not surprised later when Jimmy suggested that "Bobby was worse."[91] One June evening, the lights in Snedens Landing kept "flickering."

Later John and Jimmy realized that Julius and Ethel Rosenberg had been executed that night directly across the river.[92]

Within weeks of John and Bobby's breakup, Frank and Bobby were dating and showing up at parties together.[93] By late summer, Frank announced to friends in "confidence" that he and Bobby were living together in Snedens Landing, despite the "upheavals of several complicated lives."[94] John remained estranged from Fairfield Porter, a fact that Larry and Frank treated as juicy gossip.[95] (Frank wrote to Larry: "John . . . what do you know! is visiting Fairfield this weekend."[96] Two days later, Larry wrote to Frank: "When Ann [sic] told me little JA was coming I sort of made a face thinking about the fact that Fairfield and he are supposed to be strained. She jumped and demanded an explanation. I thought she suspected Fairfield of you know what.")[97] Larry was sometimes romantically involved with Frank and jealous of Jane, who was in a serious relationship with Joe Hazan, a handsome dancer, artist, and Hans Hofmann model. That fall, Larry Rivers, upset by various "upheavals" in his own romantic life, took an overdose of heroin, and Grace Hartigan rushed over to his apartment, "spooning him chicken broth and ice cream" all day as he recovered.[98] Even misery was competitive.

These bitter personal rivalries, however, evaporated around discussions of art, especially conversations about their own poetry. Their enthusiasm for one another's creativity was unique among artists in the city. After Ashbery's prose poem "A Dream" (1949) was published in *New Directions 14* (1953), alongside an Allen Ginsberg prose poem, Ginsberg approached Ashbery at a party to say he found his poem "too French." He wandered away before John had a chance to say (drily): "It *is* French; it takes place in Paris."[99] Whereas, among themselves, John could end an otherwise angry letter to Larry by warmly asking him to send "provocative quotations" from the long poem he was writing.[100] As John succinctly put it, "No letter would be complete without its poem."[101]

In early spring 1953, John had just finished "Petroleum Lima Beans," his longest poem to date and one with the "strangest name I could think of."[102] Inspired to write a long poem by the friendly goad of Frank's "Second Avenue" and Kenneth's "When the Sun Tries to Go On," John created the shortest of all of them, but he strove to include the

most unusual words, syntax, and phrases. In section VI, he composes
an odd list of things:

> Under the sofa-flea!
> André Messager! Mysterious
> Swaying mammoth
> Fruit-trees
> Siegfried temper
> Bulbs.[103]

His next poem, "Lieutenant Primrose," pleased him because it was
even stranger. Lines sometimes begin lyrically and end in another mood
completely. One of his favorites was "And in dry temple farting sit."[104]
Ashbery found inspiration for new words, phrases, and poems everywhere. He and Jimmy attended a Dada show at the Sidney Janis Gallery
together, where "the catalogue is printed on an enormous sheet of paper
which is all crumpled into a ball when you get it," a witty, rebellious approach to art they enjoyed so much they returned to see the show again
a few days later.[105]

In poems such as "Why," which organizes words into unlikely patterns; "Matted Hair Flowers," which includes lines such as "[t]he as-
terisked telephone needs to move"; and "Aeneas," which he wrote in
stepped quatrains (so that the poem resembles a staircase); Ashbery
kept trying new things.[106] In a very short new play, *The Coconut Milk*,
Ashbery attempted only to be "so silly" about possibilities for language,
including lines such as "Hey, Don't scream! I could radish you but these
whiskers would kinda get in the way."[107] The first scene of the play
takes place in Headquarters, but the central question is "who last had
the coconut milk." His longest and most exciting new poem was "Fortune," inspired by Carl Orff's musical setting of "O Fortuna" in *Carmina
Burana*, which Ashbery did not try to publish until 1961.[108] These poems intimated how Ashbery's experiments were already moving toward
"Europe," the defiantly novel poem that would anchor his second book,
The Tennis Court Oath (1962). As Bill Berkson declared, speaking on
behalf of a younger generation of artists, when he first read the poem
in 1960, "It immediately changed the way we thought about poetry."[109]

These friendships were spurred by not only competition but

collaboration. John and Kenneth created a pastiche of *The New York Times* by using headlines from the Sunday October 25 paper and rewriting eighteen of the articles. The result was a series of newspaper-poetry pieces:

U.S. SEEKS ACCORD OF ALLIES ON KOREA
A toy radio once spoke of mistrust
To my mother, then burst into flames upon her bust.
"The kittens are sold,"
Whispered father, "and my bare feet are cold."

Written in a rhyming, intimate first person, the poem-article undercuts the headline to highlight "mistrust" and the ongoing danger in a "cold" war. John also collaborated with Jane, who beautifully illustrated his first chapbook of poems, *Turandot and Other Poems* (1953), for the Tibor de Nagy Gallery poetry series, celebrating its release on November 11, 1953, with a packed party at the gallery. In "A Play," the best of these collaborations, Koch, O'Hara, and Ashbery created an American surrealist drama, an exaggerated, funnier, stranger version of the radio plays of their youth. A woman arrives with a can opener: "I found this on your doorstep." Soon "Jimmy and Jane" enter the house drunk. Jane says, "It was so dark in the nightclub that it was like being in a well. The air wasn't fit to breathe, but I breathed."[110]

By spring, John and Fairfield had started speaking again. In May, John visited the Porters in Southampton for the first time since the fall. His rather stilted handwritten note at the end of the weekend suggested that they all enjoyed themselves together, albeit with reservations. Despite the strain between John and Fairfield, the visit was not overly awkward because John was so good at "observing the proprieties," a detail he emphasized to Anne in the postscript to his thank-you letter:

> P.S. Ann [*sic*]—it occurs to me that you may not believe in thank-you letters since you don't in Mother's Day, but I once read one to you from John Wheelwright—we poets must stick together in observing the proprieties.[111]

If nothing else, John was determined, through the sheer force of his good manners, to make things right.

Shortly after returning to the city, he met Philippe Fecteau at a beach in Riis Park, a gay cruising ground near Breezy Point, Queens, and all summer he pursued the budding romance. Phil reminded John physically of Cégeste (played by Edouard Dermit) in Cocteau's *Orpheus*, and he had not felt so attracted to anyone in years. The relationship was immediately rocky, though. Phil, who was of Canadian ancestry, had a longtime boyfriend, and when they all met one weekend they did not get along. Phil was keen to make John jealous, which was not difficult.[112] John's friends did not like Phil, but the relationship grew more serious anyway. He was very enthusiastic about poetry, even showing Ashbery's "Petroleum Lima Beans" to his friend, the great Brechtian singer and actress Lotte Lenya. (She pronounced it "very curious.")[113] When "He" came out in *New World Writing*, Phil said he was impressed because the magazine also published work by "the great Truman Capone."[114] John repeated the malapropism to his friends, who found it less charming. Larry was jealous of John's steamy affair, and he made angry, snide comments to suggest that John was using Phil for sex (or vice versa).[115] In one letter to Frank, Larry asked if "John Ashbery invented the necessary feeling to return Philip to their nest," a blunt comment intended to get back to John and hurt him.[116] All through the fall, John and Phil kept breaking up and getting back together.

By December, though, John was alone. At Tibor de Nagy he had celebrated Nell Blaine's exhibition, and the publication of Kenneth Koch's *Poems* in September.[117] In October, Frank and Grace hosted a fête in honor of the inaugural issue of *Folder*, the new art and literary magazine. John's feelings about the magazine were mixed; he appreciated that it had enthusiastically published four of his new poems, especially since no other publication wanted to take them, though he also privately wondered why having to take material in and out of a folder was an artistic innovation.[118] He shared his feelings with Jane Freilicher, who, for reasons that had to do with Grace Hartigan's and Daisy Aldan's personalities, had not been invited to publish in *Folder*. Even those who were at the party, though, did not always feel welcome. In a letter to Larry Rivers, John Myers complained about the "party last Sat. night much enjoyed by everyone except lonesome me."[119] It was a refrain expressed by everyone on different days. Grace Hartigan felt her friendship with Frank O'Hara had run its course after seeing him very drunk one night at the Cedar Tavern viciously insulting Larry. She decided she could not "feel close to Frank, Jane, Jimmy and the other boys."[120] Even to close friends, the group seemed impenetrable, despite the internal jealousies, rivalries, and frustrations that divided them.

John also felt like an outsider. Jane Freilicher and Joe Hazan were together. Kenneth Koch and Janice Elwood were a couple. Jimmy Schuyler and Arthur Gold, and Frank O'Hara and Bobby Fizdale, remained involved. On New Year's Eve, John arrived at a party of people he did not know well, at a walk-up on Sixth Avenue and Thirteenth Street. He smoked pot for the first time, and felt nothing. At midnight each guest was asked to reveal a New Year's resolution. John declared, "I'm going to eat more in 1954." The painter Ann Truxell, whom he had not seen in a while, announced that "in 1954 when I get clap I'm going to get cured right away."[121] The emptiness of the occasion reinforced John's desire to be alone. He went back to his apartment, planning to wake up early and write something new, which was how he most liked to begin a new year.

10

"What More Is There to Do, Except Stay? And That We Cannot Do"

1954–1955

"Excitation, excitation of feeling / Excitement, mental excitement"—Ashbery typed the lines at his desk in the center of the big floor at Oxford University Press in early January. That morning, he had spotted *Roget's Thesaurus* on a reference shelf and suddenly imagined a new collage poem, "Hoboken."[1] The book was the same one he had purchased in February 1943, as he started to write poetry in Miss Klumpp's English class. Then the thesaurus had served as a tool, a helpful way to find new words for his earliest poems.[2] Eleven years later, he repurposed elements of the thesaurus (words, numbers, phrases) *as* the poem: "Work *or* operate on *or* upon / Stir, set astir, stir up, stir the blood. / Fillup, give a fillip." He kept typing, ambitiously stripping words of their usual uses and meanings. He was freeing them from "Standard, pattern, mirror etc. (prototype) 22," which was the final line of his poem. While eagerly unshackling words from their usual contexts, the poem suggests how words and ideas quickly ossify through standardization. As Kenneth put it, by beginning to "concentrate on the pleasure of words," Ashbery was letting "words act up in the way one feels most exciting."[3]

John finally found a new position that doubled his current salary, and in mid-February, after more than two years, he left Oxford University Press. Now a "research assistant" for the Council for Financial Aid to Education, an initiative created eighteen months earlier to encourage American corporations to invest in higher education, he found his new office, at 6 East Forty-Fifth Street, dignified and eerily silent. He read "pamphlets on education all day long," while "surrounded by the best quality ash trays, scotch-tape dispensers, dictionary etc." Not long after he started, he wrote to Fairfield Porter that "I miss the noise and confusion of my old office, for this one resembles a cloister." Later, he wondered why "no one ever talks to me or directs me to do anything."[4] He began to spend afternoons studying Japanese poetry and writing letters instead of reading those "trying pamphlets." "Frequently I look out of the window at a prospect of office buildings," he reported. He took long weekends to see friends in Cornwall, Connecticut, and to visit Frank, Larry, and Fairfield in Southampton. Early in June, his supervisor, Dr. Pollard, declared that the president of the foundation "has been needling me to get rid of you" and asked John to return his office key by the end of the day.[5] Ashbery spent his final few hours in the office writing a prothalamion, the last line of which was "in one minute Kenneth Koch will marry Janice Elwood."[6]

The giddy relief John felt at escaping the oppressive office was quickly replaced by extreme anxiety that he had been fired. Worse, he was now broke again, since he had used up his higher salary on rent, giving up his Morton Street studio for a "larger and grander" sublet at 219 West Fourteenth Street (a place owned by the painter Maurice Grosser, who was living in Europe). The move had been precipitated by a renewed romance with Phil Fecteau, which was going so well that John began to worry that "I am being lulled into a sense of false security."[7] Feeling exuberant about their relationship and his new apartment, they threw a party for all their friends at the beginning of May.[8] Two weeks later they had such a brutal fight about recent infidelities and jealousies that Phil moved out, ending things permanently. John learned soon after that he had been rejected from the Fulbright for the fourth time. A few days later he lost his job. He stayed at home and followed the spectacle of the televised Army–McCarthy hearings, which linked the terms *subversives* and *homosexuals* in daily testimonies and deepened John's unease.[9] At the recommendation of John Myers, John went to see a psychiatrist, Dr. Frank Hale. Dr. Hale promised not only to treat his depression, but also to provide the army with a new letter stating that Ashbery suffered from anxiety and should remain 4-F, ensuring he could avoid the draft, which continued even though the Korean War was officially over.

John Ashbery and Jane Freilicher visiting Elinor Poindexter (with Nell Blaine, not photographed) in Cornwall, Connecticut, in the spring of 1954. John developed his photographs at the Prager Camera Store, in the same building he was living in: Maurice Grosser's sublet at 219 West Fourteenth Street.

Frank O'Hara, Hal Fondren, and Fairfield Porter in Southampton in spring 1954. Photograph taken by John Ashbery.

Hal Fondren, Larry Rivers, and Frank O'Hara in Southampton in spring 1954. Photograph taken by John Ashbery.

Shortly after, Frank moved in. John described the arrangement enthusiastically to the Porters: "Frank has been staying with me and commiserating with me."[10] Frank downplayed the choice to Larry as not much fun, explaining that he was doing it only "for dear money's sake" and because "I don't seem to fuck much anymore."[11] He was still recovering from being shot in the hip during an attempted robbery in the stairway of his apartment building on East Forty-Ninth Street. Since then, he had been convalescing at Larry Rivers's Southampton home.[12] Although the violent episode had terrified his friends, Frank's response to the trauma was characteristically witty: he wrote to a friend that "my hip is no longer the impeccable mechanism it once was," but "I don't list to port when I walk and no vital functions are impaired."[13] Back in the city, Frank helped Grace Hartigan pose her friends in old costumes and clothes she had found at the Ludlow Market, for a large painting she called *Masquerade*.[14] At Frank's urging, John participated, but he preferred wandering over to talk with Jane as she worked in her "cramped tenement apartment in the far East Village" at 635 East Eleventh Street. Freilicher's 1954 Tibor de Nagy show had recently ended, and though Frank had complimented her paintings as illuminating "what the romantic poets felt about beauty," she was feeling uncertain and depressed about her newest work.[15]

Jane Freilicher painting in her
studio at 635 East Eleventh Street

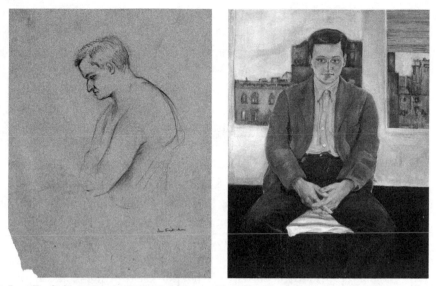

Jane Freilicher's sketch of John Ashbery and her lost oil painting of him, both done in the summer of 1954

At Jane's studio every afternoon, John observed her creating "haunting pictures" of New York City from her window.[16] Sometimes she also sketched her friend, drawings in pen, from angles that sharpened his features and showed him thinking, anxious, melancholy.[17] For several weeks, she painted in oil a *Portrait of John Ashbery*.[18] She posed John in a coat and tie, seated on a kitchen chair in front of a window. Freilicher observed him brooding, with gray New York City in the background (no flowers, no sun, no obvious signs of summer), reflecting his mood.[19]

The painting simmered with the same pensive, anxious melancholy as poems he was writing. In "Chaos," a conversation between "the sleeping river" and "the awake land," begins, "Don't ask me to go there again / The white is too painful / Better to forget it." Jimmy Schuyler recognized a "new tone" in his friend's poem, intimating "some beautiful," even darker poems to come.[20] In "Canzone," he wrote a new song with a spare, haunting sound. While people wonder "If they can / Sing the old song of can," the poem created a much more restrained song instead. Ashbery knew well Petrarch's rich Italian *canzoniere*, which he had studied in college while learning the language.[21] He also loved Auden's "Canzone," the poem that had introduced him to the form when he first saw it in 1944. In Ashbery's innovation, the repetition of five very simple words—*chill, grass, grows, can, clay*—at the end of two- to four-word lines, created much more silent space, a sense of unspoken thoughts and private intimations. In Ashbery's "Album Leaf," which also references a popular musical form, he expresses even more directly a sense of despair. The title of the poem and a few images and phrases in it recall a moment in his life at fifteen that he recorded in his diary:

> I painted the still-life a subject with an ocean background. Then downtown I got Album Leaf by Kirchner and at the library I got The Rose and the Ring and a Thackerian biography by Melville. Then through dexterous handling I stayed at Pultneyville, since Daddy wanted me to go home. (February 13, 1942)

This memory provided the origin of the poem's two questions in the opening quatrain:

> The other marigolds and the cloths
> Are crimes invented for history.
> What can we achieve, aspiring?
> And what, aspiring, can we achieve?

Was it possible to move forward? To aspire and achieve? Was his ambition—that "old song of can"—his downfall or his way forward? A year earlier he had mused, "Wouldn't it be nice to write some very simple thing that people for many centuries to come would find impossible to get out of their heads?"[22] Yet what if one's hopes for life and art, so vividly imagined in entries from his childhood diary, never materialized?[23]

He looked for a job unsuccessfully all summer. There was one promising position, at Prentice-Hall, but after taking a test to correct mistakes in "Daniel Webster's Dictionary," he realized too late that he had missed the very first error. (The title should have been "Noah Webster's Dictionary.") Most publishing firms asked what newspapers applicants read. John answered *The New York Times* and the *New York Post* and then regretted responding because he feared the *Post* would be perceived as too liberal. Questions seemed innocuous until he considered later how his answers might be misconstrued. Newspapers were full of stories detailing devastating consequences for revealing one's sexual choices and political views to the wrong person, and he felt as though he was always in some danger. The more jobs he applied for, the more he worried about what information was being gathered about him and for what purpose, since "it was the height of the McCarthy Era and homosexual propaganda. I felt afraid."[24]

Shortly after his twenty-seventh birthday, John went to update his draft status at an army office in the Financial District. The visit was supposed to be only a formality, since Dr. Hale had already sent in a letter to the draft board. When John arrived, however, the office said there was no record of any such letter, and he was required to submit to a physical and mental examination. One doctor asked if he was gay, and he said yes. Asked "to explain what you do that makes you homosexual," John "had to describe homosexual practices, acts, in detail." When the doctor stepped outside the examination room, John looked at what he had written, "Subject claims to be homosexual. He is obviously a weak character of the kind we don't need in the Army." As soon as John left the building he called Jimmy Schuyler, who immediately met him for lunch and talked with him until he felt less panicked.[25]

As his unemployment dragged on, John also felt increasingly guilty. His parents were paying his bills, which was very difficult for them. He stopped seeing Dr. Hale because of the expense.[26] Jimmy left for Europe with Gold and Fizdale. Kenneth and Janice were preparing to go abroad. Frank went to visit friends in Southampton and work on a new piece about Fairfield Porter commissioned by *ARTnews*, which had recently hired him.[27] The Porters were traveling to Maine. Jane Freilicher and Joe Hazan planned a "cruise about the Nawth," with Joe piloting their boat, followed by a visit to the Porters.[28] Lonely in the city and still with no leads on a job, John headed to Fire Island for a few days with Joe Cino, a new boyfriend prospect, but he ran out of money and had to return home to Sodus to ask for more. Jobless at nearly thirty, he listened as his mother advised him to apply more aggressively for teaching positions, mentioning friends of his she knew who were doing better professionally. Ashbery described these and other sorts of trying days much later: "These then were some hazards of the course," he wrote gently in "Soonest Mended" about the enduring pains of growing up.

Back in the city, he gave himself a new poetic project: to translate French poetry and prose into English. Working on Robert Cordier's "Une nuit . . ." for *Folder* magazine the previous year had whetted his appetite to translate better poems. He had read "tons of modern French stuff," including "Queneau, Gracq, Supervielle, Desnos, Jacob, etc.," in the fall of 1950 and returned to Max Jacob's "Littérature et Poésie," a brief prose poem he loved from *Le Cornet à dés* (The Dice-Cup I) about a child's imagined trip to Naples.[29] Working on it each afternoon in his bright living room was so engrossing that he decided to make a proposed collection of translated modern French poetry the subject of his fifth application for the Fulbright.[30] He wrote to Professor Harry Levin at Harvard, though he had not seen him in nearly six years, to ask for a recommendation. He reminded Levin that he had received "the highest mark in the class [Proust, Joyce, Mann] in the final examination" that year. Levin responded immediately, "[O]f course I remember you."[31] (Confidentially, he recalled that Ashbery "impressed me by his keen perception, his superior style, and his wide range of interests.")[32] Encouraged, John kept reading and translating prose poems, including Jacob's "To Be Continued."[33] Just as he was finally in a regular writing rhythm, he discovered that his apartment had a bedbug infestation, and Maurice Grosser wrote to say he was returning early and needed his apartment back. John had to borrow an extra seventy-five dollars from his parents to have the place professionally cleaned.

He found a tiny, inexpensive studio at 244 West Eleventh Street, but it was unavailable until the end of November. To pass the time, he visited the Porters in Southampton, though Fairfield was away. He wrote a brief poem called "In Southampton," and shared it with Anne Porter, who was also a poet. She quipped, "Maybe you should try Quogue instead?" (Quogue was a nearby town.) Her joke's sharp edge suggested that his decision to stay was a "little tone deaf."[34] He returned to Sodus and noticed that his grandfather drove unsteadily and all of a sudden spoke "with the slightest suggestion of dementia."[35] John went back to the city for another round of job interviews and was finally offered a position as a copywriter in the college textbook division at McGraw-Hill (at almost the same low salary as at Oxford University Press, but he needed the job too much to haggle). He reported to the company's tall, iconic green modernist building on Forty-Second

Street for his first day, on Monday, December 13, 1954, exactly six months since he had lost his job.[36] Later that week his grandfather died, and John went home for the funeral. The obituary in *The New York Times* identified Henry Lawrence as "a pioneer in the use of X-rays," a renown that surprised and impressed John (whose own family name was misspelled "Asbury").[37] At the church service, the open casket unnerved him. He had never seen a dead body before, and the man before him did not look like the grandfather he had loved. Sitting in the pew listening to the service, John reflected that there was no one in his family who had ever expressed his love so clearly and unconditionally as Henry Lawrence.

Returning to a noisy new office was a relief.[38] Just as at Oxford University Press, John had a desk in the middle of a big, open floor. Telephones blared and typewriters clicked. A secretary named Pat talked too loudly to her "darling daughter Tricia" every afternoon.[39] These were office work irritations (rather than interruptions) John was surprised he had missed. He assisted Argyle "Spike" Linnington, who was in charge of college advertising, and worked beside Tere Lo Prete.[40]

Addie and Henry Lawrence about 1954, shortly before Henry Lawrence's death at age ninety

In a café on Sixth Avenue near Forty-Second Street, Fall 1954. Photograph taken by John Button.

During the day, he wrote advertising copy; she set it by hand. In the evening, he accompanied Tere to the Provincetown Landing, a lesbian bar on Thompson Street in the Village. Their division worked on a series of textbooks about, among other subjects, the atomic bomb and James Boswell. John found the dull work enjoyable and once "produced a circular enumerating the virtues of the definitive textbook on feedback, which moved some of the other employees to tears."[41]

John started writing poems at the office. (He vastly preferred McGraw-Hill's nice Royal typewriter to his own Olivetti Lettera 22.) After composing "The Orioles," he reread it and decided it was "a failure, I feel, because it can't decide whether to be silly or pretty."[42] The poem was, in part, deeply nostalgic about the beautiful natural landscape of his childhood, which he had just seen again. He described how seasons were marked, not by weather, but by the arrival and departure of orioles, which anticipated shifts in weather, a fact he knew from childhood. His mother and grandmother noted in their diaries each year when they heard or saw the first bird of the season, sightings that increased after Chet built tall, handsome wooden martin houses, giving them as gifts to family and friends.[43] In Ashbery's poem, orioles arrive, and "the mad caroling" begins "as each builds his hanging nest / Of pliant twigs and softest moss and grasses." Then, one morning, "you get up" and realize the birds are leaving,

> And that night you gaze moodily
> At the moonlit blossoms

To "gaze moodily" was a phrase John took (without realizing it) directly from his childhood diary to describe how he felt when he looked out at the remarkable lake from his grandparents' Pultneyville living room.[44] The poem captures this romantic spirit, but then immediately subverts it:

> And that night you gaze moodily
> At the moonlit blossoms, for of course
> Horror and repulsion do exist! They do! And you wonder
> How long will the perfumed dung, the sunlit clouds cover my
>   heart?[45]

Although "horror and repulsion do exist," birds drive them away to once again "cluster at the feeding station." When Ashbery reread the poem much later, he felt that its overt sentimentality was actually sort of interesting because he could see the effects of a new writerly influence, the "French pre-surrealist Raymond Roussel" (1877–1933), a writer whose strange narratives John had begun reading with great excitement.[46]

Although greatly relieved to have a "pleasant though ill-paying" job at McGraw-Hill, he daydreamed about moving to Paris.[47] Kenneth and Janice were living there. Jimmy was ecstatically visiting the city on his trip with Gold and Fizdale. John read Roussel's works with increasing fervor, enjoying his "complete deodorization and objectification of the language" that followed "a commendable direction even though no tracks *do* return!"[48] Although Kenneth had introduced him to Roussel's writing, John quickly and competitively made the writer his own discovery, pertly declaring to Kenneth that "I have your copy" of *Impressions d'Afrique* "with the pages uncut!"[49] He requested every work by Roussel from the Parisian bookshop, José Corti (a place Kenneth had alerted him to), and he longed to visit the store in person. He sent Julian Beck and Judith Malina a flattering proposal to translate Roussel's plays for the Living Theatre, "the only place in New York where one can satisfy one's thirst for true theatrical entertainment."[50] They demurred, but John continued his translation work anyway. Under Roussel's influence, he wrote two more poems in quick succession. He did not like his "Winter Reveries," but he felt "Grand Abacus" achieved something new. The mysterious narrative about a valley, an abandoned meadow, and a decaying sculpture of a head begins with the uncertain word *Perhaps*.[51] The rhetorical question "Who knew it, at the beginning of the day?" appears near the end of the poem, at which point the speaker suddenly reveals that "it is already too late. The children have vanished." Everything mentioned in the poem (people, places) is left uncertain, unknown, and potentially "ghastly."

Even though he was writing, John felt upset by "life in New York," which "is depressing me right now."[52] The city seemed like "a gigantic toenail factory."[53] He was tired of even his closest friends, describing them to Kenneth as "like a lot of old Christmas trees . . . though they are all dears, to be sure."[54] At least "the New York scene" was "enlivened (though perhaps that isn't the right word)" in January by the return of Bob Hunter, John's Harvard roommate. Bob had just enrolled in Columbia University's English literature PhD program after two years in the army to fulfill his Korean War service, and he had moved to an apartment on West Seventy-Third. Sandy Gregg, who had also returned from abroad to study (Russian literature) at Columbia, lived nearby. John began to see them both more, spending his weekends lying on Bob's couch, peering into the windows of the famed Dakota apartment house, and watching for "the ghosts of Boris Karloff, Kent Smith, or Judy Holliday . . . all of whom are rumored to haunt it."[55] One afternoon while walking down Broadway together, they spotted Ted Gorey, the "tall effeminate" poet and illustrator whom they had known at Harvard.[56] Ted invited them to join him at the Theodore Huff Memorial Film Society, a group that met once or twice a month to show hard-to-find prints. John and Bob began attending "many an old film showing" together, and the "chic obscure film society" became "the joy of my life."[57]

At the very first event, he found inspiration for a new play. After watching a two-minute hand-colored film from 1900 called *The Flower Fairy*, he also saw, for the first time, the classic, full-length Rin Tin Tin feature *Where the North Begins* (1923). Afterward, he rapturously described it to Kenneth as "the greatest film ever—Rinty is a superb actor."[58] The story is set on a remote mountain, where deep snow has left a small group in almost total isolation from the rest of society for much of the year. Rin Tin Tin, raised by wolves but with the old soul of a dog, provides a lonely young family with companionship, loyalty, and wisdom. Moved by the film, Ashbery went to work that night as soon as he arrived home.

Less than three weeks later, he had a complete draft of his first three-act play.[59] The plot involves intrigue among a small group alone on a mountain. (Ashbery left the dog out of his script, further emphasizing the isolation and lack of a source or object of love.) In act 2, Mountain Lion, the chief's son, and one of the finest men, describes the problems within his tribe. He laments that "all around me I see lying, avarice, and petty bickering . . . the decay of the tribal spirit. Each begins to go his own way, no one thinks of the group any more, no one worships the old familiar gods. What is happening to us?" Other members of the tribe worry about "future unhappiness everywhere," though harmony is eventually restored because the finer nature of men surfaces at critical moments. The description of a tribe in jeopardy offered an allegory for Ashbery's own clan in New York City. He summed up his feelings in a letter to Larry: "please, please in these days of factions let there be no feelings of rancor 'twixt you and me."[60] They had sniped at each other all year about many things, but Frank had been especially "rough" with John about "the fact that I would like to publish my things . . . in a good magazine," which Frank "vaguely feels is subversive."[61] The group of friends was increasingly at its kindest when apart.[62] As soon as John showed Frank his new play, *The Compromise*, later that spring, Frank wrote to Kenneth praising the "miraculous new 3 act play . . . full of something like fresh mountain air."[63] With Frank's encouragement, John sent the play to *New World Writing* (which rejected it after a brief internal discussion by memo).[64] Because of Frank's enthusiasm, however, the play would have its first production a year later, at the Poets' Theatre in Cambridge.

As indistinguishable as one gray city winter seemed from the next, time marched forward. Kenneth Koch and Janice Elwood were visiting Tangiers, and John heard that Janice was pregnant. Jane Freilicher and Joe Hazan seemed to be moving in a similar direction of marital union and family. Jimmy Schuyler wrangled invitations for his friends (for the first and only time) to Auden's forty-eighth-birthday party. Printed cards arrived: "Martinis at 7, carriages at 9." Frank described the "nice birthday party where everyone got drunk, especially John Ashbery whom I overheard saying very seriously to Sam Barber, 'But I don't think you *should* write another major work.' Such a dear!"[65] John spoke with Robert Graves (whose poem "To Juan at the Winter Solstice" he had liked so much in college that he copied it down). He also met Edith and Osbert Sitwell, who made "kind remarks about American poetry" and expressed interest in reading *Turandot*.[66] The next day, on the way to Ted Gorey's thirtieth birthday party, John dropped off his chapbook at the Sitwells' Chelsea Hotel, along with an elaborate letter in which he apologized because "I myself have long since lost patience with most of the poems in it."[67] Despite his modesty, he felt "crushed" when they never responded.[68]

John dreamed of publishing a better book of poems. One night, he imagined he "was Tarzan and received an enormous bundle of poems on yellow paper from T.[Theodore] Weiss with this note: 'We are keeping the poem *Sestina* to round out the rather uncompromising group of your poems we are printing.'"[69] He was worrying about the poetry collection he had recently submitted to the Yale Series of Younger Poets prize. At Auden's birthday party, Auden's partner, Chester Kallman, had encouraged John and Frank to send in manuscripts to the Yale prize, which Auden had been judging since 1946. The March 1 deadline was then just a little over a week away. John had gone home and immediately arranged his poems into a book. Four years earlier, he had typed up a table of contents for a hoped-for book, a page he had been updating and reorganizing since then.[70] He began with "Two Scenes," added several of his most recent experimental poems, such as "Lieutenant Primrose," and ended with "Le livre est sur la table."[71] Both he and Frank sent in manuscripts to Yale, where a committee judged them before forwarding a small number of their favorites as finalists to Auden. While waiting to hear, John and Frank were invited to "read our own things" at the Egan gallery.[72] John was elated by the big, appreciative audience, and he told Kenneth that "Frank and I gave a poetry reading. . . . Everybody said it was very funny."[73] That night, Morris Golde, a businessman who was also a friend to young artists, threw a party for them at his West Village town house. A photograph captured a moment between Frank and John, sitting on an upholstered ottoman "and looking dreamy."[74]

A week later, though, Frank confessed to Larry that "last night I was so mean to John Ashbery I could vomit. Sometimes I feel I am some sort of furious fiend and can't even recognize myself and I can't really kid myself that it's just the liquor either."[75] Part of Frank's frustration was that he "got a book of poems ready for Yale at Wystan's suggestion and of course they were too late for the deadline, isn't that a laugh?"[76] Soon after, he heard that both their manuscripts had been rejected. Frank explained to Kenneth: "Mine was returned because it arrived too late and then John's was returned because they are so stupid."[77] In fact, the poetry prize committee officially "had thrown out Ashbery's manuscript because it was under length," though no one ever told him the reason.[78] He only knew that "when I first sent *Some Trees* to Yale—the manuscript was then called *Poems*—it was rejected in the first round. It was sent back to me and never made it to

Auden. I was told that Auden hadn't liked any manuscript that he had been sent and wasn't going to give a prize."[79]

When Chester Kallman informed Auden that both Ashbery's and O'Hara's manuscripts had been rejected in the first round by Yale, Auden asked them to resend their manuscripts directly to him in Italy, where he lived in the summer.[80] This request was not unusual, since the press, since the inception of the prize, had strongly encouraged judges to solicit manuscripts and discover winners on their own.[81] Auden's particular desire to find a winner in 1955, though, was driven by his experience judging the previous year. For the first time, he had not awarded a prize to any of the finalists (although Galway Kinnell's and Donald Hall's manuscripts were among them), but then he had been surprised to discover that $100 of his $250 salary was withheld since it had been allocated specifically for writing an introduction to the winning book.[82] In 1955, however, these discussions were occurring unusually late in the process. On May 30 an interoffice memo at the press reported that Auden "is again unwilling to pick a publishable manuscript from among this year's candidates for the Yale Series of Younger Poets."[83]

By that point, both John's and Frank's manuscripts had just arrived in Italy. John sent his off in the middle of May, just after he was rejected by the Fulbright committee for a fifth time, news he took especially hard because he wished to travel. He had "not been literally anywhere."[84] Jane and Joe were planning to drive to Mexico so that Joe could obtain a divorce from his first wife and marry Jane.[85] Grace Hartigan and her boyfriend, Walt Silver, wanted to join them. Jane wanted John to go, too. On May 28 the group got into Joe Hazan's car and left New York City.

For months, and years, afterward the "staggeringly beautiful" Mexican landscape changed Ashbery's color palette in poems and letters.[86] Monterrey had "low hills and shrubs" so that one could see far in the distance. Mexico City "was fabulous, my first foreign metropolis. Life was going on everywhere."[87] A new poem began to form in his mind, though he did not yet begin to jot phrases for what would become "The Instruction Manual" until he returned to New York City. On June 6, Jane, Joe, and John left Mexico City for Acapulco, but Grace and Walt wanted to see the "artists' ghetto" at Guanajuato and

John Ashbery's still life of Fairfield Porter's mantelpiece in his Southampton home. Frank O'Hara's essay "Porter Paints a Picture" had just been published in *ARTnews* in January 1955, and Ashbery and Porter began discussing painting technique: "Fairfield felt about my painting the way I felt about his poetry."

In Acapulco, June 1955. "Joe, Jane, and I were there watching boys diving off the cliff."

took off by themselves, a decision that created a permanent rift in their already fragile friendships.[88]

As John was leisurely sightseeing, life-changing news raced to catch up with him. The Fulbright foundation had unexpectedly reversed its decision after someone declined an award. The official acceptance letter, dated June 3, 1955, was mailed to Sodus, New York, along with details concerning the SS *Queen Mary*'s September 21 departure for France.[89] Then Auden chose Ashbery's manuscript as the winner of the Yale Younger Poets prize. Frank wrote to Larry on June 8 that "the other great news of the season is that John Ashbery is the Yale Younger Poet this year. Isn't that sweet? Wystan wrote me yesterday about it and I telegrammed JA in Mexico City, I hope he hasn't already left for Acapulco."[90] Frank's telegram had just missed him.

Having left New York City with a long future of dull office work stretching out ahead of him, John felt it was nearly a miracle to return three weeks later to a book contract and a steamer ticket to France. The Fulbright was supposed to be for only a year, but from the moment John heard he had received the award, he began plotting how to extend his stay in France.[91] Sitting in his hot office over the next three days, he wrote "The Instruction Manual," despite "the interruption of a watchful superior (a Whitmanesque phrase)."[92] He had Whitman's long prose-y lines of poetry in his head as he wrote the new poem, which was the longest narrative with the longest lines he had ever written, an utterly new form of expression for him. Just before leaving for Mexico, he had discovered "how great old Walt is," copying some of Whitman's long, expressive lines from "Song of Myself" into his letters.[93] Nineteen fifty-five was, after all, the hundredth anniversary of the publication of *Leaves of Grass*, and Whitman's poetry was in the air after a translation of Federico García Lorca's "Ode to Walt Whitman" appeared in *Poetry* in January. (The translation also inspired Ginsberg's "A Supermarket in California," in which the speaker follows Whitman into a contemporary grocery where Lorca lurks "by the watermelons.")

The joy in Ashbery's poem, communicated through its freely expressive long lines and vibrant colors, reflects his ecstatic mood. It begins at a desk in an office somewhere, the speaker longing to be someplace else: "As I sit looking out of a window of the building . . .

I begin to dream." When his "dim" dream of Guadalajara begins to feel real, he becomes so happy. He sees a great deal, so much that he feels he has seen almost everything: "We have seen young love, married love, and the love of an aged mother for her son. / We have heard the music, tasted the drinks, and looked at colored houses." In the poem, the speaker finally forces himself to abandon the exuberant daydream. Before leaving the wonderful dream, he asks and answers, "What more is there to do, except stay? And that we cannot do." So he returns to the stifling office, trapped by the dull work of writing an instruction manual. Ashbery, however, understood as he wrote the question and answer that it had a parallel meaning in his own life. Of course life in the city among his friends would continue without him, but he had to leave. John wrote something similar to Jimmy Schuyler: "How can I bear a year away from it all? Still, I suppose there are ways."[94]

He gave notice at McGraw-Hill.[95] Full of new energy, Ashbery began to turn the manuscript he had sent to Auden into a book, published by Yale University Press. The publications department had been surprised to learn at the beginning of July that Auden had named Ashbery the winner of the prize, sending an internal memo: "Auden didn't exactly reverse himself. He reversed us."[96] (That the members of Yale University Press seemed not only surprised but irritated at Auden's choice suggests that perhaps "under length" was not the only reason Ashbery's manuscript was eliminated in the first round. In his subsequent correspondence with the press, John liked to allude to the fact that they had not sanctioned Auden's choice.)[97] Ashbery, meanwhile, added "The Instruction Manual" to his manuscript and fiddled with the order of the poems. Auden, however, wanted him to reshape the manuscript in more significant ways. Ashbery had called it *Poems*, which was the title of two first books he most admired by Auden (1928) and F. T. Prince (1938). Auden insisted he pick a title from one of the poems in the volume, and thought *Some Trees* best, a decision about which John was ambivalent.[98] Ashbery had included his best experimental poems in the manuscript, but Auden removed any poem that had objectionable language, including "White" (because of "masturbation") and "Lieutenant Primrose" (because of "farting"). Ashbery accepted all Auden's changes, but he privately objected.[99]

Just before John returned for a final visit to Sodus, Frank visited him at his apartment to read aloud his new play, *The Thirties*, which he had dedicated to John, "a wonderful play and one of the best things he wrote—all the characters were Hollywood actors."[100] In Sodus, John's parents were also uncharacteristically gentle as he prepared to leave. The *Sodus Record* published an article, "John Ashbery Received Auden Poetry Award," and papers in Pultneyville and Rochester were printing similar pieces. To Chet an old friend wrote, "You must be very proud! . . . it would appear that John has mastered 'sliders' and 'fast breaks' in the word business."[101] His parents saved these congratulatory notes in an album, and seemed both relieved and perplexed by his sudden success. For three weeks they let their son do as he pleased. He stayed busy by learning how to drive and by taking daily Spanish lessons in Rochester, for he planned to travel while in Europe.

Shortly before leaving, the *Some Trees* galleys arrived in Sodus with Auden's new introduction, and John finally got to read it. He had been anticipating what Auden might say about his poems, and he was disappointed. In "Wystan's quite splendidly distant introduction," he told Jimmy Schuyler, "my name crops up several times (usually in phrases like 'poets from Rimbaud to Ashbery'—it would seem I'm the last of a dissolute line)." He was philosophical about the essay, however, because he understood that "it fills the bill: since I've his sanction I guess I don't need his approval." Ashbery had wished for Auden's approval since falling in love with his poems in college. Reading his essay was a useful if still painful exercise. Auden "seems to portray me as a very responsible poet who goes to extremes only to ask if he is right to do so. One almost sniffs the smoke of the burning library of Alexandria as one reads it." Seeing his poetry from this perspective immediately made Ashbery want to alter it, especially given "how insatiable my thirst for novelty is."[102] He ended his analysis of Auden's introduction by imploring Jimmy, Auden's former secretary, not to "tell *anybody* what I've said about the introduction or even that I've read it, or it will somehow get back to Wystan that I don't like it."[103] Perhaps Ashbery's comments did get back to Auden, who confided to a friend a few years later that Ashbery was "the most ambitious person" he had ever known.[104] In any case, Auden's essay served as a spur. Ashbery began thinking about the kind of book he would have published without Auden's involvement. In its rawest form, the beginnings of *The Tennis Court Oath* (1962) began to take shape in his mind.

Reviews for *Some Trees* trickled in over the next few years.[105] In June 1956, *The New York Times* listed *Some Trees* as one of the 100 "Outstanding Books for Summer Reading" (one of only seven volumes of poetry chosen).[106] William Meredith's *New York Times* book review (one of five poetry volumes reviewed together) was brief but positive. While Meredith preferred Chester Kallman's new volume of poetry, *Storm at Castelfranco*, he praised Ashbery's "derring-do" and "eight or ten beautiful and accomplished poems."[107] Other reviewers were more sharply negative. The poet Louise Bogan, in a very brief *New Yorker* review, called the volume "contrived" and "therefore somewhat boring."[108] Even family members weighed in. Helen Ashbery complained that the phrase "the sun pissed on a rock" from "The Way They Took" was neither necessary nor appropriate.[109] For the next decade, the volume remained on an upstairs bookshelf at the farmhouse, where only family saw it.[110]

The warmest words arrived from friends. Fairfield Porter responded to William Arrowsmith's very negative review in *The Hudson Review*. Arrowsmith had accused Ashbery of "intolerable vagueness" and suggested that Auden's preface proved that the elder poet felt the same way.[111] Porter wrote that Arrowsmith had misread the introduction, and Ashbery's poetry gave great pleasure from its "new rhetoric" and "a kind of music new to poetry."[112] Frank O'Hara's review in *Poetry* magazine suggested that readers ought to recognize Ashbery's "dry wit," and "difficult attention to calling things and events by their true qualities." As O'Hara put it, linking Ashbery's poetry to Stevens rather than Auden, his friend had written "the finest first book to appear in America since *Harmonium*." In the late 1950s, Kenneth Koch expressed his sincerest praise to his friend: "What news is there to write you except that I just reread the entire *Some Trees* and was overwhelmed, unhelmeted, surprised by joy, impatient as the wind—to get to my own typewriter. You're great!"[113] Ashbery also critiqued his book over time, shifting which poems he liked—and did not—from year to year.[114]

The Fulbright Commission had sent John a train ticket to New York City, but his parents and grandmother insisted on driving him to the ship. For some time, they had all been anticipating the opening of the New York State Thruway and were eager to test it.[115] As they sped toward the city, they discussed John's "going away" party at Morris Golde's place that evening at ten. All week, John had been reminding his friends to come. Chet was afraid that no one would talk to him. John was worried his mother would realize "just how many couples were not married." That night, Helen Ashbery was so pleased and relieved to see Sandy Gregg's and Bob Hunter's familiar faces that John had trouble introducing her to anyone else.[116] Jane, meeting John's parents for the first time, thought Chet was "a really impressive person."[117] Fairfield Porter engaged Chet in a long discussion on apples and cherries, a conversation that resulted in an invitation to visit the Ashbery farm, which Fairfield "hoped to do." Fairfield concluded that John's "appearance" and "his nasal voice" came from his mother. As a parent, he understood just how much John's parents would miss their son, for "they are lonely now without even John's laundry every week."[118]

On the morning of September 21, Helen, Chet, and Addie brought John to the ship, settling him into his cabin. Jane arrived; then Bob, Sandy, Frank, and Jimmy crowded in. They opened a bottle of champagne and toasted John and his journey. Later in the day, John left his cabin to explore. He stood on the deck and looked out at the sea, a scene as vast and mysterious as his childhood view. He contemplated its depths, its current promise in bringing him to another shore and to a new way of seeing what he had just left behind. In *Three Poems* (1972), he apologizes for staring endlessly at the same view:

> I'm sorry—in staring too long out over this elaborate view one begins to forget that one is looking inside, taking in the familiar interior which has always been there, reciting the only alphabet one knows.[119]

He had recognized the beginning of this idea first as a child, and it was one he would have to forget and relearn many more times before he could articulate it fully for himself. He needed the drama of a new shore in order to remember that "it is the personal / Interior life that gives us something to think about. / The rest is only drama."[120] He was twenty-eight years old and finally getting a chance to discover thoroughly all the things he already knew.

After arriving in Montpellier, France, to begin his Fulbright, fall 1955

Notes

JF Papers–Houghton	Jane Freilicher Papers, Houghton Library, Harvard University
JF	Jane Freilicher
JS	James Schuyler
JS mss–uncatalogued	Uncatalogued James Schuyler Manuscripts, Henry W. and Albert A. Berg Collection of English and American Literature, New York
JS Papers–Mandeville	James Schuyler Papers, Mandeville Special Collections and Archives, University of California at San Diego
KK	Kenneth Koch
Living Theatre Records	Living Theatre Records, Beinecke Rare Book and Manuscript Library
LR	Larry Rivers
LR Papers	Larry Rivers Papers, Fales Library and Special Collections, New York University
MW	Mary Wellington
MW Letters	John Ashbery letters to Mary Wellington, Houghton Library, Harvard University
RHPC	Robert Hunter Private Collection, Thetford, VT
SG	Sandy Gregg
Typewriter-paper Box	a sheaf of early poems that survived unknown for years in a typewriter-paper box, John Ashbery Private Collection
WH	William Haddock
YUP Records	Yale University Press, Manuscripts and Archives, Yale University, New Haven, CT

Preface
1. Author interviews with JA, July 2009, Hudson, NY.
2. Guggenheim correspondence, AM6 Box 24, JA Papers, Houghton Library, Harvard University, Cambridge, MA; Knopf correspondence (1961–62), Alfred A. Knopf, Inc., Records, Harry Ransom Center.

"My Grand Party"
1. Author interview with JA, September 22, 2012, Hudson, NY. This sublet at 21 Jones Street was the third apartment JA had lived in already during the summer of 1949. He shared the tiny place with Richard Shaw, a coworker from the Brooklyn Library, and they were not friendly. "It was in the basement, below street level. We had to walk up steps to get out. People walking past could look down and in."
2. Letter from JA to KK, September 13, 1949, JAPC.
3. Author interview with JA, September 21, 2014, New York.
4. Letter from JA to Robert Hunter, June 30, 1949, RHPC.
5. Letter from FO to Edward Gorey. Frank O'Hara wrote to Ted Gorey from Grafton, MA, that "I have a beastly cold but plan to visit John Ashbery in New York this weekend if I live" (September 1, 1949). Edward Gorey Papers, Harry Ransom Center.
6. Author interview with JA, April 6, 2013, Hudson, NY.
7. Author interview with Pat Hoey Cooper, April 24, 2013, New York.

8. Author interview with JA, September 13, 2014, Hudson, NY.
9. Author interview with Albert Kresch, May 13, 2013, Brooklyn, NY.
10. Author interview with JF, May 21, 2013, New York.
11. Letter from JA to KK, September 13, 1949, JAPC.
12. Robert Motherwell gave his Provincetown lecture naming a "School of New York" on August 11, 1949.
13. Author interview with JA, November 25, 2012, Hudson, NY.

1. "The Pleasant Early Years" (1927–1935)

1. Elizabeth (Betty) Sherwood, Mary Roberts Rinehart's daughter-in-law, read Ashbery's poem aloud. Elizabeth's grandmother was Mary Lawrence Gordon, the older sister of HEL, John's grandfather. Helen Ashbery's much younger sister, Janet, and Elizabeth were almost exactly the same age and as close as sisters, though they were, in fact, second cousins. On December 14, 1929, Elizabeth Sherwood married Frederick Robert Rinehart. Clippings on the wedding in JAPC.
2. John Farrar, a partner in Farrar and Rinehart, who was soon to launch Farrar and Straus, Ashbery's future publisher, was most likely present.
3. In interviews, John Ashbery has often repeated that his poem was read aloud at the "Fifth Avenue" apartment of Mary Roberts Rinehart. In fact, her address was the slightly less romantic and mildly less grand 630 Park Avenue. Since neither John nor his family knew New York City, "Fifth Avenue" simply symbolized wealth and success and, at some point, became part of the mythology of the family tale.
4. His parents' closest friends were the Meulendyke, Gaylord, and Boller families, all of whom lived nearby.
5. Author interview with JA, November 27, 2013, Hudson, NY.
6. Addie and HEL permanently moved from 69 Dartmouth Street to the Washington Throop house in Pultneyville on September 20, 1934. The date was noted by Addie Lawrence in her datebook. JAPC.
7. Both John's much younger cousins mentioned that HEL read constantly and that they shared childhood memories of quietly watching him read. Author telephone interview with Larry Taft, December 8, 2011; and author interview with Deborah Taft Perry, October 10, 2011, Farmington, CT.
8. Chet Ashbery had been an indifferent high school student, with poor grades and a thin schedule, but he also ran his father's small five-acre farm in Alden. During two consecutive winters (1911–13), he took courses at the Cornell Agricultural College winter program, designed specifically for farmers who wanted to learn the latest agricultural technologies during their off season. Chet Ashbery's Cornell transcript shows that he completed a winter course, Horticulture, in 1911–12, and General Agriculture in 1912–13. At Cornell he met Arthur Boller from Rochester, who told him about large tracts of inexpensive and extraordinary farmland in the village of Sodus. Eager to see if those rumors about the land were true, Chet left Alden temporarily to run the Boyd Farm in Sodus. When he discovered that the Hiram Barnes farm and vineyard, a seventy-five-acre fruit farm directly across the street, at the intersection of Maple Avenue and Lake Road, was up for sale, he encouraged his family to buy it. In the summer of 1914, shortly before the outbreak of World War I, Henry Ashbery purchased the land for $150 an acre, a higher price than other farms

in the area had gotten, "but at present considered a very moderate figure," according to the local paper, the *Sodus Record*. Henry Ashbery immediately sold his rubber stamp and stenciling business to his brother-in-law Frederick Koehler, put the Alden farmhouse on the market, and moved his family in March 1915.

9. Chet Ashbery became such a sought-after furniture maker that locals bid on his elegant coffee tables and martin birdhouses in community auctions. He turned part of his barn into a woodworking shop. In the late 1940s he even built a boat in the garage. Author interview with Deborah Taft Perry, October 10, 2011, Farmington, CT. Chet Ashbery's boat drawings and building notebook, JAPC.

10. By 1924, Chet Ashbery had been voted chairman of the local Fruit Growers' Cooperative (*Sodus Record*, April 11, 1924). He probably had a romance with a popular local woman who worked as a secretary in a Sodus law office. The only record of this relationship was a photograph that family friend Art Boller saved of two young couples in their bathing suits at the Sodus Point Beach, smiling broadly, their arms around each other. Handwritten on the back of the small photo: "Chet Ashbery, Margaret Toor, Castelle G. Boller, Art Boller, Sodus Point." Whatever the nature of Chet and Margaret Toor's friendship, it ended very suddenly, on February 8, 1922, when the twenty-eight-year-old Margaret died very unexpectedly only a few days after contracting the flu. Margaret Toor's obituary and the chronicle of her sudden illness was published in the *Sodus Record*, "Fatal Termination to Short Illness," February 22, 1922.

11. *Sodus Record*, September 11, 1925, front page.

12. Helen Ashbery's attitude toward farm work shifted completely over the next thirty years. By the early 1960s, she was admonishing John for not fairly crediting his Sodus roots: "The write up about you is wonderful—but wish you had said you came from Sodus instead of Rochester," she wrote on March 25, 1962. In AM6 Box 2, JA Papers.

13. Events noted in JA's baby book: Chet gave John a first haircut; took John and Helen for an afternoon at Sodus Point Beach; and arranged for his first sleigh ride, just before Christmas 1928. JAPC.

14. Author interview with Nancy Meulendyke Schopf, January 10, 2012, Sodus, NY.

15. Lawrence (Addie and Henry Lawrence) checkbook receipts, JAPC.

16. Author interview with Nancy Meulendyke Schopf, January 10, 2012, Sodus, NY.

17. Author interview with JA, November 27, 2013, Hudson, NY.

18. Author interview with JA, January 31, 2014, Hudson, NY. JA remembers walking across the field holding the hand of Ann, Elizabeth Koehler Ashbery's older sister, who lived with the family on and off for several years after Henry Ashbery died.

19. Author interview with JA, November 27, 2013, Hudson, NY.

20. Author interview with JA, November 2, 2011, Hudson, NY.

21. Author interview with JA, July 2, 2015, Hudson, NY.

22. Author interview with JA, inside 69 Dartmouth Street, October 3, 2009, Rochester, NY.

23. "Take out my tricycle . . ." from *Flow Chart* (New York: Alfred A. Knopf, 1991), 165; "The Children," undated, unpublished poem, AM6 Box 27, JA Papers.

24. Letter from Chet Ashbery to Frank Boyden, May 18, 1943, JA Alumni File.

25. The school was built in 1905 by a favorite local architect, J. Foster Warner, in the Classical Revival style.

26. Author interview with JA, October 3, 2009, Rochester, NY. JA remembers having a crush on a kindergarten classmate named Barbara, and he remembers friendships that year with Eleanor Hill, Patricia Lawn, Sydney Cohen, Jay Freeman, and a boy named Lester.

27. Author interview with JA, August 9, 2013, Hudson, NY. Evelyn Weller lived at 95 Dartmouth Street. They had all seen Claire Tree Major and her troupe perform, probably *Snow White*, during one of several performances at the Eastman Theatre.

28. This section was often written as recipes, almost in verse as well, and was an inspiration much later for parts of JA's poem "The Skaters."

29. Author interview with JA, October 3, 2009, Rochester, NY.

30. Author interview with JA, February 8, 2014, Hudson, NY.

31. Addie Lawrence became increasingly religious as an adult. On Good Friday, April 9, 1909, both she and Helen Lawrence were confirmed at St. Paul's Church by Rev. Wm. D. Walker. Details in Clark (her mother, Jeanette Clark's) family Bible, JAPC.

32. Author interview with JA inside 69 Dartmouth Street, October 3, 2009, Rochester, NY.

33. From "Soonest Mended," in *The Double Dream of Spring*: "Better, you said, to stay cowering / Like this in the early lessons, since the promise of learning / Is a delusion, and I agreed . . ." (1970; reprint New York: Library of America, 2008).

34. At the time of HEL's birth, his parents, Ruth Ann Throop Holling and Edmund Wilson (E. W.) Lawrence, had recently purchased the hotel. It was considered quite elegant then, and its sitting room had even served as a voting booth in the 1860 presidential election. Wayne County Historical Society, Lyons, NY.

35. "Congestion of the stomach" was listed as cause of death in the Wayne County Office of the County Historian, Lyons, NY.

36. Addie was a top student, passing state exams to teach history and literature before abandoning her studies to marry. She attended the three-year college preparatory teacher-training program at Marian Collegiate Institute, receiving grades in the high nineties. She received a New York State Teaching Certificate in February 1888, but never used it. In 1888–89, she attended "Mr. and Mrs. Kingsley's School for Young Ladies," on East Avenue in Rochester, which offered certificates for admission to the freshman class at Smith, Wellesley, or Vassar, or served as a finishing school in "the principles of Christian courtesy." Addie was nearly a perfect student and was school editor of the *School Times*; her report cards included marks of 100 in English, History, Spelling, French, and Composition. She returned home after a year and performed with a local acting troupe, the Cheerful Gleaners, until her marriage in 1892. JAPC.

37. Author interview with JA, January 20, 2012, Hudson, NY.

38. Author interview with JA, October 3, 2009, Rochester, NY.

39. Author interview with JA, October 4, 2009, Sodus, NY.

40. Author interview with JA, July 2, 2015, Hudson, NY.

41. Ibid.

42. Author interview with Mary Wellington Martin, October 17, 2010, Vero Beach, FL.

43. JA, *Flow Chart*, 4.

44. From the *Williamson Sun*, "Pultneyville Honors Its Early Heroes in Old Church Now Hall," JAPC.

45. Herman Melville, *Moby-Dick*, chap. 54, "The Town-Ho's Story."

46. Sarah Throop Miller's scrapbook, JAPC.

47. "Fragment," *The Double Dream of Spring*, 238.

48. Chet Ashbery's cigarette smoking bothered Helen as well. In her job as a biology and health instructor in the Albion School just after college, she was quoted by her students: "Miss Lawrence says a boy who smokes cigarettes weakens his health." From *The Chevron* (yearbook), Graduation 1920, Albion, NY.

49. Author interview with JA, June 3, 2011, Sodus, NY.

50. A friend of the family recalled that "everybody knew that Richard was unbelievably coordinated." Author telephone interview with Preston "Buddy" Gaylord, December 27, 2012, Salt Lake City, UT.

51. Author interview with JA, February 8, 2014, Hudson, NY.

52. Author interview with JA at farmhouse, June 3, 2011, Sodus, NY.

53. Town Line, NY, was a rural village less than twenty miles east of Buffalo with a large German immigrant population. Chet Ashbery went to school in nearby Alden and was so closely allied with his mother's German ancestry that his nationality was listed as "German" on his Alden High School transcript.

54. Author interview with JA, July 6, 2013, Hudson, NY.

55. Ashbery recalls beginning first grade at the Francis Parker School in Rochester before transferring to Sodus in midyear; Sodus school records, however, reveal that he was there from the beginning, in September 1933, but first grade was clearly not very memorable. Sodus official school transcript, Sodus, NY.

56. Author telephone interview with Preston "Buddy" Gaylord, December 27, 2012, Salt Lake City, UT.

57. Author interview with Mary Ann Boller Henderson, November 21, 2011, Rochester, NY; author telephone interview with Preston "Buddy" Gaylord, December 27, 2012, Salt Lake City, UT.

58. Author interview with Mary Ann Boller Henderson, November 21, 2011, Rochester, NY.

59. Author interview with Margaret Jordan Wahl, October 26, 2011, Sodus, NY. Margaret Wahl recalled that John kicked her in the shin quite hard for no reason one day; Ashbery remembered her, but did not recall the event she recounted in detail.

60. JA made this comment at a Boston University poetry reading on October 3, 2013, and at the Beinecke Library, November 12, 2013, in a reading that included "The Ritz Brothers on Moonlight Bay," a poem that invoked those films.

61. Author interview with JA, January 31, 2014, Hudson, NY.

62. Author interview with JA, September 21, 2014, Hudson, NY.

63. Author telephone interview with Preston "Buddy" Gaylord, December 27, 2012, Salt Lake City, UT.

64. Author interview with JA, December 26, 2013, Hudson, NY.

65. Author interview with JA, July 8, 2012, Hudson, NY.

66. Author interview with JA, July 2, 2015, Hudson, NY.

67. Author interview with JA, September 21, 2014, Hudson, NY.

68. Letter from HEL to JA, October 7, 1935, AM6 Box 11, JA Papers.

69. Author interview with JA, June 3, 2010, Rochester, NY. JA told a slightly different story in a recent e-mail to Peter Holbrook, writing, "I remember . . . 'motoring' with my parents to the nearby city of Rochester to see the Max Reinhardt film of *A Midsummer Night's Dream* . . ." (July 11, 2015).

70. Author interview with JA, July 15, 2015, Hudson, NY.

71. *New York Times* review, October 10, 1935, by Andre Sennwald. Sennwald praised "its fun and haunting beauty" without actually giving it a positive appraisal.

72. Author interview with JA, September 21, 2014, Hudson, NY.

73. "The Battle," in AM6 Box 27, JA Papers. (There are multiple copies of this poem and some in scrapbooks. JAPC.)

74. Addie Lawrence, Autograph Book, JAPC.

75. Examples that Addie Lawrence kept in her files. JAPC.

76. William Shakespeare, *A Midsummer Night's Dream*, 4.1.183–84.

77. *Poems for Boys and Girls* with typed drafts of "The Battle" and nothing else. JAPC, New York.

78. JA, "Robert Frost Medal Address," *Selected Prose*, ed. Eugene Richie (Ann Arbor: University of Michigan Press, 2004).

79. "In the Garden" is dated May 1936:

> Yellow daffodils, bright and gay.
> Greet with joy the new born day;
> Forget-me-nots poke their heads
> From their freshly moisture beds;
> And the gentle pansies, sweet
> Smile demurely at my feet.
> Stately tulips, tall and fine,
> Go to sleep at even time
> What, so lovely in all the world,
> As a garden with buds unfurled?

Addie reused this final couplet as the opening lines for a poem she sent to a friend the following year, suggesting that the poem was more hers. Addie Lawrence Scrapbook, JAPC.

2. Blue Mountain (1936–1940)

1. Author interview with JA, September 13, 2014, Hudson, NY.

2. A check for Camp Cory was cashed in 1938, but Ashbery also remembers saying he felt ill, so camp was canceled that year. Lawrence checkbook receipts, JAPC.

3. Author interview with JA, July 15, 2015, Hudson, NY.

4. Letter from JA to Addie and HEL, July 12, 1939, AM6 Box 24, JA Papers.

5. Letter from Helen Ashbery to JA, October 9, 1960, AM6 Box 2, JA Papers. Helen Ashbery wrote that she and Addie Lawrence found this old letter: "Nana was reading a letter from you—written from camp—and you said 'The food is very good—more so than at home'—we have had a good laugh over that. You were 12, I think."

6. Author interview with JA, December 6, 2011, Hudson, NY.

7. It was not for another four years, in 1942, that Ashbery began to think formally about parody in verse. That year, he borrowed Carolyn Wells's *A Parody Anthology* (1904), an anthology of poetry. JA Diary II, October 23, 1942, JAPC.

8. All quotations in this paragraph from author interview with JA, March 16, 2013, Hudson, NY.

9. Florence Klumpp (later Florence Klumpp Anson) graduated with a BA from the College of Wooster on June 14, 1937. Wooster College Transcript, Anson Private Collection.

10. Author interview with JA, July 2, 2015, Hudson, NY.

11. *God's Board: A Manual for Holy Communion.* On the inside front cover is written, "John Lawrence Ashbery confirmed the Second Sunday after Trinity June 6th 1937 by R. Rev. D. L. Ferris DD Bishop of Rochester in Saint John's Church Sodus NY John S. Williamson Rector." JAPC.

12. Letter from JA to MW, February 12, 1940, MW Letters.

13. John missed seventy-two days of school that year, and Richard missed eighty-four, according to Sodus school official records, Sodus, NY.

14. Author interview with JA, September 13, 2014, Hudson, NY.

15. From the episode "Sade Can Keep a Secret" (66–67), in *Vic and Sade: The Best Radio Plays of Paul Rhymer*, ed. Mary Frances Rhymer (New York: Seabury Press, 1976).

16. Author interview with JA, August 9, 2013, Hudson, NY.

17. Author interview with Mary Wellington Martin, October 17, 2010, Vero Beach, FL.

18. Author interview with JA, August 6, 2012, Hudson, NY.

19. Author interview with CRD, January 10, 2012, Rochester, NY.

20. Letter from JA to MW, April 3, 1940, MW Letters.

21. "Soonest Mended," from *The Double Dream of Spring* (1970); *Flow Chart*, 22.

22. *Flow Chart*, 25–26.

23. John Ashbery, *Planisphere* (New York: HarperCollins, 2009).

24. Author interview with JA, June 4, 2014, Hudson, NY.

25. *Life* magazine, December 14, 1936.

26. John Ashbery, "Preface" to Alvin Levin's *Love Is Like Park Avenue*, ed. James Reidel (New York: New Directions, 2009), quotation from p. vii.

27. Julien Levy's *Surrealism* (New York: Marstan Press, 1936). A photograph of Joseph Cornell's "The Soap Bubble Set" appears on page 183.

28. John Ashbery's "Memorial to Joseph Cornell," delivered on January 15, 1973. Draft of speech in AM6 Box 31, JA Papers.

29. Letter from JA to Betsy Myers Exner, March 10, 1978, AM6 Houghton Box 23, JA Papers.

30. Author interview with JA, March 20, 2011, Hudson, NY.

31. Ford Madox Hueffer, *Hans Holbein the Younger: A Critical Monograph* (London: Duckworth and Co., 1905).

32. Author interview with Mary Wellington Martin, October 17, 2010, Vero Beach, FL.

33. Author telephone interview with Jinny Gilbert, January 19, 2012, Sun City Center, FL.

34. Author interview with JA, July 15, 2015, Hudson, NY.

35. Letters from JA to MW, January 18 and February 12, 1940, MW Letters.

36. Patrick Brownbridge was from Ireland, and he was originally trained as a butler. He lived with Paul and Lillian Holling from at least 1921 on. In the 1940 census, he was listed as Paul and Lillian's brother-in-law, though each was also listed as single. Wayne County Historical Society, Lyons, NY.

37. Letter from JA to MW, March 28, 1940, MW Letters.

38. Letter from JA to MW, April 24, 1940, MW Letters.

39. This diagnosis was eventually confirmed by the doctor on Richard Ashbery's death certificate, Sodus City Records, Sodus, NY.
40. Author interview with Nancy Meulendyke Schopf, January 10, 2012, Sodus, NY.
41. Letter from JA to MW, April 1, 1940, MW Letters.
42. Letter from JA to MW, April 24, 1940, MW Letters.
43. Lawrence checkbook receipts, June 5, 1940, JAPC.
44. A year earlier, on June 5, 1939, at the end of seventh grade, John tied Mary Ann Boller for third place in the spelling bee.
45. *Sodus Record*, Thursday, June 27, 1940 (front page): "PRIZES AWARDED AT CLASS DAY EXERCISES."
46. Author interviews with CRD, October 5, 2011, and January 10, 2012, Rochester, NY.
47. Richard Ashbery's death certificate lists the death at 3:00 p.m. in Sodus and is signed by Chester Ashbery. Author interview with CRD, June 28, 2012, Rochester, NY.
48. Author interview with Deborah Taft Perry, October 10, 2011, in Farmington, CT. Debby was not yet born when Richard died, but she remembered her mother mentioning the flowers.
49. Author interview inside the farmhouse with JA, June 3, 2011, Sodus, NY.
50. The Gaylord family gave the book to Richard.
51. Marie-Catherine D'Aulnoy, "The White Cat," in *Wonder Tales*, ed. Marina Warner, trans. John Ashbery (London: Chatto and Windus, 1994; New York: Farrar, Straus and Giroux, 1996; New York: Vintage, 1996). Reprinted in John Ashbery's *Collected French Translations: Prose*, ed. Rosanne Wasserman and Eugene Richie (New York: Farrar, Straus and Giroux, 2014).
52. Author interview with JA, February 8, 2014, Hudson, NY.
53. Author interview with JA, January 31, 2014, Hudson, NY.
54. Author interview with JA, March 16, 2013, Hudson, NY.
55. *Flow Chart*, 6–7.
56. Author interview with JA, March 16, 2013, Hudson, NY.
57. Ashbery's handwritten copy of the play, in Typewriter Paper Box (see note 22 for chapter 3), JAPC. I never found the original play that CRD's mother described to JA, and Carol also had a copy of the play from 1940, in Ashbery's handwriting.
58. In multiple interviews with MW, CRD, and JA, they spoke often and affectionately about the play long before it became clear to me precisely when the play took place and why.
59. Author interview with CRD, January 10, 2012, Rochester, NY.
60. "Avant de Quitter ces Lieux," in *Hotel Lautréamont*; "Plainness in Diversity," in *The Double Dream of Spring*; "Meditations of a Parrot," in *Some Trees*; "Popular Songs," in *Some Trees*.
61. Author interview with Joan Buckman Micha, October 26, 2011, Ontario, NY.
62. For example: "Nine years ago my only child was hovering between life and death. . . . It was while he was in what seemed to be his greatest agony, and when I was in the darkest despair, that I first heard of Christian Science. . . . I read it silently and audibly, day and night, in my home, and although I could not seem to understand it, yet the healing commenced to take place at once. . . . [T]he child was soon able to be up, playing and romping about the house as any child should."

Testimonial by M. T. W., Los Angeles (Mary Baker Eddy's *Science and Health with Key to the Scriptures* (Boston: Christian Scientist publishing company, 1875), p. 607.

63. Author interview with JA, July 15, 2015, Hudson, NY.
64. "Definition of Blue," in *The Double Dream of Spring* (1970; reprint New York: Library of America, 2008).
65. *A Wave* (1984; reprint New York: Library of America, 2008).
66. Author interview with JA, July 8, 2012, Hudson, NY.

3. Quiz Kid (1940–1941)

1. From interviews with several Sodus families who were friends with the Ashberys and had memories of Richard's death and its aftermath, including the Parsons, Malchoff, Boller, Micha, and Meulendyke families.
2. JA Diary I, January 1, 1941, JAPC.
3. JA Diary I, January 2, 1941, JAPC.
4. Throop sailing log, Pultneyville Historical Society, Pultneyville, NY.
5. Sarah Throop Miller, 1916 Diary, JAPC.
6. JA Diary I, January 8, 1941, JAPC.
7. JA Diary I, January 10, 1941, JAPC.
8. JA Diary I, January 20, 1941, JAPC.
9. JA Diary I, January 28, 1941, JAPC.
10. JA Diary I, January 26, 1941, JAPC.
11. JA Diary I, January 12, 1941, JAPC.
12. JA Diary I, January 10, 1941, JAPC.
13. Author interview with JA, July 15, 2015, Hudson, NY.
14. JA Diary I, January 11, 1941, JAPC.
15. Author interview with JA, July 15, 2015, Hudson, NY.
16. "The New Spirit" in *Three Poems* (1972, reprint New York: Library of America, 2008), 251. The reference to the "fountain" is also a reference to the Memorial Art Gallery's most beautiful room, called the Fountain Court, part of the gallery's recent expansion in 1926.
17. JA Diary I, January 18, 1941, JAPC.
18. JA Diary I, January 28, 1941, JAPC.
19. JA Diary I, February 6, 1941, JAPC.
20. JA Diary I, March 7, 1941, JAPC.
21. "The New Spirit," in *Three Poems*, 256.
22. A sheaf of these earliest pieces survived for years unknown in Typewriter-paper Box, JAPC.
23. JA Diary I, March 3, 1941, JAPC.
24. JA Diary I, January 31, 1941, JAPC.
25. JA Diary I, March 4, 1941, JAPC.
26. "Sertus," in Typewriter-paper Box, JAPC.
27. JA Diary I, March 12, 1941, JAPC.
28. JA Diary I, February 23, 1941, JAPC.
29. JA Diary I, June 5, 1941, JAPC.
30. JA Diary I, March 18, 1941, JAPC.

31. JA Diary I, April 5 and 20, 1941, JAPC.

32. JA Diary I, April 13, 1941, JAPC.

33. JA Diary I, April 21, 1941, JAPC.

34. JA Diary I, May 4, 1941, JAPC.

35. JA kept the iron parrot always, eventually affixing it to the door of his upstairs library in his Hudson, NY, home.

36. JA Diary I, May 2–16, 1941, JAPC.

37. JA Diary I, May 23, 1941, last art class with Miss Cook. Also the comment about Miss Cook's reaction to Richard's death from author interview with JA, July 8, 2012, Hudson, NY.

38. JA Diary I, June 24, 1941, JAPC.

39. Author interview with JA, December 31, 2011, Hudson, NY.

40. JA Diary I, June 26, 1941, JAPC.

41. JA Diary I, July 5–13, 1941, JAPC.

42. JA Diary I, October 14, 1941, JAPC.

43. "Nothing to do at noon," JA Diary I, Tuesday, January 14, 1941, JAPC.

44. JA Diary I, September 2, 1941, JAPC.

45. Author interview with JA, November 24, 2014, Hudson, NY.

46. JA Diary I, entries during period September 23–October 18, 1941, JAPC.

47. JA Diary I, entries during September 17–October 21, 1941, JAPC. Author interview with JA on early study of Latin, November 27, 2013, Hudson, NY. During this interview, Ashbery suggested that his penchant for playing with pronouns in his mature poems developed out of this early Latin translation practice, for he discovered that English pronouns had much less tying them down than did Latin pronouns (which were declined).

48. JA Diary I, entries September 5–19, 1941, JAPC.

49. JA Diary I, October 10, 1941, JAPC.

50. JA Diary I, October 31, 1941, JAPC.

51. According to one of the show's producers, who later wrote a book on her experience putting the show together, children rarely applied on their own—a parent or a teacher wrote to the show first. Eliza Merrill Hickok, *The Quiz Kids* (Cambridge, MA: The Riverside Press, 1947).

52. JA Diary I, October 26, 1941, JAPC.

53. *Life* magazine, September 29, 1941.

54. *The Century Book of Facts, Standard Edition* (Springfield, MA: King-Richardson Company, 1906), 50–51.

55. Including Mr. Dobbins from *Tom Sawyer*, Creakle from *David Copperfield*, and Mr. Crane from *The Legend of Sleepy Hollow*. JA Diary I, April 23, 1941, JAPC.

56. Hickok, *The Quiz Kids*. Ruth Duskin, *Whatever Happened to the Quiz Kids?: Perils and Profits of Growing Up Gifted* (Chicago: Chicago Review Press, 1982), 16.

57. JA Diary I, October 26, 1941, JAPC.

58. JA Diary I, October 29, 1941, JAPC.

59. JA Diary I, November 1, 1941, JAPC.

60. JA Diary I, week of November 3–8, 1941, JAPC.

61. Author interview with MW, October 17, 2010, Vero Beach, FL.

62. JA Diary I, November 8, 1941, JAPC.

63. JA Diary I, November 8–December 9, 1941, JAPC.

64. JA Diary I, November 9, 1941, JAPC.

65. JA Diary 1, December 8, 1941, JAPC.

66. The Claude Bragdon–designed depot has since been torn down.

67. JA Diary I, December 10, 1941, JAPC.

68. *Life* magazine, November 29, 1937.

69. JA Diary I. Although he did not win in Chicago, he was asked to write a three-hundred-word article on the subject of "defense" for *Quiz Kids* magazine in January and discovered in May that his article had won a prize of seven dollars. Diary entry on assignment: January 25, 1941. Diary entry on prize: May 7, 1941, JAPC.

70. JA Diary I, December 10, 1941, JAPC.

71. JA Diary I, December 14, 1941, JAPC.

72. JA Diary I, December 24, 1941, JAPC.

73. Nancy Meulendyke mentioned that "Chet would often shout up to John's bedroom, 'John we have company,' and then he would not come down." Author interview with Nancy Meulendyke Schopf, January 10, 2012, Sodus, NY.

74. The term *genius* was a refrain in most of my interviews with local families. The first person to explain what he meant about John Ashbery as a genius—and to explain that he was proved to be a "genius" when he became the Rochester Quiz Kid—was Chester Peters, author interview, June 16, 2009, Pultneyville, NY.

75. Author interview with JA, May 30, 2013, Hudson, NY.

76. JA Diary I, December 16, 1941, JAPC.

77. "The History of My Life," *Your Name Here* (New York: Farrar, Straus and Giroux, 2000).

78. JA Diary I, entries for December 1941, JAPC.

4. The Art of Self-Education (1942–1943)

1. JA Diary II, January 1, 1942, JAPC.

2. JA Diary II, January 12, 1942, JAPC.

3. JA Diary II, August 10, 1942, JAPC.

4. JA Diary II, January 5, 1942, JAPC.

5. Author interview with JA, July 15, 2015, Hudson, NY.

6. JA Diary II, February 13, 1942, JAPC.

7. Letter JA to MW, February 14, 1942, MW Letters.

8. Author interview with CRD, January 10, 2012, Rochester, NY.

9. JA letter to MW, August 6, 1942, MW Letters.

10. "Syringa," *Houseboat Days* (1977, reprint New York: Library of America, 2008).

11. The film had been released in a limited fashion in 1940 but had arrived in the area only recently.

12. Author interview with JA, November 27, 2013, Hudson, NY.

13. JA Diary II, September 1, 1942, JAPC.

14. JA Diary II, [September 10, 1942], AM6, Box 31, JA Papers. At the beginning of September 1942, John lost his diary for several weeks and started to write on loose-leaf pages, which he dated more haphazardly, by days of the week. This date is a likely guess.

15. In the late 1940s, a few years after John was her student, Miss Klumpp attended Bread Loaf for several consecutive summers, to study with Robert Frost.

16. Author telephone interview with Betty Lou Burden Warrington, June 13, 2011, Pinellas Park, FL.

17. In my correspondence with two of Anson's four sons in 2011, they shared the assignments she had kept, including a book report. She kept a few of John Ashbery's written assignments from her class in a safe, with her most important family papers.

18. These loose pages of the diary are in AM6 Box 31, JA Papers.

19. JA Diary II, October 25, 1942, JAPC.

20. JA Diary III, January 3, 1943, JAPC.

21. JA Diary II, October 27, 1942, JAPC.

22. JA Diary II, October 26, 1942, JAPC.

23. JA Diary II, January 15, 1943, JAPC.

24. JA Diary II, May 22, 1942, JAPC.

25. JA Diary II, February 17, 1942, JAPC.

26. JA Diary II, March 5, 1942, JAPC.

27. JA Diary II, October 24, 1942, JAPC.

28. JA Diary III, January 28, 1943, JAPC.

29. "The New Spirit" (1970, reprint New York: Library of America, 2008), 255.

30. Alvin Levin, *Love Is Like Park Avenue*, ed. James Reidel, preface by John Ashbery (New York: New Directions, 2009), quotation from p. viii. In 1942, New Directions promised another installment of the story, but it was not published until 2009.

31. JA Diary III, February 25, 1943, JAPC.

32. Typewriter Paper Box, JAPC.

33. JA Diary III, February 28–March 2, 1943, JAPC.

34. JA Diary III, May 27, 1943, JAPC.

35. JA Diary III, March 3, 1943, JAPC.

36. JA copied the poem into his April 13 diary entry. He also won a copy of this anthology in a current-events test competition on May 20, 1943. He discovered that he had won a "5 dollar book" on May 25, 1943. Untermeyer's anthology was one choice, which he received at the class day awards ceremony on June 21, 1943. In interviews, JA remembers discovering modern poetry from Untermeyer's book and attributes his interest in modern poetry to winning that competition, but in fact he already had been reading the book for two months when he received his copy. That night, he wrote in his diary, "The book is swell. I regret that Hermann Hagedorn's 'Doors' is not in it, though." (The copy at the library was the 1943 edition and the copy he took home was the 1939 edition, with notable poems missing.)

37. JA Diary III, January 18, 1943, JAPC.

38. JA Diary III, April 16, 1943, JAPC.

39. JA Diary III, April 15, 1943, JAPC.

40. Author interview with JA, September 12, 2015, New York.

41. JA Diary III, April 8, 1943, JAPC. No copy of the poem exists, though Ashbery might have reshaped it at that time into "The Ocean: Midnight." Spiral Notebook, JAPC.

42. Author interview with Marie Wells, Mrs. Wells's daughter-in-law, February 29, 2012, Rochester, NY.

43. John McPhee, *The Headmaster: Frank L. Boyden, of Deerfield* (New York: Farrar, Straus and Giroux, 1966).

44. Handwritten letter from Mrs. Margaret Wells to FB, February 6, 1943, JA Alumni File.

45. Mr. Boyden's offer, though quickly made, was significant and suggested how much he respected Mrs. Wells's recommendation. In the fall of 1944, for example, the class of 150 students was chosen from more than 1,000 applicants. From an essay on "Deerfield Academy in a World at War" (dated August 1, 1945). Boyden Wartime File, Deerfield Academy Library, Deerfield, MA.

46. JA Diary III, April 21, 1943, JAPC.

47. JA Diary III, April 30, 1943, JAPC.

48. Letter from Chester Ashbery to FB, May 18, 1943 (handwritten on Ashbery Farm stationery), JA Alumni File.

49. Letter from FB to Mr. Donald Fenn, Unitarian Service Committee, February 13, 1942. Boyden Wartime File, Deerfield Archive, Deerfield Academy Library.

50. Letter from FB to Chester Ashbery, May 26, 1943, JA Alumni File.

51. From HEL to FB, May 11, 1943, JA Alumni File.

52. Author interview with JA, March 17, 2014, New York.

53. JA Diary III, April 28, 1943, JAPC.

54. JA Diary III, May 4, 1943, JAPC.

55. JA Diary III, June 11, 1943, JAPC.

56. JA Diary III, January 9, 1943, JAPC.

57. JA Diary III, May 6, 1943, JAPC.

58. JA Diary III, June 11, 1943, JAPC.

59. JA Diary III, May 10, 1943, JAPC.

60. JA Diary III, May 11, 1943, JAPC.

61. "In the Time of Cherries," *Where Shall I Wander* (New York: Ecco Press, 2005).

62. Author interview with Malcolm White, April 22, 2012, Palo Alto, CA. Several interviews were also conducted on the telephone between 2011 and 2016.

63. JA Diary III, June 12, 1943, JAPC.

64. JA Diary III, July 28, 1943, JAPC.

65. During the spring of his freshman year, just before being drafted and leaving Amherst for good, White beat his Amherst classmate, future poet James Merrill, in a recitation competition. The *Gazette of Amherst College*, June 2, 1944, 1: "White is Kellogg Poetry Reading Contest Winner": "Malcolm White '48 [*sic*], Amherst, Mass. was the winner of the poetry reading contest for the Kellogg Prizes, held at the Jones Library, May, 26. White read *End of the World and Epistle to Be Left in the Earth*, by Archibald MacLeish. Second place went to James I. Merrill, '47, who read an original poem entitled, *Theory of Vision*. . . . [J]udges of the contest were Mr. Clyde W. Dow and Dr. Maxwell H. Goldberg of Massachusetts State College and Professor Robert Dewey, of Smith College. Professor Lee Garrison presided."

66. Author telephone interview with JA, December 1, 2011, Hudson, NY. Author interview with Malcolm White, April 22, 2012, Palo Alto, CA.

67. JA Diary III, August 7, 1943, JAPC.

68. JA Diary III, August 4, 1943, JAPC.

69. JA Diary III, August 8, 1943, JAPC.

70. JA Diary III, August 13, 1943, JAPC.

71. They never saw each other again. Beginning a few months after I contacted Malcolm White for an interview in 2012, they began corresponding by letter and phone.

72. JA Diary III, August 31, 1943, JAPC.

73. JA Diary III, June 21, 1943, JAPC.

74. JA Diary III, July 2, 1943, JAPC.
75. Philip Horton's *Hart Crane: The Life of an American Poet* (New York: Viking Press, 1937; reprint New York: Compass Books, 1957), 80–81.
76. Author interview with JA, July 15, 2015, Hudson, NY.
77. JA Diary III, August 7, 1943, JAPC.
78. JA Diary III, August 17, 1943, JAPC.
79. JA Diary III, September 4, 1943, JAPC.
80. JA Diary III, July 14, 1943, JAPC.
81. My ellipses. Letter from JA to MW, July 9, 1943, MW Letters.
82. JA Diary III, May 22, 1943, JAPC.
83. JA Diary III, June 28, 1943, JAPC.
84. Although JA has discussed that he discovered while at Deerfield that Mrs. Wells had paid for his tuition, the school's records indicate clearly that the tuition check came directly from Chet Ashbery and not Mrs. Wells. See especially letters dated 5/18/43, 5/26/43, and 9/20/44, Ashbery Alumni File, OAL.
85. JA Diary III, September 9, 1943, JAPC.
86. JA Diary III, September 14 and 20, 1943, JAPC.
87. JA Diary III, September 21, 1943, JAPC.

5. Self-Portrait at Deerfield (1943–1945)

1. JA Diary III, September 22, 1943, JAPC.
2. JA Diary III, September 22, 1943, JAPC.
3. Malcolm White continued to write letters, but John stopped answering them; at the time, he associated the relationship with his former immaturity, which he was trying to rise above. In fact, he felt embarrassed both by evidence of his homosexuality and by his lower class.
4. Others living in the house included Brad Bond, "Mike" Michelson, and Stephen Prager.
5. He had begun the morning at the "very lovely" church on campus. JA Diary III, September 26, 1943, JAPC. Attendance at the service was compulsory for all students, a rule at which other students often balked, but Ashbery did not mind, finding the place peaceful and the sermons of the Reverend Tileston neither better nor worse than any other he had heard.
6. Donald Carlisle Greason was hired by FB a year earlier. Claude Fuess, the headmaster of Andover, suggested to Boyden that Deerfield students needed more access to high-quality instruction in the arts. Greason felt that he did not really fit into the existing sports culture at the school, but he made every attempt to conform. He created a slogan "Art as a Sport, not a Study!" and encouraged the club's inclusiveness, declaring "that the best possible system was that which followed no particular system, promoted no one theory, but encouraged each boy to follow his own bent" (*Deerfield Scroll*, February 20, 1943). Greason could extemporize at length on modern art; he had lived in Paris in 1923 and painted in a studio Delacroix was reputed to have used a hundred years earlier. Delacroix, "the patrician painter, aristocratic and dignified," was his "ideal." In private, he felt depressed about his new job at Deerfield because "for over a year now I have made a living—but I have made no art—Production does not require privacy but creation does" (Donald Carlisle Greason Journals, February

8, 1943, Deerfield Academy Library). In public, however, he kept these feelings to himself and concentrated on the students, who responded with genuine affection most apparent in their thank-you notes, which he kept. He was extremely proud of the "favorable attention—and justly—the progress" made by students in the Studio Club. In the fall of 1943, Greason was quite excited about the "new members [who] show signs of potential" (Donald Carlisle Greason Journals, July 8 and October 5, 1943, Deerfield Academy Library). He invited club members to his home almost every Sunday, where he and his wife would talk to the students about literature and painting over coffee and cake, an evening to which Ashbery looked forward each week.

7. James Wilder Green, though, mentioned he liked Ashbery's painting. Green was already a student at Deerfield. He graduated in 1945 and went to Yale. He studied architecture and eventually became an assistant to Alfred Barr, in 1956, and then to Philip Johnson, in the Department of Architecture at the Museum of Modern Art. Later he became the director of MoMA's exhibition program. DAL.

8. JA Diary III, September 24, 1943, JAPC.

9. JA Diary III, October 5, 1943, JAPC.

10. "Deerfield Academy in a World at War" (August 1, 1945), Boyden Wartime File, DAL.

11. JA Diary III, October 1, 1943, JAPC.

12. *Deerfield Scroll*, October 24, 1942.

13. Letter from FB to Deerfield alumni POW, March 18, 1944. Boyden Wartime File, Deerfield Archive, DAL. In addition to helping local farmers several times a week, Boyden arranged for students to plant eighty acres of potatoes; in the fall of 1943, this additional farming created a five-thousand-bushel surplus.

14. JA Diary III, October 1943, JAPC.

15. Picture of the week, November 19–24, 1943. Beginning on the 24th, the painting was hung for a week in an open area by FB's office.

16. JA Diary III, October 25, 1943, JAPC.

17. Author interview, September 12, 2015, New York.

18. In WH's Deerfield file, his excellent ability in literature is noted several times. Haddock Alumni File, DAL. Author interview with JA, September 12, 2015, New York.

19. JA Diary III, November 3, 1943, JAPC.

20. JA Diary III, November 8 and December 11, 1943, JAPC.

21. Among the poems from the anthology studied in class were Dylan Thomas's "Among Those Killed in the Dawn Raid," and works by Edwin Arlington Robinson and Elinor Wylie.

22. Author interview with JA, September 12, 2015, New York.

23. JA Diary III, November 8, 1943, JAPC.

24. JA Diary III, November 6, 1943, JAPC.

25. JA Diary III, December 19, 1943, JAPC.

26. JA Diary III, December 23, 1943, JAPC.

27. JA had the idea for this poem, "Not Normal," on December 24, 1943. Handwritten copy in "Miss Klumpp Spiral Notebook," JAPC.

28. Horton, *Hart Crane*, 80–81.

29. From JA sonnet, "Inmates of the Palace," written between December 31, 1943, and January 5, 1944, JAPC.

30. JA Diary III, December 30, 1943, JAPC.

31. JA, "Miss Klumpp Spiral Notebook," JAPC.

32. JA Diary IV, January 7, 1944, JAPC.

33. JA Diary IV, 1944 Horoscope, JAPC. Underlining is Ashbery's.

34. JA Diary IV, January 11, 1944, JAPC.

35. The painting is lost.

36. JA Diary IV, January 9, 1944, JAPC.

37. JA Diary IV, January 11, 1944, JAPC.

38. JA Diary IV, January 10, 1944, JAPC.

39. JA Diary IV, February 3, 1944, JAPC.

40. In WH's Deerfield file, his poor character is noted, especially in an unsigned letter written to Boyden from the master in his senior dorm, Nathan West, discussed later in the chapter. Haddock Alumni File, DAL.

41. "The Daunted," unpublished story, dated June 28, 1948, JAPC, New York. The existing typed draft, with additional handwritten pages, is incomplete.

42. JA Diary I, February 20, 1941, JAPC.

43. His earlier poetry had already generated some interest. In December the student editor at the *Deerfield Scroll* accepted two of his imagist-like poems, written the previous spring. In February the *Scroll* accepted two more of John's old poems, including the brief and evocative "January Twilight."

44. "Poem," AM6 Box 30, JA Papers.

45. In his study of John Ashbery, *On the Outside Looking Out* (1994), John Shoptaw noticed this connection between the two poems. After reprinting the 1944 poem, Shoptaw wrote, "It is amazing to see how precisely the long poem exfoliates from this compendious metaphysical lyric. 'Poem' anticipates 'Self-Portrait' in the interchange of attributes (eyes flicker, hands grope and strike); the outstretched, tensile gaze . . . the opaque, translucent face enclosed within its protective (handlike) frame; and, above all, the introverted, narcissistic eros . . . the enigma of the self confronting another as (the other within) itself. This speculative affair involves the gazer and his image, the poet's writing hand and seeing eye. The aptness of the description makes one wonder if the young Ashbery might not already have had the seductive dualisms of Parmigianino's *Self-Portrait* in mind" (178–79).

46. John Ashbery borrowed the phrase once again in "A Sweet Disorder" (*Breezeway*, 2015), which begins, "Pardon my sarong. I'll have a Shirley Temple."

47. JA Diary III, May 15, 1943, JAPC.

48. Author interview with JA, March 9, 2015, New York.

49. John Ashbery's Deerfield classmate, W. Ford Schumann, was enthusiastic about Gertrude Stein and recommended her work to JA, who began to read it in the Deerfield library.

50. JA Diary IV, February 10, 1944, JAPC.

51. Boyden advised boys to remain in prep school for as long as possible and not to rush to college both in order to mature and for their safety. Since John was a year ahead because he had skipped a grade, Boyden felt strongly that one more year of Deerfield would better prepare him to be successful in college.

52. Author interview with Gillett Griffin, August 20, 2011, Colrain, MA.

53. Author interview with JA, September 12, 2015, New York.

54. This memory is from Malcolm White, who went to campus from the Amherst clothing store where he worked to bring tuxedos to Deerfield students for their formal. John Ashbery has no recollection that he ever saw Malcolm at Deerfield.

55. Lawrence checkbook receipts, JAPC. Author interview with Deborah Taft Perry, October 10, 2011, Farmington, CT.

56. "Railway Catastrophe," AM6 Box 28, JA Papers.

57. "The Long Game," AM6 Box 28 (typed on the back of "The Railway Catastrophe" in "The Long Game" folder), JA Papers.

58. AM6 Box 27, JA Papers.

59. Dated August 3, 1944, AM6 Box 30, JA Papers.

60. "Dark River" was published in *Voices* under the name William C. Haddock (Summer, 1947). "Dark River" drafts in AM6 Box 27, JA Papers.

61. Author interview with JA, September 12, 2015, New York.

62. Ibid.

63. Letter from Henry Lawrence to JA, September 29, 1944, AM6 Box 11, JA Papers.

64. Letter from JA to MW, November 27, 1944, MW Letters.

65. William Haddock Alumni File, DAL.

66. Letter from HEL to JA, January 29, 1945, AM6 Box 11, JA Papers.

67. William Haddock Alumni File, DAL.

68. Ibid.

69. John's parents even drove up to see his performance.

70. The costume John wore in the play, a silk taffeta gown from the 1890s, had been borrowed from family friend Mrs. Bess Adams, who kept it in her attic. Letter from JA to MW, January 3, 1945, MW Papers. Author interview with JA, September 21, 2014, Hudson, NY.

71. Letter from FB to Chester Ashbery, April 15, 1945, JA Alumni File: "I was very much pleased that he wanted to move into the senior dormitory with the larger group and that it worked out so well. I am also very glad that he has decided to take the extra year, and I am sure he will never regret it."

72. Author interview with JA, September 12, 2015, New York.

73. Author interview with JA, August 6, 2012, Hudson, NY. In Mark Ford's interview with JA, published in 2003, Ashbery says, "On my first trip to New York I rushed to the Gotham Book Mart and bought all kinds of things, and one of them was a little Poet of the Month pamphlet of [Frank] Prince's poems published by New Directions in 1939. I immediately fell in love with his poems, and after that would look out for them in magazines" (42).

74. Author interview with JA, August 24, 2013, Hudson, NY.

75. Letter from JA to MW, January 3, 1945, MW Letters.

76. JA with JS, *A Nest of Ninnies* (New York: E. P. Dutton and Co., 1969), 25.

77. Author interview with Deborah Taft Perry, October 10, 2011, Farmington, CT.

78. Letter from JA to MW, January 3, 1945, MW Letters.

79. SG diary, January 23, 1945, Gregg Papers.

80. SG diary, February 8, 1945, Gregg Papers.

81. Author interview with JA, May 8, 2014, New York.

82. Author interview with Jonathan Gregg, January 28, 2012, New York.

83. The daughter and son-in-law of Addie and Henry Lawrence's neighbor, the Merrells, in Pultneyville, worked at MIT and told JA they "suspected he would thrive" at Harvard.

84. FB, undated admission recommendation to Harvard, JA Alumni File.
85. In 1945 the application was due at about the end of January, and acceptances were sent out in May, according to SG's letters to his sister about applying to Harvard, 1945, Jonathan Gregg Private Papers, New York.
86. Letter from HEL to JA, May 16, 1945, AM6 Box 11, JA Papers.
87. Letter from HEL to JA, May 16, 1945, AM6 Box 11, JA Papers.
88. Author interview with JA, May 8, 2014, New York. In Ashbery's private Harvard University File, JA requests an application for financial aid in March, and Chet and Helen Ashbery initially applied for financial aid in April 1945. JA withdrew the application in May 1945, citing sufficient funds to pay for college (Harvard University Office of the Registrar).
89. Author interview with JA, January 2, 2015, Hudson, NY. The poems of Robert Frost were taught, but there was no interest at that time in more recent poets. English faculty member Robert McGlynn did have such an interest, but he arrived just before JA graduated, and JA did not have him as a teacher.
90. "Recent Tendencies in Poetry," February 13, 1945, AM6 Box 31, JA Papers.
91. The essay referenced the following poets he had read during the previous two years: Whitman, Tennyson, Longfellow, Whittier, Robinson, Pound, Eliot, Auden, Spender, and the "Agrarian" School: John Crowe Ransom, Robert Penn Warren, and Allen Tate.
92. Author interview with JA, January 20, 2012, Hudson, NY.
93. Both poems published in *Poetry: A Magazine of Verse*, November 1945, under the name Joel Michael Symington (66–67). A further discussion of the publication of these poems occurs in chap. 6. Both poems are reprinted in the Library of America Volume I under "Uncollected Poems." The versions I include here are from Ashbery's original manuscripts, AM6 Boxes 28 and 29, JA Papers.
94. JA postcard to Helen Ashbery, May 16, 1945, AM6 Box 23, JA Papers.
95. In a letter from Morton to Boyden, he wrote of "a post as resident Writer (somewhat analogous to Mr. Grayson's [sic] post as Resident artist) wherein I should make myself useful in the encouragement of boys who want to write, and in the direction of their efforts through individual conferences. This could be combined with such lectures in modern poetry as might be useful and practicable." Letter from David Morton to FB, November 22, 1944, Morton Teaching File, DAL.
96. Postcard from JA to Helen Ashbery, May 9, 1945, AM6 Box 23, JA Papers.
97. In the John Ashbery Papers at the Houghton Library, the following copies of these poems were saved: "Seasonal"; one handwritten draft called "Poem," on loose-leaf paper; and one typed draft dated April 28, 1945, signed by JA, AM6 Box 29; "Lost Cove," dated April 25, 1945, one typed draft, AM6 Box 28; and "Dark River," originally typed on the back of "Salvage from Love," AM6 Box 27.
98. John Ashbery never knew that Morton wrote this letter in praise of the poems until I showed him a copy in 2015. *Poetry: A Magazine of Verse* Records, Box 63, Folder 7 (May 11, 1945), University of Chicago Special Collections.
99. Letters from *Poetry* magazine to WH at 8216 Seminole Avenue, Philadelphia, June 5, 1945, and July 13, 1945, AM6 Box 15, JA Papers.
100. *Poetry: A Magazine of Verse* Records, Box 75, Folder 16, University of Chicago Special Collections.
101. Letter from *Poetry* magazine to WH at 8216 Seminole Avenue, Philadelphia, July 13, 1945, AM6 Box 15, JA Papers.

102. *Poetry: A Magazine of Verse* Records, Box 75, Folder 16 (July 23, 1945), University of Chicago Special Collections.

103. Letter from *Poetry* magazine to WH at 8216 Seminole Avenue, Philadelphia, August 22, 1945, AM6 Box 15, JA Papers.

104. Author interview with JA, December 31, 2011, Hudson, NY.

105. John Kendall, younger brother of Nobel Prize–winning physicist Henry Kendall, was on this committee, but he responded to my request for an interview about his Deerfield days by saying that "he had known no one named John Ashbery at Deerfield," though JA and Henry were good friends and JA remembered John.

106. Author interview with JA, December 31, 2011, Hudson, NY.

107. Letter from Chester Ashbery to FB, May 31, 1945, JA Alumni File.

108. Given Boyden's intimate knowledge of the personal lives of all his students and their families, there is no question that he knew about Richard's death, but there is no mention of it in Ashbery's Deerfield Alumni File.

109. Chet Ashbery stopped raising turkeys in 1953. After that, he sent only apples. The last gift was at Thanksgiving 1964, shortly before Chet Ashbery passed away.

110. Letter from Chet Ashbery to FB, JA Alumni File.

111. Letter from Chet Ashbery to Dean of Freshmen, Harvard College, May 31, 1945, Private Ashbery File, Harvard Registrar, Cambridge, MA.

112. Letter from JA to SG, June 8 or 9, 1945, Gregg Papers.

113. Ibid.

114. Letter from JA to MW, June 2, 1945, MW Letters.

6. "Undergraduate Reflections" (1945–1947)

1. Letter from JA to SG, June 19, 1945, Gregg Papers.

2. Letter from Henry Lawrence to JA, May 16, 1945, AM6 Box 11, JA Papers.

3. Letter from JA to SG, June 19, 1945, Gregg Papers.

4. Author interview with JA, November 18, 2015, New York.

5. Author interview with JA, February 23, 2012, Hudson, NY.

6. Author interview with JA, September 12, 2015, New York.

7. Author interview with JA, February 23, 2012, Hudson, NY.

8. Author interview with JA, June 4, 2014, Hudson, NY.

9. "The Daunted," unpublished story, dated June 28, 1948, JAPC, New York.

10. Author interview with JA, February 23, 2012, Hudson, NY.

11. "In News, Echoes of Crash at Empire State Building," *New York Times*, October 13, 2006.

12. Author interview with JA, September 12 and November 18, 2015, New York. The party was held in Bob Gardner's room.

13. August 6, 1945, Harry Truman's "Statement by the President of the United States" announcing the bombing of Hiroshima, www.pbs.org.

14. JA's assigned freshman adviser reported that he would "probably develop with maturity into a good student. Fairly wide academic interests, serious in intent, studious" (Freshman Adviser's Report, dated August 27, 1945, signed by B. D. Thompson).

15. Known as Joel Dorius, he was a favorite fourth-year graduate student of the modernist literary critic and professor Harry Levin. He would later become famous at Smith College when he was fired from his professorship for homosexuality, though Ashbery

saw him only once in the 1960s. Correspondence between Harry Levin and Joel Dorius, MS AM2461, Folder 254, HL Papers.

16. Author interview with JA, September 12, 2015, New York.

17. AM6 Box 28, JA Papers.

18. Theodore Spencer gave few comments on John Ashbery's poetry during that semester. He occasionally marked a missing foot or other metrical irregularities. He singled out Ashbery's poem "Image of the Swan," written (as per the assignment) with limited, repeated vowel sounds. Both John Hawkes and Robert Creeley were in the class, but the future writers rarely spoke to one another. The seats were assigned alphabetically, and another student sat between Ashbery and Creeley.

19. Letter from HEL to JA, November 2, 1945, AM6 Box 11, JA Papers.

20. Author interview with JA, October 7, 2013, Hudson, NY. JA said that as close as they were, he never asked Bubsy about her arm, and he felt she did not want to discuss it.

21. Haddock also submitted five of his own original poems (July 23, 1945), but *Poetry* magazine rejected them in an August 22, 1945, letter. *Poetry* kept both Ashbery's poems, "Lost Cove" (April 25, 1945) and "Poem" (which Ashbery called "Seasonal"; April 28, 1945). However, when Haddock retyped it to send to *Poetry*, he left out line thirteen—"Is still the understanding of silences"—not realizing that Ashbery's original poem was a sonnet. (The Library of America edition uses *Poetry* magazine as its source for "Seasonal," so carries this error. See page 889.)

22. Quoted in *Dear Editor: A History of Poetry in Letters, The First Fifty Years, 1912–62*, ed. and comp. Joseph Parisi and Stephen Young (New York: W. W. Norton, 2002), 362. Quoted from *Poetry*'s seventy-fifth-anniversary issue. Author interviews on the subject as well, 2012.

23. According to the *Poetry* magazine archives (at the University of Chicago), no such confession was ever sent. And since Haddock claimed in *Voices* magazine a year later that the poems were written by him, it is unlikely that he actually sent in a confession. Multiple author interviews with JA on this subject, 2012.

24. On his death certificate, which I obtained from state offices in Buffalo, NY, Wallace Ashbery's death was attributed to an epileptic seizure at seven fifty on the morning of December 10, which caused him to fall down a cement staircase at his campus dorm. University of Buffalo students knew that he had epilepsy, but if John's parents knew, no one ever told John. He had never heard that Wallace suffered from seizures, though it would explain Wallace's rejection from the navy in 1943 (and Ashbery knew Wallace had been rejected). At the University of Buffalo, students reacted to Wallace's death with outrage. Students deemed his death preventable had emergency medical attention been provided faster, highlighting the dearth of high-quality health care on campus. Several students sent a signed letter and petition to *The Buffalo Bee* to protest (October 25, 1946).

25. "Local Anesthesia," draft dated January 1946, AM6 Box 28, JA Papers.

26. Author interview with JA, December 31, 2011, Hudson, NY.

27. Author interview with Bob Hunter, August 9, 2011, Thetford Hill, VT.

28. In December, Ashbery attended a reading by Tennessee Williams, who was "goofy, obviously gay, and probably inebriated." The small audience in Sever Hall had been hoping to hear his celebrated new plays, especially *The Glass Menagerie*, which had recently opened, but Williams read only poems. *Harvard Crimson*, November 9, 1945; Ashbery interview, December 31, 2011, Hudson, NY.

29. *Harvard Crimson*, March 15, 1946; author interview with JA, December 31, 2011, Hudson, NY.

30. W. H. Auden, *Collected Poems* (New York: Random House, 1945), JAPC.

31. Letter from JA to Bob Hunter, September 3, 1946, RHPC.

32. Letter from JA to Miss Cordingly in the Poetry Room about the whereabouts of "Auden's *Dog Beneath the Skin* (PR 5175.34)," June 15, 1946, Poetry Room Correspondence, Harvard University Archives.

33. Handwritten in his green freshman-year notebook, JAPC.

34. Essay dated April 23, 1946, AM6 Box 31, JA Papers.

35. Letter from JA to Bob Hunter, June 16, 1946, RHPC.

36. Letter from JA to Bob Hunter, July 27, 1946, RHPC.

37. Ibid.

38. Letter from JA to Bob Hunter, August 15, 1946, RHPC.

39. Author interview with CRD, January 10, 2012, Rochester, NY. Chet never spoke to John about homosexuality, and John never knew that his father was aware he was gay until Carol Rupert told me about Chet's visit to her father. She was aware of their conversation and heard bits and pieces of it, but she was not in the kitchen. Afterward, her father talked about how upset Chet had been. She had been unaware up until then that her friend was gay. I told JA on February 23, 2012, about my conversation with Carol, and JA said he had "always wondered what his father knew."

40. Letter from JA to Bob Hunter, June 16, 1946, RHPC.

41. Ibid.

42. Letter from JA to Bob Hunter, August 15, 1946, and June 16, 1946, RHPC.

43. Letter from JA to Bob Hunter, July 27, 1946, RHPC.

44. "A Sermon: Amos 8:11–14" was the first poem Ashbery published in the *Harvard Advocate*. It appeared on Tuesday, March 25, 1947, in the April issue. He also chose to read the poem to the class of 1949 when chosen as class poet in the spring of 1949.

45. Letter from JA to Bob Hunter, August 15, 1946, RHCP.

46. From "The Daunted," unpublished story, dated June 28, 1948, JAPC, New York. The full sentence is, "It was not often that Wilfred had the opportunity to realize so clearly the vast contradictions that existed within his soul."

47. Letter from JA to Bob Hunter, September 3, 1946, RHPC.

48. Letter from JA to Bob Hunter, August 15, 1946, RHPC.

49. Letter from JA to Bob Hunter, July 27, 1946, RHPC.

50. Ibid.

51. Ibid.

52. Letter from JA to Bob Hunter, August 15, 1946, RHPC.

53. Letter from JA to Bob Hunter, July 27, 1946, RHPC.

54. Letter from JA to SG, November 26, 1946, Gregg Papers.

55. Author interview with JA, December 31, 2011, Hudson, NY.

56. Letter from JA to SG, November 26, 1946, Gregg Papers.

57. Author interview with Bob Hunter, December 11, 2011, Hanover, NH; author interview with JA, December 31, 2011, Hudson, NY.

58. Author interview with JA, August 2, 2011, Hudson, NY.

59. Author interview with JA, March 17, 2014, New York.

60. Letter from JA to SG, March 8, 1947, Gregg Papers.
61. His grandmother died on February 20, 1947.
62. Letter from JA to SG, August 13, 1946, Gregg Papers.
63. Author interview with JA, June 4, 2014, Hudson, NY.
64. Letter from Richard Eberhart to Kenneth Rexroth, February 16, 1947, Box 31, Folder 38, "Correspondence 1947," Eberhart Papers, Rauner Library, Special Collections, Dartmouth College.
65. *Harvard Crimson*, February 11, 1947; author interview with JA, December 31, 2011, Hudson, NY.
66. Letter from JA to Bob Hunter, September 6, 1946, RHPC. Typographic errors on the word *it* in the letter have been corrected so as not to distract from the point.
67. Ashbery's note-taking system was such that the largest number of notes created and saved were for science courses that he found difficult to pass. He rarely took notes in English class unless he was working out an idea, disagreed with the lecture (in which he usually included a wry aside in parentheses), or did not know the information.
68. "Dull" from author interview with JA, January 1, 2013, Hudson, NY; notes on Donne from AM6 Box 31, JA Papers.
69. JA notes on the courses English Literature Since 1890 60A and Humanities [in General Education] 2A: The Epic, both dated September 26, 1946, AM6 Box 31, JA Papers.
70. Essay: "Modern Implications of Dante's Inferno," Fall 1946, for Professor John Finley's General Education course Humanities 2A: The Epic, AM6 Box 31, JA Papers.
71. Letter from JA to SG, March 8, 1947, Gregg Papers.
72. Letter from JA to SG, July 9, 1947, Gregg Papers.
73. Ibid.
74. Letter from JA to SG, June 20, 1947, Gregg Papers.
75. Letter from JA to SG, July 9, 1947, Gregg Papers.
76. Ibid.
77. Letter from JA to SG, undated, Gregg Papers.
78. John McC. Howison, *Harvard Crimson*, Tuesday, March 25, 1947; Anonymous, *Harvard Crimson*, March 27, 1947.
79. Letter from JA to KK, March 20, 1955, JAPC.
80. Letter from KK to Daisy Aldan, August 29, 1953 (Koch includes his own biography) Box 3, Folder 7, DAP.
81. Harvard University Archives, Box 18, HUD 3121. Relevant correspondence includes: May 7, 1946, from Samuel H. Ordway to Hoffman Nickerson: "I am inclined to think that if the returning editors can state and enforce a set of objectives and standards and policies which meet the Trustees' desires . . . provided the editors are of the right sort"; September 11, 1946, from A. G. Hanford, Dean's Office, Harvard College, 4 University Hall, to Hoffman Nickerson: "I am glad to know that a person like yourself is taking an interest in the *Advocate* and a hand in its present affairs. . . . Recently I have had complaints from students and parents regarding the goings on at the *Advocate* before and during the early part of the war—the heavy drinking, obscene initiations, and over-interest in abnormal sex matters"; March 1, 1947, from Nickerson: "The one point on which I definitely disagree with you is the Jew-Nigger business.

As I am sure you already know, I see no good reason for mentioning that matter in the way that you suggest in connection with the *Advocate*, and many good reasons for not doing so"; March 29, 1947, from 40 Bow Street, from Donald B. Watt Jr. to Nickerson: "Obviously it will be impossible to write into this constitution anything along the lines which you advised in our private talk. Howison, Gilmour, and I have talked about this matter at some length and have agreed that, as a matter of policy, it would be extremely dangerous to follow the course outlined. We do not feel, in the first place, that we can support such a principle; but more than that, we know that the *Advocate* would be wrecked if such a policy became known, for a large part of our public would withdraw support."

82. Letter from JA to SG, June 1, 1947, Gregg Papers.
83. Letter from JA to SG, April 8, 1947, Gregg Papers.
84. Letter from JA to SG, June 1, 1947, Gregg Papers.
85. The *Advocate*'s Commencement Issue (May 21, 1947), in which he published "all old things," including "Elegy," "A Fable," and "The Perfect Orange." Letter from JA to SG, June 1, 1947, Gregg Papers.
86. Letter from JA to Bob Hunter, May 30, 1947, RHPC.
87. Letter from JA to SG, June 1, [1947], Gregg Papers.
88. Letter from JA to SG, June 16, 1947, Gregg Papers.
89. Letter from JA to SG, June 20, 1947, Gregg Papers.
90. Letter from JA to Bob Hunter, May 30, 1947, RHPC.
91. Ibid.
92. Ibid.
93. Ibid.
94. Letter from JA to Bob Hunter, June 8, 1947, RHPC.
95. In *Poetry New York Number Two*, 1950; author interview with Bob Hunter, August 9, 2011, Thetford Hill, VT.
96. "Dreams," July 4, 1947, AM6 Box 31, JA Papers.
97. "Undergraduate Reflections" (later draft called "Undergraduate Stanzas"), June 7, 1947, AM6 Box 29, JA Papers.
98. Letter from JA to Bob Hunter, September 3, 1946, RHPC.
99. Author conversation with Professor Edwin Duval about "the forty occurrences of dolor in the *Aeneid*," and who wrote in an e-mail afterward: "(beginning in the High Middle Ages) 'dolor' might have had an inescapable association with the death of a son because of the huge success of the thirteenth-century hymn Stabat Mater (Mary at the cross of her crucified son), which begins "Stabat mater dolorosa . . ." October 28, 2015. In Finley's class, Ashbery took notes on related materials, for example: "But Virgil and Aeneas are somehow mystical—closer to coming Christianity than Classical Greece. Inwardness, pity, individualism." AM6 Box 31, JA Papers.
100. Letter from JA to Bob Hunter, undated, the beginning of which has been lost, signed "Artemus Ward," RHPC. Poem drafts are dated June 22, 1947, AM6 Box 27, JA Papers.
101. Letter from JA to Bob Hunter, August 24, 1947, RHPC.
102. Letter from JA to SG, June 20, 1947, Gregg Papers.
103. Letter from JA to Bob Hunter, August 24, 1947, RHPC.
104. Ibid.
105. Ibid.

106. *Voices: A Quarterly of Poets* 131 (Fall 1947). Although WH told John Ashbery about the promised correction, Ashbery never actually saw it in print with all these additional mistakes.
107. Letter from JA to Bob Hunter, August 24, 1947, RHPC.
108. Ibid.
109. Ibid.
110. The poem's two sources, Jean Antoine Watteau's painting *L'Embarquement pour Cythère* (1717) and Claude Debussy's "L'Isle Joyeuse" (1904) for solo piano, had long been familiar to Ashbery. Poem dated September 13, 1947, AM6 Box 27, JA Papers.
111. "The Embarkation for Cythera," September 13, 1947 (there are slightly earlier undated partial drafts), AM6 Box 27, JA Papers.
112. Letter from JA to SG, September 2, 1947, Gregg Papers. Second quotation from letter from JA to Bob Hunter, August 15, 1946, RHPC.

7. *"Some Trees" (1947–1949)*

1. Norman Mailer's reputed old room. "Women stopped by to take a look": author interview with JA, February 8, 2014.
2. AM6 Box 27, JA Papers. Also the *Harvard Advocate* (November 1947). In the *Advocate* version, the last paragraph is in all caps.
3. "*The Harvard Advocate*: On the Shelf," *Harvard Crimson*, November 10, 1947 (no writer attributed).
4. JA Diary 1948, May 10 and 11, JAPC.
5. Author interview with JA, October 2013. Signet member Palmer Dixon told JA he was particularly pleased with his performance.
6. This was the first and only public reading JA gave for five years. Beginning in the early 1940s, John Sweeney encouraged more established poets at Harvard, and even those he knew in Cambridge and Boston, to support talented younger poets and to attend student readings. In the spring of 1947, about eight poets gave mini-readings, including Richard Wilbur, Ralph Nash, and Ruth Stone. HUD 2946.71, Harvard University Archives. Some flyers announcing readings exist, though not for JA. No exact date is known, though given the audience present, which included SG, this approximate date is most likely.
7. Author interview with Bob Hunter, September 18, 2013, Thetford Hill, VT. There is no mention of this event in any of the extant papers of Eberhart, Ciardi, or Sweeney that I have found. In Eberhart's papers, however, his correspondence with Kenneth Rexroth details how John Sweeney encouraged him to help younger poets whenever he could. Eberhart also mentioned being impressed by Kenneth Koch (June 27, 1948, letter to Ted Weiss), but he does not mention John Ashbery.
8. "For a European Child" (draft dated July 13, 1947), AM6 Box 27, JA Papers. The poem was later published in the *Harvard Advocate*, April 1949.
9. Author interview with Bob Hunter, September 18, 2013, Thetford Hill, VT.
10. Ibid.
11. Author interview with JA, December 28, 2015, Hudson, NY.
12. Ibid. Also a reference to the love poem "Paradoxes and Oxymorons," which was the original working title of *Shadow Train* (1981) and includes the lines "You miss it, it

misses you. You miss each other / The poem is sad because it wants to be yours, and cannot."

13. While John's reference to homosexuality was daring for him, it was also encouraged by a new, slightly more open view on homosexuality developing at Harvard. The *Advocate* had recently run a mixed review, by John Snow, one of the *Advocate*'s board members, of Gore Vidal's openly gay novel, *The City and the Pillar* (1948), review of *The City and the Pillar*, 24–36. In the *Harvard Advocate* 131, no. 5 (March 1948).

14. Author interview with JA, October 7, 2013, and March 24, 2014, Hudson, NY. In a subsequent draft, John changed the phrase to "Fortunate Alphonse, the shy homosexual."

15. Author interview with JA, October 7, 2013, Hudson, NY. Author interview with Bob Hunter, December 12, 2012, Lyme, NH.

16. These two lines also allude to Richard Wilbur's first volume of poetry, *The Beautiful Changes*, which JA read and admired when it was published in September, and which Kenneth Koch reviewed favorably in the *Advocate*. Kenneth Koch, "The Beautiful Changes," *Harvard Advocate* 131, no. 3 (December 1947): 28–30.

17. JA Diary 1948, May 10, JAPC.

18. JA Diary 1948, May 28, JAPC.

19. Letter from JA to Bob Hunter, June 10, 1948, RHPC.

20. Typed index cards, JAPC.

21. JA Diary 1948, May 14, JAPC.

22. JA Diary 1948, May 12, JAPC.

23. JA Diary 1948, May 15, JAPC.

24. Letter from JA to Bob Hunter, June 10, 1948, RHPC.

25. "Song from a Play," Garrison competition, Honorable Mention, *Harvard Advocate*, Commencement Issue, 1948, 7.

26. JA Diary 1948, May 29, JAPC.

27. JA Diary 1948, June 4, JAPC. This Bonnard exhibit was "already affecting a generation of young painters who would be my friends," though JA was "unaware" of this rapturous reaction until he met Jane Freilicher, Larry Rivers, Nell Blaine, Al Kresch, and others a year later. See *Reported Sightings: Art Chronicles 1957–1987* (New York: Alfred A. Knopf, 1989), 241.

28. Letter from JA to Bob Hunter, June 10, 1948, RHPC.

29. Ibid.

30. JA Diary 1948, June 9, JAPC.

31. Ibid.

32. JA Diary 1948, June 10, JAPC.

33. John Ashbery's essay "Nature Images in the Poetry of Vaughan and Marvell," for Douglas Bush's English course 130b, AM6 Box 31, JA Papers.

34. JA Diary 1948, June 10, JAPC.

35. Letter from JA to Bob Hunter, June 10, 1948, RHPC.

36. JA Diary 1948, June 15, JAPC.

37. JA Diary 1948, June 16, JAPC.

38. Library of America. JA wrote several drafts of the poem in June 1948, with minor changes: AM6 Box 28, JA Papers.

39. JA Diary III, June 29, 1943, JAPC.

40. Letter from JA to Bob Hunter, July 9, 1948, RHPC.
41. Ibid.
42. Ibid.
43. Ibid.
44. Author interview with JA, December 31, 2011, Hudson, NY.
45. Author interview with JA, March 24, 2014, Hudson, NY.
46. Recent collages, especially those created in 2014, return to this image of a cat, in an unconscious homage to his very first collage.
47. John Simon, who later became a film and culture critic, served as Levin's graduate teaching assistant and grader. Adrienne Rich, a sophomore, and Robert Bly, a junior, were also in the course. JA did not talk to either there, though Rich and Bly became friends that semester. Bly was the "Pegasus" that semester, the *Advocate*'s name for the student elected to lead the literary aspects of the magazine, a position that was considered rather important among those involved in literary politics on campus. Letter from Adrienne Rich to her parents, October 21, 1948, Carton 4, AR Papers.
48. Later letters in which he mentioned Proust testify to how well he knew the novel by the end of college: letter from JA to JF, August 28, 1950; letter from JA to JF, May 7, 1956; letter from JA to JF, November 22, 1956. In each of these letters he corrects Freilicher on some small detail from her discussion of the novel. JF Papers–Houghton.
49. Robert Bly, however, was not a fan of the cover art, and he confided his anxieties about it to Adrienne Rich. Letter from Adrienne Rich to her parents, November 7, 1948: "I saw Bob Bly in the Yard yesterday. . . . He was much concerned over the new Advocate cover." Carton 4, AR Papers.
50. Author interview with JA, December 28, 2015, Hudson, NY.
51. "3 A.M." (draft dated October 6, 1948), AM6 Box 29, JA Papers.
52. "Poem About Autumn" (draft dated November 8, 1948), JA Papers.
53. "From a Diary" (draft dated August 6, 1948), AM6 Box 28, JA Papers.
54. Author interview with JA, March 9, 2015, New York.
55. Marianne Moore's recording is dated 1944 in files, but she initially recorded it in 1941.
56. *The Nation*, October 16, 1948, 167, no. 16, Ashbery's handwritten copy, JAPC, New York.
57. "The Statues" would in 1950 become one of his earliest professionally published poems. "The Statues," *Poetry New York: A Magazine of Verse* 2 (1950).
58. Author interview with JA, March 8, 2015, New York.
59. Stevens later reprinted the essay in *The Necessary Angel* (1951).
60. Wallace Stevens, "About One of Marianne Moore's Poems," *The Quarterly Review of Literature* 4, no. 2 (Fall 1948).
61. Author interview with Bob Hunter, August 9, 2011, Thetford Hill, VT.
62. "Some Trees" (draft dated November 16, without a title), AM6 Box 29, JA Papers. There are three typed drafts and one handwritten draft of the poem with two identical handwritten copies. Note that this early draft differs in some small ways from the version later published in *Some Trees* and reprinted in Library of America, 26.
63. Author interview with JA, September 12, 2012, Hudson, NY.

64. "'Some Trees' . . . was definitely written about somebody I was in love with" was the closest he ever came to explaining its creation. JA, in an interview with John Tranter for *Scripsi* in 1985, MS Box 4, JA Papers. In his "Robert Frost Medal Address" (April 28, 1995; reprinted in *Selected Prose*), Ashbery also said about "Some Trees," "This poem, I think, was quite influenced by Marianne Moore, whose work I still love; her poem 'An Octopus' is as fine as anything written in this century" (248).

65. "Some Trees" was published in the *Advocate* (April 1949, p. 10), Harvard University Archives. Author interview with JA, 2013. In his "Robert Frost Medal Address" (April 28, 1995; reprinted in *Selected Prose*), Ashbery said, "'Some Trees' . . . elicited a compliment from Richard Wilbur, a tremendous thrill."

66. Letter from Chet Ashbery to FB, JA Alumni File.

67. Author interview with JA, November 27, 2013, Hudson, NY.

68. Author interview with JA, March 9, 2015, New York.

69. *Harvard Crimson*, December 11, 1948; author interview with Bob Hunter, August 10, 2011, Thetford Hill, VT; author interview with JA, December 31, 2011, Hudson, NY.

70. Author interview with JA, November 18, 2015, New York. JA was shocked by the sudden death of his former professor Theodore Spencer (who was only forty-six years old) on January 18, 1949.

71. JA Diary 1949, February 7 and 8, 1949, JAPC.

72. Author interview with JA, December 28, 2015, Hudson, NY.

73. Ibid. JA was also reading romantic English poetry in senior spring classes for Howard Mumford Jones (English 152: English Lit 1850 to 1901) and Renato Poggioli (Comp Lit 251: European Romanticism), but this intensive, private reading of Keats was much more important to him.

74. Author interview with JA, March 17, 2014, Hudson, NY.

75. Notes to English 178 course (February 24, 1949), AM6 Box 31, JA Papers.

76. John Ashbery's paper has been lost, but his copy of Stevens's *Transport to Summer* (1947) contains his marginal notes and markings on "Chocorua to Its Neighbor" (16–23) as he worked on this paper, JAPC. Matthiessen's assignment to students to create an imagined anthology was inspired by his own work on an anthology due to Oxford University Press, which he was working on at the same time.

77. John Ashbery's essay "W. H. Auden and Marianne Moore College Paper," for F. O. Matthiessen's English 278, AM6 Box 31, JA Papers.

78. "The Egoist" (February 21, 1949), AM6 Box 27, JA Papers.

79. Letter from SG to Nancy Gregg, February 25, 1949. In the letter, he also mentions that JA is just starting to write his paper on Auden. Jonathan Gregg Private Papers, New York.

80. Author interview with Bob Hunter, December 17, 2012, Lyme, NH. Author interview with JA, January 1, 2013, Hudson, NY.

81. Author interview with JA, June 4, 2014, Hudson, NY. Note that he was able to use this private study later in the semester, in a paper for Renato Poggioli's course on European Romanticism. In the essay, Ashbery wrote, "All those poets [English romantics] were poets mainly of vision: to Keats, merely to *see* the world on a summer day was the luxury to be valued above all others; to Coleridge, seeing was synonymous with perceiving moral truth; to Wordsworth, it was a synonym for thought. The world burst in upon these poets through their eyes, and mingling in them, caused

them to see spiritual beauty everywhere. They positively thirsted to '. . . see the world in a grain of sand / and eternity in a wild flower.' Which is what every poet ought to do.' . . . The romantic movement, finally, was merely a reawakening of the imagination, 'which adds strangeness to beauty,' and whose discoveries have always been the most important part of any poetry." "Arthur Symons Paper," AM6 Box 31, JA Papers.

82. Author interview with JA, June 4, 2014, Hudson, NY.
83. Ashbery, Auden thesis, p. 28, JAPC.
84. Ibid., 29.
85. His grandparents sent him twenty dollars to pay for the typist. Lawrence checkbook receipts, JAPC.
86. The Mandrake Book Store was located at 82 Mount Auburn Street.
87. Author interview with JA, May 14, 2013, and September 21, 2014, Hudson, NY. Also, John has said in several published interviews that he thought Frank O'Hara seemed pugnacious just by the look on his face, including in an interview on Frank O'Hara with Ron Padgett at Harvard University, April 4, 2010.
88. Notes on Frank O'Hara, AM6, Carton 31, JA Papers. Published in *Homage to Frank O'Hara*.
89. Letter from JA to Bob Hunter, June 30, 1949, RHPC.
90. FO later gave JA's composition manuscript as a gift to Gerrit Lansing, who sold the original (after asking Ashbery's permission) to a rare book and art dealer in Boston. Although titled "Op.1, No. 1," the work was actually JA's second. He composed "Desert Music" (now lost) at age twelve.
91. Author interview with JA, December 28, 2015, Hudson, NY.
92. Author interview with JA, May 14, 2013, and September 21, 2014, Hudson, NY.
93. Ashbery's reminiscences of Barbara Epstein appeared in *The New York Review of Books* (2006). The poetic line is from "The Perfect Orange" (drafted June 1946 and published in the *Harvard Advocate* Commencement Issue, 1947).
94. Author interview with JA, October 7, 2013, Hudson, NY.
95. Letter from Henry Lawrence to JA, March 13, 1949, AM6 Box 11, JA Papers.
96. Northrop Frye borrowed the phrase "green world" from Keats's "Endymion" (1.16), and applied it (later) to Shakespeare. Ashbery's "The Calendar" uses the phrase "green areas," a version of Keats's phrase, which suggests a similar feeling.
97. Draft July 3, 1949, AM6 Box 27, JA Papers. The poem in an earlier draft is called "These Are Merely Suggestions."
98. Letter from JA to JF, September 18, 1950, JF Papers–Houghton.

8. "Darkness Falls Like a Wet Sponge" (1949–1951)

1. Letter from HEL to JA, July 19, 1949, JA Papers.
2. Letter from HEL to JA, January 29, 1949, and July 19, 1949, JA Papers.
3. Author interview with Alfred Leslie, June 1, 2013, New York. He offered a verbal history of the period to express fully "the world John was walking into."
4. Author interview with JA, April 6, 2014, New York.
5. Letter from JA to FB, September 25, 1949, JA Alumni File.
6. Author interview with JA, December 28, 2015, Hudson, NY. Richard Elliott briefly lived at 7 Middagh Street with writers, the Brooklyn town house shared by Auden

and others. Sherill Tippins's *February House* (2005) describes the house shortly before Elliott moved in.

7. Letter from JA to KK, September 13, 1949, JAPC.
8. Letter from JA to Richard Elliott, September 17, 1950, Richard Elliott Papers, Houghton Library. Ashbery's dislike of Jean Rhys was short-lived, and her work was published in the first issue of his literary journal, *Art and Literature*.
9. Letter from JA to FO, December 25, 1949, JAPC.
10. Letter from JA to F. O. Matthiessen, July 31, 1949, Matthiessen Papers, YCAL MSS 495, Box 1, Beinecke Rare Book and Manuscript Library.
11. They talked on the beach in Water Mill in August. (Although Matthiessen spent most of the summer in Maine, he told Ashbery he would be in the Hamptons that weekend.) JA stayed with Lyon Phelps, an acquaintance from Harvard, and they met near Phelps's house. They discovered that JA's Deerfield English teacher Mr. Bogues had been Matthiessen's English teacher at Hackley Prep. Author interview with JA, December 31, 2011, Hudson, NY. Ashbery certainly did not know that throughout 1949, Matthiessen was arguing with the Harvard English Department over course allocations and other matters. See particularly August 16, 1949, Harry Levin to F. O. Matthiessen, Matthiessen Papers, YCAL MSS 495, Box 3, Beinecke Rare Book and Manuscript Library, Yale University.
12. Author interview with JA, December 31, 2011, Hudson, NY.
13. Letter from JA to KK, September 13, 1949, JAPC.
14. Author interview with JA, December 28, 2015, Hudson, NY.
15. Letter from JA to FO, December 25, 1949, JAPC.
16. Letter from JA to KK, September 13, 1949, JAPC.
17. Ashbery would remove the reference to Rachmaninoff before publishing the prose poem in *New Directions* 14 (February 11, 1953).
18. "A Dream" (draft dated September 18, 1949), AM6 Box 27, JA Papers. The version that would eventually be published in *New Directions* 14 was significantly revised.
19. JA, "Introduction to the Collected Poems of Frank O'Hara," ed. Donald Allen (Berkeley: University of California Press, 1995).
20. Author interview with Alfred Leslie, June 1, 2013, New York.
21. Letter from JA to SG, September 10, 1950, Gregg Papers.
22. "Splendors of 60 W. 12th," in letter from JA to SG, Gregg Papers. Author interview with Les Brown, May 12, 2012, Amherst, MA.
23. Letter from JA to KK, September 13, 1949, JAPC.
24. Author interview with JA, September 22, 2012, Hudson, NY.
25. Ibid.
26. Ibid. Later, in his study of twentieth-century British writers, Tindall relegated Firbank to a footnote: "Both before and after the war, Ronald Firbank, a corrupt dandy, composed arabesques in the most decadent style of the nineties" (William York Tindall, *Forces in Modern British Literature 1885–1946* [New York: Knopf, 1947], 127n).
27. Author interview with JA, September 22, 2012, Hudson, NY. JA always wished he had replied, "I'm glad you think it is an abyss."
28. Letter from JA to FO, March 21, 1951, JAPC. In this letter, JA specifically refers to "IC-B," though in others he compares Green to Auden.

29. Letter from JA to SG, September 10, [1950], Gregg Papers.

30. Letter from JA to JF, July 12, 1951, JF Papers–Houghton.

31. Author interview with JA, April 6, 2013, Hudson, NY.

32. Author interview with JA, December 28, 2015, Hudson, NY.

33. Nell Blaine said that "there was something wistful about John in those years." Martica Sawin, *Nell Blaine, Her Art and Life* (New York: Hudson Hills Press, 1998), 45.

34. Letter from HEL to JA, October 25, 1949, AM6 Box 11, JA Papers.

35. Author interview with JA, August 9, 2012, Hudson, NY. The painting was lost.

36. Letter from JA to FO, December 25, 1949, JAPC.

37. Ibid.

38. Author interview with JA, December 28, 2015, Hudson, NY. Porter, though, "was not at home."

39. Letter from FO to JA, September 22, 1958, AM6 Box 14, JA Papers. O'Hara reminisced, writing, "How sweet you were to me, it really seemed just like when I first used to visit New York. I wonder what other capital cities of the world you will guide me around for the first time?"

40. Letter from JA to KK, May 2, 1951. Reflecting on this period in 1950, JA wrote, "Everything repeats last year, without the vitality of the poetry I read and wrote then." JAPC.

41. Letter from JA to Richard Elliott, September 17, 1950, Houghton Library.

42. Hadas was about to publish his first book, *History of Greek Literature* (1950). Moses Hadas, *A History of Greek Literature* (New York: Columbia University Press, 1950).

43. JA Letter to JF, August 8, 1950, JF Papers–Houghton.

44. JA had already liked the story when it appeared earlier in *Partisan Review*.

45. John Ashbery, *Three Plays* (Calais, VT: Z Press, 1978), 15.

46. Author interview with JA, December 28, 2015, Hudson, NY.

47. Letter from JA to JF, September 18, 1950, JF Papers–Houghton.

48. This phrase is Auden's in his introduction to the poems in *Some Trees*, 1956. Michael W. Clune discusses the phrase in *Writing Against Time* (Palo Alto, CA: Stanford University Press, 2013).

49. Five years later, in a letter to KK, apropos of John's seeing Kenneth's poem in *Poetry* magazine, he explained that "the word empiricism jars me; just as I changed 'paraphrase' to 'bed' in 'Meditations of a Parrot.'" Letter from JA to KK, April 13, 1955, JAPC.

50. Draft, March 27, 1950, AM6 Box 28, JA Papers.

51. The short obituary "Prof. F. O. Matthiessen Dies in Boston Plunge," which appeared on the bottom of page 32 in *The New York Times*, hardly addressed Matthiessen's intellect or teaching.

52. Draft dated April 15, 1950, Box 28 AM6, JA Papers. All drafts dated that day and one with a significantly different second section.

53. Letter from JA to FO, October 11, 1950, JAPC.

54. Letter from JF to LR, July 1, 1950, LR Papers.

55. For example, articles and photographs of "The 'Emergency Kit' in Event of Atomic Disaster" and other articles about atomic disaster preparedness, *New York Times*, June 6, 1950, Section 1, p. 5.

56. "The Cool Head," draft dated June 1, 1950, AM6 Box 27, JA Papers.

57. Author interview with JA, November 29, 2013, Hudson, NY.

58. Author interview with JA, December 28, 2015, Hudson, NY.

59. Letter from JA to KK, July 29, 1950, JAPC.

60. Letter from JA to JF, August 8, 1950, JF Papers–Houghton. The poem is dated July 23 and 24, 1950, AM6 Box 28, JA Papers. Author interview with JA, November 10, 2012, Hudson, NY.

61. "Mencius in Milk Street," draft dated July 23 and 24, 1950, AM6 Box 28, JA Papers.

62. Letter from JA to JF, September 8, 1960, JF Papers–Houghton.

63. Letter from JA to JF, September 18, 1950, JF Papers–Houghton.

64. Letter from JA to Donald Allen, June 30, 1969, MSS 3, Box 56, Folder 15, DA Collection–Mandeville.

65. *New York Times*, July 16, 1950.

66. In the fall of JA's senior year at Harvard (1948–49), in Professor Kuhn's course Fine Arts 165a: 15th and 16th Century Painting in Northern Europe. Nov 19: "15th C. a change. Classical learning brought back. A desire to represent human body as it is." In margins, JA wrote "Parmagianino" [*sic*].

67. Letter from JA to JF, August 8, 1950, JF Papers–Houghton.

68. Letter from JA to JF, no date [September 1950], JF Papers–Houghton.

69. Letter from JA to JF, September 18, 1950, JF Papers–Houghton.

70. JA's handwritten homework assignment on loose-leaf paper, left inside his *Prose and Poetry for Appreciation* textbook, JAPC.

71. Letter from JA to FO, May 30, 1951, JAPC.

72. "Le livre est sur la table," draft dated August 31, 1950, AM6 Box 28, JA Papers.

73. JA, Introduction, *The Collected Poems of Frank O'Hara*, ed. Donald Allen (Berkeley: University of California Press, 1995).

74. Letter from JA to JF, September 18, 1950, JF Papers–Houghton.

75. Ibid.

76. Letter from JA to FO, October 11, 1950, JAPC.

77. Letter from JA to JF, August 8, 1950, JF Papers–Houghton.

78. Letter from JA to JF, August 14, 1951, JF Papers–Houghton.

79. Letter from JA to JF, September 18, 1950, JF Papers–Houghton.

80. Letter from JA to KK, May 2, 1951, JAPC.

81. Ibid.

82. AM6 Box 29, JA Papers. One of the sonnets ("The young darling says to his wife . . .") is dated October 12, 1950. The others are undated, but JA remembers writing all four at approximately the same time. They begin: "Each servant stamps the reader with a look"; "The barber at his chair"; "Each day the sky lets out."

83. Letter from JA to Bob Hunter, June 30, 1949, RHPC.

84. During the summer of 1950, LR wrote Jane Freilicher a twenty-four-page handwritten letter, which served as both a complaint about Jane's desire to break up and a plea not to. JF Papers–Houghton.

85. Letter from JA to KK, May 2, 1951, JAPC.

86. The inaugural group included Richard Eberhart, Bunny Lang, Hugh Amory, Frank O'Hara, Ted Gorey, Lyon Phelps, and Alison Lurie.

87. In addition to John's and Frank's plays, Richard Eberhart's *The Apparition*, starring Donald Hall; and Lyon Phelps's *3 Words in No Time*, with Jerry Kilty playing

Herman Melville, were all being performed on the same program. "How wonderful your music was," JA wrote in a letter to FO, March 21, 1951, JAPC.

88. Author interview with Freddy English, June 1, 2013, New York. Freddy English felt that Wilder misunderstood the youthful audience with its own sense of humor: "his [Wilder's] comment was unnecessary and kind of crazy."

89. Christina Davis, curator of the Woodberry Poetry Room at Harvard University, unearthed the original reel of Wilder's impromptu speech, which had been cut from the recording of the four plays made that evening. While certain words are difficult to hear, we listened together multiple times to determine what he said. October 6, 2014. For more details, see Karin Roffman, Woodberry Poetry Room Blog, January 2015.

90. Letter from JA to FO, March 21, 1951, JAPC.

91. Letter from JA to JF, July 26, 1951, JF Papers–Houghton.

92. Letter from JA to FO, March 21, 1951, JAPC.

93. Ibid.

94. He submitted "Epilogue to Experience" for a grade and received a B+ and the comment "Fine individual phrases and lines—I'd like more cohesion, more aim."

95. Columbia Notebook, JAPC.

96. Letter from JA to KK, May 2, 1951, JAPC.

97. Letter from JA to FO, May 30, 1951, JAPC.

98. "A Long Novel," earliest draft dated July 11, 1951, AM6 Box 28, JA Papers.

99. Letter from JA to Jane Freilicher, July 12, 1951, JF Papers–Houghton; *Partisan Review* (July/August 1951).

100. Letter from JA to JF, July 12, 1951, JF Papers–Houghton.

101. Ibid.

102. Ibid.

103. Letter from JA to JF, [1951], JF Papers–Houghton.

104. Ibid.

105. Author interview with JA, December 28, 2015, Hudson, NY.

106. Handwritten draft of the letter in Columbia University Notebook, JAPC. Letter from JA to JF, July 28, 1951, JF Papers–Houghton.

107. Letter from JA to KK, May 2, 1951, JAPC. Letter from JA to JF, August 14, 1951, JF Papers–Houghton.

108. Postcard from JA to JF, August 28, 1951, JF Papers–Houghton.

109. Letter from JA to JF, August 14, 1951, JF Papers–Houghton.

110. Author interview with JA, May 14, 2013, and September 21, 2014, Hudson, NY. In an interview with Ron Padgett at Harvard, April 4, 2010, JA made a similar comment about his mother having mistaken Frank's voice for his.

111. Author interview with JA, January 1, 2013, Hudson, NY.

112. "Still feel a wreck," from letter from JA to JF, August 14, 1951, JF Papers–Houghton. "Crisping my veils," from postcard from JA to JF, August 28, 1951, JF Papers–Houghton.

9. *"Greetings, Friends!" (1951–1953)*

1. Postcard from JA to JF, September 8, 1950, JF Papers–Houghton.

2. Letter from JA to FO, March 21, 1951, JAPC.

3. FO, "A Party Full of Friends" (Ann Arbor, April 1951), in *Poems Retrieved*, ed. Don Allen (San Francisco: City Lights, 1955–2013).

4. JA, *Selected Prose*, ed. Eugene Richie. "A Reminiscence: Frank O'Hara." Ann Arbor: University of Michigan Press, 2004, 174.

5. Kenneth Koch, "A Note on Frank O'Hara in the Early Fifties," in Bill Berkson and Joe LeSueur, eds. *Homage to Frank O'Hara* (Bolinas, CA: Big Sky, 1978).

6. "A Reminiscence: Frank O'Hara," in JA, *Selected Prose*, ed. Eugene Richie (Ann Arbor: University of Michigan Press, 2004, 174).

7. Letter from JA to JF, September 18, 1950, JF Papers–Houghton.

8. Author interview with Gerrit Lansing, December 1, 2012, Gloucester, MA; interview with JA, December 16, 2012, Hudson, NY.

9. From 1952 tax return, JAPC.

10. Letter from Chet Ashbery to FB, February 6, 1953, JA Alumni File.

11. Letter from JA to Helen and Chet Ashbery, January 31, 1952, JAPC.

12. Letter from JA to JF, August 14, 1951, JF Papers–Houghton.

13. Author interview with JA, October 16, 2012, New York.

14. Author interview with JA, September 15, 2012, New York. The discussion was prompted by the presence of a new copy of that book, which Ashbery had ordered after it was recently reissued.

15. Author interview with JA, November 29, 2013, Hudson, NY.

16. Author interview with JA, October 16, 2012, New York.

17. See especially David K. Johnson, *The Lavender Scare: The Cold War Persecution of Gays and Lesbians in the Federal Government* (Chicago: University of Chicago Press: 2004).

18. AM6 Box 27, nd, JA Papers.

19. After more than a decade of silence between Ashbery and Howard Wamsley, Wamsley wrote a sympathetic, serious review of *Rivers and Mountains* (1966), especially "The Skaters," explaining that Ashbery's poetry suggested that "the tensions existing between man's perennial desire to grasp the essential secret of the universe, and his desire to remain comfortably, if anxiously, earth-bound, can be resolved in a multi-dimensional vision of reality. . . . [I]t is a vast, wide-ranging, poignant, beautifully modulated, irrepressibly comic occasion [that demonstrates how] the man has found his range and hit his stride" (Howard Wamsley, "Speeding Hackney Cabriolet," *Poetry*, December 1966).

20. Author interview with Judith Malina, April 13, 2013, Englewood, NJ. From Judith Malina's unpublished essay "The Living Theatre" (written 2012–13), which she showed to me during the interview. John Tytell also discusses this meeting in *The Living Theatre: Art, Exile, and Outrage* (New York: Grove Press, 1995), 79, though the accounts differ slightly.

21. Author interview with Judith Malina, April 13, 2013, Englewood, NJ. Picasso's *Desire Caught by a Tail* in a 1948 translation by Herma Briffault.

22. Not long after meeting them, she wrote in her diary that "Frank is more sophisticated than John," February 28, 1952. In manuscript draft in the Living Theatre Records; author interview with Judith Malina, April 13, 2013, Englewood, NJ.

23. Box 99, Living Theatre Records.

24. Author interview with Judith Malina, April 13, 2013, Englewood, NJ.

25. From uncatalogued Box s5a, Cashed Checks to JA from the Living Theatre, JA mss–uncatalogued.

26. Audio recording from the 92nd Street Y of Brinnin's introduction, April 3, 1952, 92nd Street Y Archives.

27. JA read fifteen poems first, before the other two winners, Gray Burr and Harvey Shapiro, and then each read one more poem as an encore at the very end. The list of poems read (in order): "Eclogue," "Meditations of a Parrot," "Mythological Poet," "Pied Piper," "From a Diary," "The Painter," "Jane," "Some Trees," "Errors," "Friar Laurence's Cell," "The Picture of Little J.A. in a Prospect of Flowers," "A Dream," "A Speech," "The Dolors of Columbine," "The Grapevine," "Why We Forget Dreams," 92nd Street Y Archives.

28. Letter from KK to JF, "Easter Sunday," 1952, JF Papers–Houghton.

29. "The Year's Midnight," draft dated September 19, 1948, AM6 Box 30, JA Papers.

30. "Jane" (draft dated February 1952), AM6 Box 28, JA Papers.

31. Box 16, Folder 401, YCAL MSS 388, New World Writing, Yale Collection of American Literature, Beinecke Rare Book and Manuscript Library, Yale University, New Haven, CT.

32. "Jane Freilicher," ARTnews, May 1952, p. 47.

33. Letter from Fairfield Porter to Aline Porter (his sister-in-law), Christmas Day 1951, published in Material Witness: The Selected Letters of Fairfield Porter, ed. Ted Leigh (Ann Arbor: University of Michigan Press, 2005), 123.

34. JF interview with Barbara Shikler, Tuesday, August 4, 1987, Water Mill, NY, Jane Freilicher Papers, Archives of American Art.

35. "Presenting Jane," JS mss–uncatalogued. This play manuscript was first identified by Schuyler biographer Nathan Kernan.

36. One afternoon, shortly after beginning his job at Oxford University Press in October 1951, Ashbery spotted Guest at an outdoor café near the office and uncharacteristically introduced himself, complimenting her on two recent poems, "People in Wartime" and especially "This Way to Pity" ("On the way to your house / I was followed by a bear, a rhinoceros, / and a pigeon"), which he had just read in Partisan Review and really liked. They started talking, and he introduced her soon after to Frank O'Hara and Jane Freilicher. She had similar interests and was especially captivated by contemporary painting, and Frank immediately began inviting her to gatherings ("Two Poems" in Partisan Review [September–October 1951]. Author interview with JA, November 27, 2013, Hudson, NY).

37. Brad Gooch offers a specific date for this event: May 14, 1952. John Ashbery remembered the event not as a panel but as a reading, from author interview with JA, May 30, 2013, Hudson, NY. Brad Gooch discusses the details of the play's disappearance in A City Poet: The Life and Times of Frank O'Hara (New York: Alfred A. Knopf, 1993), 263–65.

38. From Kenward Elmslie's "Fifties Probe," in New American Writing 18 (2000): 123. In January 1953, John Malcolm Brinnin accepted "He" for New World Writing's third mentor edition.

39. Author telephone interview with Harrison Starr, May 5, 2013.

40. Author telephone interviews with Harrison Starr, 2013; author interview with Harrison Starr and JA, May 9, 2014, New York.

41. Author interview with JF, October 21, 2011, New York.

42. Kenward Elmslie also recalled that "cast and crew shared a Hamptons house . . . one morning. . . . I spied three people in the same bed: Frank, J.A., and Holy Moly, Jane in the middle." From Elmslie's "Fifties Probe," 129.

43. JA interview with Barbara Shikler, Tuesday, August 4, 1987, Water Mill, NY; and 33 of the Jane Freilicher Papers, Archives of American Art.

44. Harrison edited the film in Maya Deren's apartment and created a four-minute rough cut to screen on February 25, 1953, at the Theatre de Lys after a staged reading of Jimmy Schuyler's play (from Box 38, Grace Hartigan Papers, Syracuse Rare Book and Manuscript Library, Syracuse University Libraries, Special Collections Research Center, Syracuse, NY.) After the event, Harrison took the film back, to work on it some more, and kept it while waiting for Latouche to pay him the final promised installment. Latouche never paid. Harrison Starr and Maya Deren broke up not long after, and Starr moved back to California and took the film reels with him, where they remained in their original tins for the next sixty years.

45. Author interview with JF, March 29, 2013, New York.

46. Ibid.

47. Kenneth Koch, "A Note on Frank O'Hara in the Early Fifties," AM6 Box 46, JA Papers.

48. Letter from LR to FO, August 12, 1952, Box 11, Folder 7, LR Papers.

49. In *Audit* (featuring Frank O'Hara) 4, no. 1, ed. Michael Anania and Charles Doria: 32–33. Kenneth Koch's "A Note on Frank O'Hara in the Early Fifties," AM6 Box 46, JA Papers.

50. James Schuyler, "At the Beach," *The New Yorker*, July 5, 1952, p. 45.

51. Author interview with JA, June 4, 2014, Hudson, NY.

52. Author interview with JA, April 6, 2013, Hudson, NY. Also, JA discussed the beginning of the novel with Bill Berkson in an unpublished interview for *The Paris Review*, Bill Berkson Papers, Dodd Rare Book and Manuscript Library, University of Connecticut.

53. James Schuyler's biographer, Nathan Kernan, notes that Schuyler commented on Fairfield Porter's sister-in-law Aline Porter: "She's very *Nest*." *The Diary of James Schuyler* (Santa Rosa, CA: Black Sparrow Press, 1997), 312. Another line in *Nest*, which Ashbery took from a comment made by Mrs. Meulendyke at a dinner she attended at the Ashbery Farm in the late 1950s, p. 38: Mrs. Kelso says, "They think I'm funny . . . but I never take sugar in my coffee after a sweet dessert." Author interview with JA, April 6, 2013, Hudson, NY.

54. "Presenting Jane," JS mss–uncatalogued.

55. Author interview with JA, November 29, 2013, Hudson, NY.

56. On April 3, 1952, at the 92nd Street Y, Brinnin had announced *The Heroes* would be produced in June, but at some point between April and the end of May, the production was delayed until August.

57. The cast of *The Heroes*: Julian Beck designed sets and played Theseus in a white suit. Herbert Hartig was Achilles, Shirley Gleaner was Circe, Jackson Mac Low played Ulysses, Ruth Kaner the Chorus, and Tchouki Mataj played Astyanax.

58. Author interview with Judith Malina, April 13, 2013, Englewood, NJ.

59. Judith Malina diary, June 17, 1952, Judith Malina diary draft, Box 9, p. 537, Living Theatre Records.

60. Author interview with Judith Malina, April 13, 2013, Englewood, NJ.

61. Vernon Rice, "Summer Madness Goes on Too Long," *New York Post*, August 6, 1952, p. 44.

62. Author interview with JA, March 17, 2014, Hudson, NY.

63. Judith Malina diary draft, p. 696, August 13, 1952. The entry begins: "A world ends."

64. May 18, 1953, p. 78, Grace Hartigan Journals.

65. JA met them at the very beginning of September 1952. JA wrote Gold and Fizdale a thank-you note that included four poems ("The Painter," "Illustration," "Le livre est sur la table," and "Sestina from *Turandot*") on September 4, 1952, Gold and Fizdale Private Collection, New York.

66. Author interview with JA, January 1, 2013, Hudson, NY.

67. JA to Gold and Fizdale, September 4, 1952, Gold and Fizdale Private Collection.

68. On October 15, 1952, p. 47, Grace Hartigan Journals.

69. Letter from JA to Arthur Gold, October 20, 1952, Gold and Fizdale Private Collection.

70. Author interview with JA, April 6, 2013, Hudson, NY.

71. Ibid.

72. Author interview with JF, March 29, 2013, New York.

73. October 10, 1952, Box 7, JS Papers–Mandeville.

74. Dated October 20, 1952, Gold and Fizdale Private Collection.

75. The play, rediscovered recently, is dated November 1, 1952, JAPC, New York.

76. Author interview with JA, December 16, 2012, Hudson, NY. In 1967, after visiting the Hearst Castle in San Simeon, JA wrote to JS: "The Hearst Chateau was quite lovely—the interiors in the Arthur Weinstein tradition as you can see." Postcard from JA to JS, August 16, 1967, Box 1, Folder 15, JS Papers–Mandeville.

77. Author interview with JA, December 16, 2012, Hudson, NY.

78. Author interview with JA, August 6, 2012, Hudson, NY.

79. Ibid.

80. Fairfield Porter gave the painting to JA in the mid-sixties. It took John many more decades to begin to warm (and he never warmed fully) to the work. Quotation from Letter from JA to the Porters, May 11, 1953, JAPC.

81. Letter from JA to Fairfield Porter (on Oxford University Press stationery), 1952, JAPC.

82. Author interview with JA, August 6, 2012, Hudson, NY.

83. In an interview Nathan Kernan conducted with Jane Freilicher and her husband, Joe Hazan, October 18, 1994, New York. JF Papers–Houghton.

84. Author interview with JA, December 16, 2012, Hudson, NY.

85. "Pantoum," from *Some Trees* (New York: Library of America, 2008). No early drafts with changes exist. Note "clay pipes" that begin and end the poem were, among their other uses, also materials used in Joseph Cornell's "Soap Bubble Set."

86. Letter from FO to LR, December 30, 1952, Box 11, Folder 7, LR Papers.

87. Author interview with JA, November 29, 2013, Hudson, NY.

88. The poem begins: "May Christmas goodies go in tins / To Charles Campisi and Katherine Hinz / And roast turkey and pudding (plum) / To Robert Cram and Esther Blum . . ." In JA Oxford University Press files, JAPC.

89. AM6 Box 29, January 1953, JA Papers.

90. Letter from JS to Arthur Gold, April 19, 1953, Gold and Fizdale Private Collection, New York.

91. Author interview with JA, December 16, 2012, Hudson, NY.

92. Author interview with JA, December 28, 2015, Hudson, NY. The execution took place on June 19, 1953.

93. One such party was held at Jane Freilicher's: October 17, 1953, p. 101, Grace Hartigan Journals.

94. Letter from FO to LR, August 10, 1953, Box 11, Folder 7, LR Papers.

95. According to a letter Schuyler wrote to John Button several years later, Larry never knew for certain about John and Fairfield. JS wrote to Button: "What is most serious (if true) is that you told Larry about Fairfield's private affairs. No matter what Larry may have surmised, he did not really know anything (I got this from Jane). I don't imply at all that you were motivated by malice, but you do provide people who are malicious with weapons: would you really care to take the responsibility for what Larry is capable of saying to Anne Porter, and do you think she deserves having it said to her? (Not that her nature isn't large enough to encompass it.) And what about the obligations your friendship with Fairfield, John Ashbery and with me place on you?" (JS to John Button, [approx. 1956], JS Papers–Mandeville).

96. Letter from FO to LR, May 6, 1953, Box 11, Folder 7, LR Papers.

97. Letter from LR to FO, May 8, 1953, Box 11, Folder 7, LR Papers.

98. September 17, 1953, p. 96, Grace Hartigan Journals.

99. Author interview with JA, November 29, 2013, Hudson, NY.

100. Letter from JA to LR, June 15, 1953, Box 1, Folder 19, LR Papers.

101. Letter from JA to LR, May 28, 1953, Box 1, Folder 19, LR Papers.

102. Author interview with JA, April 6, 2013, Hudson, NY. He had discarded the titles "The White Ball" and "The White Heron."

103. "Petroleum Lima Beans," AM6 Box 28, JA Papers.

104. No date on draft; JA dates it to spring 1953. AM6 Box 28, JA Papers.

105. Letter from JS to Arthur Gold on Periscope Bookstore stationery, Wednesday, April 15, 1953, Gold and Fizdale Private Collection.

106. "Aeneas," unpublished draft dated May 1953, AM6 Box 27, JA Papers.

107. Author interview with JA, May 7, 2013, Hudson, NY. *The Coconut Milk* was published in John Myers's short-lived literary magazine *Semi-Colon*.

108. Author interview with JA, June 4, 2014, Hudson, NY.

109. Author interview with Bill Berkson, November 9, 2012, New York.

110. AM6 Box 30, JA Papers. Act 1 was written in 1953; act 2 was written in 1966, shortly before Frank O'Hara's death.

111. Letter from JA to Anne and Fairfield Porter, May 11, 1953. JAPC.

112. Author interview with JA, June 4, 2014, Hudson, NY.

113. Author interview with JA, April 6, 2013, Hudson, NY.

114. Author interview with JA, November 25, 2012, Hudson, NY.

115. Letter from LR to FO, July 30, 1953, Box 11, Folder 7, LR Papers.

116. Letter from LR to FO, September 3, 1953, Box 11, Folder 7, LR Papers.

117. KK dates the publication as September 15, 1953, in a letter to Daisy Aldan, August 29, 1953, Box 3, Folder 7, Daisy Aldan Papers.

118. Author interview with JA, January 4, 2014, Hudson, NY. Folder 1 published: "Grapevine," "Errors," "White," and "The Way They Took."

119. Letter from John Myers to LR, October 5, 1953, Box 10, Folder 11, LR Papers.

120. December 21, 1953, p. 111, Grace Hartigan Journals.

121. Author interview with JA, May 7, 2013, Hudson, NY.

10. *"What More Is There to Do, Except Stay? And That We Cannot Do"* (*1954–1955*)

1. He referred to the poem later as "my Thesaurus poem." Letter from JA to KK, April 13, 1955, JAPC.

2. *Roget's Thesaurus* signed "John Lawrence Ashbery February 29 1943," JAPC. Quotation from author interview with JA, May 7, 2013, Hudson, NY.

3. *Semi-Colon* 1, no. 3. John Myers's brief magazine was never dated, but this issue, from context, probably was published in 1955. Flow Chart Foundation and Ashbery Resource Center, Hudson, NY. Ashbery's poem especially excited KK, who in correspondence with the poet Daisy Aldan about the next issue of her journal, *Folder*, explained that "it seems so evident that poetry has not been using the full resources of its medium (words) in the way that modern painting & music have been using and experimenting with theirs." He argued that "there is a great deal of pleasure and excitement to be gotten from language which can only be released by concentrating one's attention on that pleasure of words, and which can't be captured and made to serve as a 'texture' for a poem whose apparent logical aim is to make some explicit psychological, historical, etc. point." He felt that John's newest poetic experiments encapsulated these thoughts about a future direction of American poetry, that "when one lets the words act up in the way one feels most exciting . . . they suggest a new kind of structure." Letter from KK to Daisy Aldan, February 24, 1954, Box 3, Folder 7, Daisy Aldan Papers.

4. Letter from JA to the Porters, February 17, 1954, JAPC.

5. Author interview with JA, January 4, 2014, Hudson, NY.

6. Ibid. The prothalamion is lost. (They married on June 13, 1954.)

7. Letter from JA to FO c/o LR, March 18, 1954, Box 11, Folder 8, LR Papers.

8. Frank O'Hara mentions it in a letter to the Porters on May 1, 1954, Box 1, Folder 3, typescript, DA Collection–Dodd.

9. *New York Times*, May 14, 1954, front page: "Adams Disavows Threats or 'Bait' to Halt M'Carthy." In the Army-McCarthy transcripts printed on page 12, Jenkins asks Adams: "[Y]ou offered up a bigger bait from time to time—to wit—subversives, homosexuals, in the Air Force and in the Navy." A central issue in the case had been the question of whether McCarthy was promised names of homosexuals in the army and navy as a means of stopping his investigation of the army.

10. Letter from JA to the Porters, June 3, 1954, Box 1, Fairfield Porter Papers, Archives of American Art, Smithsonian Institution, Washington, DC.

11. Letter from FO to LR, June 14, 1954, Box 11, Folder 8, LR Papers.

12. Letter from LR to FO, March 9, 1954, LR Papers.

13. FO in Southampton to the composer Ben Weber, March 20, 1954, typescript, DA Collection–Mandeville.

14. The painting would be bought, and later auctioned off, by the Art Institute of Chicago.

15. FO quote from April 1954 typescript, DA Collection–Dodd.

16. JA on Jane Freilicher in Klaus Kertess's *Jane Freilicher*, p. 10, painting on p. 23.

17. Two of these drawings, recently discovered, were published in a catalogue by Tibor de Nagy, *Painter Among Poets*, 2013.

18. The painting is presumed lost.

19. During Jane Freilicher's 1955 Tibor de Nagy exhibition, *The New York Times* singled out her "almost hallucinatory" portrait of Ashbery with a "Foujita gaze." Ashbery, who deeply admired the painter Tsuguharu Foujita's ability to capture a figure's combination of innocence and intensity, loved the comment (Stuart Preston, "Artists of Personal Vision," *New York Times*, April 10, 1955). Five years earlier, Freilicher had sent Ashbery a postcard of a Foujita painting, for which he profusely thanked her: "Your postcard was greeted by shrieks of approval in Sodus. As you have guessed, Foujita is one of my twelve favorite artists" (letter from JA to Jane Freilicher, August 8, 1950, JF Papers–Houghton).

20. *Just the Thing: The Selected Letters of James Schuyler.* He said, "[W]hat I like best . . . is the emerging of a new tone . . . in the poem "Chaos" . . . that might betoken some beautiful yet unwritten poems" (9). Letter from JS to Fairfield Porter, July 16, 1954.

21. JA studied Petrarch in History 316 (Italian Renaissance) and the roots of the Canzone form in English 316 (Milton), both in spring 1947.

22. Letter from JA to LR, May 28, [1953], Box 1, Folder 19, LR Papers.

23. During the six-month period he sublet Grosser's apartment, he wrote a prose poem, "Novel," and six new poems: "Chaos," "Album Leaf," "Poem" (a sestina, "While we were walking under the top"), "Two Brothers on the Phone," "Canzone," and "The Minstrel Boy." "Two Brothers" he initially liked, as did Jimmy Schuyler and Kenneth Koch, but he changed his mind about it. "Two Brothers on the Phone" was never published, and all drafts are currently lost. Author interview with JA, May 7, 2013, Hudson, NY.

24. Author interview with JA, December 16, 2012, Hudson, NY.

25. Ibid.

26. John began to read the works of psychoanalyst Karen Horney instead, as a less expensive alternative to seeing Dr. Hale. Letter from FO to KK, August 14, 1954, typescript, DA–Dodd.

27. FO, "Porter Paints a Picture," published in *ARTnews*, January 1955.

28. FO mentions the trip in a letter to Fairfield Porter, August 5, 1954, typescript, DA–Dodd.

29. Letter from JA to SG, September 10, 1950, Gregg Papers. JA published this translation of Max Jacob in John Myers's *Semi-Colon* 1, no. 1 (undated, but approx. 1955), a new literary magazine.

30. JA's original translation began, "It was in the vicinity of the Orient . . ." Later, when he revised his translation, he realized "de Lorient" meant "near Lorient," a town in France.

31. Correspondence between JA and Harry Levin, October 1954, HL Papers.

32. Harry Levin, letter to the Guggenheim Foundation, November 30, 1955, HL Papers. This recommendation was for the Guggenheim (a year later), not the Fulbright—no other recommendation letter exists in Levin's files—but they were probably very similar letters.

33. "To Be Continued," draft dated October 19, 1953, JAPC.

34. Author interview with JA, December 16, 2012, Hudson, NY.

35. Author interview with JA, November 29, 2013, Hudson, NY.

36. The start date listed on JA's 1954 filed income tax return, JAPC.

37. December 20, 1954, "Dr. Henry," obituary, *New York Times*.

38. Letter from JA to LR, March 8, 1955, Box 1, Folder 19, LR Papers. Shortly after beginning the job, he sent a note to Larry Rivers on McGraw-Hill stationery, marking an X next to the image of the building to denote the middle floor he was on. The building's location: 330 West Forty-Second Street.

39. Author interview with JA, December 28, 2015, Hudson, NY.

40. Author interview with Tere Lo Prete, January 23, 2013, Wainscott, NY.

41. JA, "A Statement on Poetry," undated but written in the late 1960s or '70s, Box 111, JA mss–uncatalogued.

42. Letter from JA to KK, January 16, 1955, JAPC.

43. Helen Lawrence's Five-Year Diary, 1963–67: written at the top of the page for "Dec 19" (Cardinal) "March 16" (Robin), JAPC.

44. JA Diary I, May 10, 1941, JAPC.

45. "The Orioles" was published in *The New York Times Book Review*, March 31, 1957.

46. Letter from JA to Judith Malina and Julian Beck, February 21, 1955, Box 104, Living Theatre Records.

47. Letter from JA to KK, January 16, 1955, JAPC.

48. Ibid.

49. Ibid.

50. Letter from JA to Judith Malina and Julian Beck, February 21, 1955, Box 104, Living Theatre Records.

51. Letter from JA to KK, January 16, 1955, JAPC.

52. Ibid.

53. Letter from JA to the Porters, June 3, 1954, JAPC.

54. Letter from JA to KK, January 16, 1955, JAPC.

55. JA described the Dakota to JS in a letter, September 6, 1955, when Jimmy was thinking of moving uptown, near where Bob Hunter had lived, JS Papers–Mandeville.

56. Letter from JA to Bob Hunter, June 30, 1949, RHPC.

57. Letter from JA to KK, April 13, 1955 (for first quotation). Second two quotations: Letter from JA to KK, March 20, 1955, JAPC.

58. Letter from JA to KK, March 20, 1955, JAPC.

59. Letter from JA to KK, April 13, 1955, JAPC.

60. Comments on FO in a letter from JA to KK, January 16, 1955, JAPC; and letter from JA to Larry Rivers, May 18, 1955, Box 1, Folder 19, LR Papers.

61. Letter from JA to KK, January 16, 1955, JAPC.

62. For example: Letter from FO to JF, February 23, 1954, typescript, DA Collection–Dodd.

63. Letter from FO to KK, May 9, 1955, typescript, DA Collection–Dodd.

64. JA submitted the play on May 11, 1955. The memo read, "I am dubious." MSS 388, Box 1, Folder 27, Yale Collection of American Literature (YCAL), Beinecke Rare Book and Manuscript Library, Yale University, New Haven, CT.

65. Letter from FO to Ned Rorem, April 8, 1955, DA Collection–Dodd.

66. Letter from JA to "Dame Edith" Sitwell, February 23, 1955. Box 90, Folder 2, Edith Sitwell Papers, Harry Ransom Center, University of Texas at Austin (hereafter

"Edith Sitwell Papers"). JA on Edith Sitwell: "I love her early stuff more and more." In letter from JA to JF, July 6, 1950, JF Papers–Houghton.

67. Letter from JA to Dame Edith and Sir Osbert Sitwell, February 23, 1955, Box 90, Folder 2, Edith Sitwell Papers.

68. Author interview with JA, December 16, 2012, Hudson, NY.

69. Letter from JA to KK, April 13, 1955, JAPC.

70. No date, though Ashbery remembers creating the document around 1950, JAPC.

71. Undated typed draft, AM6 Box 28, JA Papers.

72. Letter from FO to KK, April 22, 1955, typescript, DA Collection–Dodd.

73. Letter from JA to KK, from an April 14, 1955, section of April 13, 1955, letter, JAPC.

74. Author interview with JA, November 25, 2012, Hudson, NY. John Ashbery said this photo was mislabeled in the past as having been taken at a *Folder* event. The Egan reading probably occurred on Sunday, April 10, 1955. A young poet, Edward Field, was present that night and jotted down his recollections: "[Frank] and John Ashbery gave a joint poetry reading [at the Egan gallery] one Sunday afternoon. . . . There was a feeling of 'important occasion' in the air, as there always was around Frank's doings. . . . Frank and John read consecutively, sitting at a table, not performing at all, just reading from the papers on the desk. . . . The audience was attentive. At the time I didn't understand the sense of unity that world had, the sense of being a world they had" (Edward Field, from "Some Memories of Frank O'Hara," in Bill Berkson's Papers, Dodd Research Center, University of Connecticut).

75. Letter from FO to LR, April 28, 1955, Box 11, Folder 8, LR Papers.

76. Ibid.

77. In a letter from FO to KK, May 9, 1955, Box 1, Folder 4, typescript, DA Collection–Dodd.

78. Interoffice memo from RY (Roberta Yerkes) to Mr. Chester Kerr, July 5, 1955, YUP Records.

79. Author interview with JA, May 7, 2013, Hudson, NY.

80. Yale University Press minutes reveal that Auden's choice to ask for manuscripts directly was discussed since Ashbery's had already been officially rejected. Meeting took place on Monday, June 27, 1955: "A Meeting of the Committee on Publications of the Governing Board of the Yale University Press." YUP Records.

81. Box 12, Folder "YSYP Managements 1946–54," YUP Records. In his introduction to the *Anthology of Yale Younger Poets*, editor George Bradley suggests this happened regularly during Auden's tenure as judge for the competition.

82. Box 12, "Folder YSYP Management 1946–54," YUP Records.

83. Box 11, "Folder YSYP Publications Committee," YUP Records.

84. Author interview with JA, November 27, 2013, Hudson, NY.

85. Jane Freilicher Private Papers, New York.

86. Letter from JA to JF, September 1, 1960, JF Papers–Houghton.

87. Author interview with JA, November 27, 2013, Hudson, NY.

88. Author interview with JF, March 29, 2013, New York.

89. Letter from the U.S. Educational Commission for France to JA in Sodus, NY, June 3, 1955, AM6 Box 19, JA Papers.

90. Letter from FO to LR on MoMA stationery, LR Papers.

91. In October 1955, John took the first step toward this by applying for the first (of eleven applications) to receive a Guggenheim Fellowship. He also applied to extend the Fulbright for an additional year, a request that came through.

92. Letter from JA to LR, May 18, 1955, Box 1, Folder 19, LR Papers. Author interview with JA on writing "The Instruction Manual" in the McGraw-Hill office. FO, "Rare Modern," *Poetry*, February 1957, p. 313. FO intuitively noted that "The Instruction Manual" was John Ashbery's most Whitmanesque poem.

93. Letter from JA to LR, May 18, 1955, Box 1, Folder 19, LR Papers.

94. Letter from JA to JS, September 6, [1955], JAPC.

95. August 5 was his last day of work.

96. Interoffice memo from RY (Roberta Yerkes) to Mr. Chester Kerr, July 5, 1955, YUP Records.

97. Author interview with JA, June 4, 2014, Hudson, NY.

98. Letter from JA to JS, September 6, [1955], JAPC.

99. Author interview with JA, May 7, 2013, Hudson, NY.

100. Author interview with JA, February 8, 2014, Hudson, NY. Gooch, *A City Bet*, 263–65.

101. Typed letter from Rex M. Johnson to Chet Ashbery, July 27, 1955, and preserved in a scrapbook of John Ashbery's life that Helen Ashbery put together, JAPC.

102. Letter from JA to KK, January 16, 1955, JAPC.

103. Letter from JA to JS, September 6, [1955], JAPC.

104. Auden said this to Sonia Orwell, who told her friend, the painter Anne Dunn. Author interview with Anne Dunn, April 22, 2013, New York. In 1945, FB, the Deerfield headmaster, was asked by Harvard University, "[E]xpress your opinion as to whether the candidate is motivated primarily by intellectual curiosity or ambition?" Boyden answered: "[I]ntellectual curiosity." In Private Ashbery File, Harvard Registrar, Cambridge, MA.

105. *Some Trees* was published (817 copies) on March 28, 1956. Over the next four years, 456 copies were sold. Royalty ledger for John Ashbery, Box 12, Folder 305, YUP Records.

106. *New York Times*, June 3, 1956.

107. William Meredith, "Images and Meaning," *New York Times*, April 15, 1956.

108. Louise Bogan, *The New Yorker*, September 1, 1956.

109. Author interview with JA, November 25, 2012, New York.

110. Author interview with CRD, January 10, 2012, Rochester, NY.

111. William Arrowsmith, "Nine New Poets," in *The Hudson Review* (Summer 1956).

112. Letter from Fairfield Porter to William Arrowsmith, July 23, 1956, in Porter, *Material Witness*, 150–53.

113. Letter from KK to JA, Sunday [nd] 1959, AM6 Box 11, JA Papers.

114. Letter from JA to Donald Allen, September 1, 1958, MSS3, Box 60, Folder 6, DA Collection–Mandeville.

115. HEL kept a list of the updated Thruway exits in his wallet, though he died before trying out the new roadway. HEL's wallet in JAPC.

116. Author interview with Bob Hunter, September 18, 2013, Thetford Hill, VT.

117. Author interview with JA, May 30, 2013, New York.

118. Fairfield Porter to Lawrence Porter, September 26, 1955; and Porter, *Material Witness*, 134–35.
119. "The New Spirit," 252, in *Three Poems* (1972, reprinted New York: Library of America, 2008).
120. "But What Is the Reader to Make of This?" from *A Wave* (1984, reprinted New York: Library of America, 2008).

Selected Bibliography

Primary Sources
Works by John Ashbery

POETRY
Breezeway. New York: Ecco, 2015.
Flow Chart. New York: Alfred A. Knopf, 1991.
Hotel Lautréamont. New York: Alfred A. Knopf, 1992.
Planisphere. New York: HarperCollins, 2009.
Some Trees. New Haven, CT: Yale University Press, 1956.
Turandot and Other Poems. New York: Tibor de Nagy Gallery, 1953.
Where Shall I Wander. New York: Ecco, 2005.
Your Name Here. New York: Farrar, Straus and Giroux, 2002.

COLLECTED POETRY
Collected Poems: 1956–87. Ed. Mark Ford. New York: The Library of America, 2008.

PROSE
"Introduction." In Donald Allen, ed., *Collected Poems of Frank O'Hara*. Berkeley: University of California Press, 1995.
"Introduction." In Klaus Kertess, *Jane Freilicher*. New York: Harry N. Abrams, 2004.
A Nest of Ninnies. With James Schuyler. New York: E. P. Dutton and Co., 1969.
Other Traditions (The Charles Eliot Norton Lectures). Cambridge, MA: Harvard University Press, 2000.
"Preface." In Alvin Levin, *Love Is Like Park Avenue*. James Reidel, ed. New York: New Directions, 2009.
Reported Sightings: Art Chronicles 1957–1987. David Bergman, ed. New York: Alfred A. Knopf, 1989.
Selected Prose. Eugene Richie, ed. Ann Arbor: University of Michigan Press, 2004.

PLAYS
Three Plays. Calais, VT: Z Press, 1978.

TRANSLATIONS
Collected French Translations. Ed. Rosanne Wasserman and Eugene Richie. New York: Farrar, Straus and Giroux, 2014.

PUBLISHED INTERVIEWS
John Ashbery in Conversation with Mark Ford. London: Between the Lines, 2003.

Bibliography
Kermani, David K. *John Ashbery: A Comprehensive Bibliography, Including His Art Criticism and with Selected Notes from Unpublished Materials*. New York: Garland Publishing, 1976.

Archives
Archives and Special Collections. Thomas J. Dodd Research Center. University of Connecticut. Storrs, CT.
    The (Donald) Allen Collection of Frank O'Hara Letters, 1950–1966
    Bill Berkson Papers
Archives of American Art. Smithsonian Institution. Washington, DC.
    Fairfield Porter Papers
    Jane Freilicher Papers
    John Bernard Myers Papers
    Tibor de Nagy Gallery Records
Arthur and Elizabeth Schlesinger Library on the History of Women in America. Harvard University. Cambridge, MA.
    Papers of Adrienne Rich
Beinecke Rare Book and Manuscript Library. Yale University. New Haven, CT.
    Barbara Guest Papers
    F. O. Matthiessen Papers
    Living Theatre Records
    New World Writing Records
Deerfield Academy Library. Deerfield, MA.
    Ashbery Alumni File
    Boyden Wartime File
The Fales Library and Special Collections. New York University. New York.
    Larry Rivers Papers
Harry Ransom Center. University of Texas at Austin. Austin, TX.
    Alfred A. Knopf, Inc., Records
    Daisy Aldan Papers
    Edith Sitwell Papers
    Edward Gorey Papers. Harvard University Archives Records of *The Harvard Advocate*.
    Woodberry Poetry Room (Harvard College Library) Papers
Henry W. and Albert A. Berg Collection of English and American Literature.
    New York Public Library.

Uncatalogued James Schuyler Manuscripts
Uncatalogued John Ashbery Manuscripts
Houghton Library. Harvard University. Cambridge, MA.
  Harry Levin Papers
  James Laughlin Papers
  Jane Freilicher Papers
  John Ashbery Letters to Mary Wellington
  John Ashbery Papers
  Richard Elliott Papers
  Richard A. "Sandy" Gregg Papers
Mandeville Special Collections and Archives. University of California at San Diego. San
  Diego, CA.
  Donald Allen Collection
  James Schuyler Papers
Manuscripts and Archives. Yale University. New Haven, CT.
  Yale University Press Records (YUP Records)
92nd Street Y Archives
Peter Jay Sharp Special Collections. Juilliard School. New York.
  Gold and Fizdale Collection
Rauner Special Collections Library. Dartmouth College. Hanover, NH.
  Richard Eberhart Papers
Syracuse University Libraries Special Collections Research Center. Syracuse, NY.
  Grace Hartigan Papers
University of Chicago Special Collections
  Poetry: A Magazine of Verse records, 1912–1961

Local History Collections
Albion High School Library. Albion, NY.
Alden Historical Society. Alden, NY.
Francis Parker School. Rochester, NY.
Pultneyville Historical Society. Pultneyville, NY.
Sodus City Records. Sodus, NY.
Sodus Free Library. Sodus, NY.
Wayne County Office of the County Historian. Lyons, NY.

Private Collections
Anson Family Papers. Solon, OH.
Ashbery Resource Center. Hudson, NY.
Gold and Fizdale Papers. New York.
Harvard University Registrar. Cambridge, MA.
John Ashbery Private Collection. Hudson, NY, and New York.
Jonathan Gregg Private Papers. New York.
Robert Hunter Private Collection. Thetford Hill, VT.

Journals, Newspapers, and Magazines
Art and Literature: An International Review (1964–67).
ARTnews. Frank O'Hara, "Porter Paints a Picture," January 1955.
The Buffalo Bee. October 25, 1946.

The Deerfield Scroll. Issues referenced:
   October 24, 1942.
   February 20, 1943.
Folder magazine (1953–55).
The Harvard Advocate
   "A Sermon: Amos 8:11–14," March 25, 1947.
   John Ashbery Poems. May 21, 1947.
   Kenneth Koch's review of *The Beautiful Changes*, December 1947.
   "For a European Child," April 1949.
The Harvard Crimson
   On Tennessee Williams reading, November 9, 1945.
   On W. H. Auden reading, March 15, 1946.
   On Wallace Stevens reading, February 11, 1947.
   Review of *The Harvard Advocate*, March 27, 1947.
   Review of *The Harvard Advocate*, November 10, 1947.
   On Marianne Moore reading, December 11, 1948.
Life. "Surrealism on Parade," December 14, 1936 (24–27).
New Directions 14 (February 11, 1953).
The New Yorker. Louise Bogan, review of *Some Trees*, September 1, 1956.
The New York Review of Books. "John Ashbery Remembers Barbara Epstein," August 10, 2006.
The New York Times
   Film review by Andre Sennwald, October 10, 1935.
   "Prof. Matthiessen Dies in Boston Plunge," April 15, 1950.
   "Adams Disavows Threats or 'Bait' to Halt McCarthy," May 14, 1954.
   "Dr. Henry," December 20, 1954.
   "Artists of Personal Vision." Review of Jane Freilicher at Tibor de Nagy Gallery, April 10, 1955.
   William Meredith, "Images and Meaning." Review of *Some Trees*, April 15, 1956.
   "In News, Echoes of Crash at Empire State Building," October 13, 2006.
The New York Times Book Review. "The Orioles," March 31, 1957.
Partisan Review. "The Picture of Little J.A. in a Prospect of Flowers," July/August 1951.
Poetry: A Magazine of Verse
   November 1945 (66–67).
   Frank O'Hara, "Rare Modern." Review of *Some Trees*, February 1957.
   Joel Michael Symington, review of *Rivers and Mountains*, December 1966.
Poetry New York. "The Statues," 1950 (p. 2).
Semi-Colon. John Myers, ed. (1955).
The Sodus Record. "Prizes Awarded at Class Day Exercises," June 27, 1940.
Voices: A Quarterly of Poets 131 (Fall 1947).

Secondary Sources
General Sources
Allen, Donald, ed. *Collected Poems of Frank O'Hara*. Berkeley: University of California Press, 1995.
———. *New American Poetry, 1945–1960*. New York: Grove Press, 1960.
Auden, W. H. *Collected Poems*. New York: Random House, 1945.

Berkson, Bill, and Joe LeSueur, eds. *Homage to Frank O'Hara*. Bolinas, CA: Big Sky, 1978.

Bradley, George, ed. *Anthology of Yale Younger Poets*. New Haven, CT: Yale University Press, 1998.

Brinnin, John Malcolm, ed. *New World Writing. Third Mentor Selection*. New York: New American Library, 1953.

Chauncey, George. *Gay New York: Gender, Urban Culture, and the Making of the Gay Male World: 1890–1940*. New York: Basic Books, 1994.

Cocteau, Jean, dir. *Orpheus (Orphée)*. Comité Cocteau, 1950. Film.

Corbett, William, ed. *Just the Thing: Selected Letters of James Schuyler: 1951–1991*. New York: Turtle Point Press, 2004.

———. *The Letters of James Schuyler to Frank O'Hara*. New York: Turtle Point Press, 2006.

Cornwall, Barry, ed. *The Complete Works of Shakespeare, Vol. 1: Comedies*. London and New York: Printing and Publishing Co., 1864.

Duskin, Ruth. *Whatever Happened to the Quiz Kids?: Perils and Profits of Growing Up Gifted*. Chicago: Chicago Review Press, 1982.

Eddy, Mark Baker. *Science and Health with Key to the Scriptures*. Boston: Christian Science Publishing Company, 1875.

Edgar, Natalie. *Club Without Walls: Selections from the Journals of Philip Pavia*. New York: Midmarch Arts Press, 2007.

Elmslie, Kenward. "Fifties Probe." In *New American Writing: 18*. Chicago: Columbia College, 2000.

Freedberg, Sydney J. *Parmigianino: His Works in Painting*. Westport, CT: Greenwood Press, 1950.

Gooch, Brad. *City Poet: The Life and Times of Frank O'Hara*. New York: Alfred A. Knopf, 1993.

Hadas, Moses. *A History of Greek Literature*. New York: Columbia University Press, 1950.

Halberstam, David. *The Fifties*. New York: Ballantine Books, 1993.

Hickok, Eliza Merrill. *The Quiz Kids*. Cambridge, MA: The Riverside Press, 1947.

Horton, Philip. *Hart Crane: The Life of an American Poet*. New York: Viking Press, 1937. Reprint: Compass Books, 1957.

Hueffer, Ford Maddox. *Hans Holbein the Younger: A Critical Monograph*. London: Duckworth and Co., 1905.

Imagist Anthology, 1930. London: Chatto and Windus, 1930.

Johnson, Denis K. *The Lavender Scare: The Cold War Persecution of Gays and Lesbians in the Federal Government*. Chicago: University of Chicago Press, 2004.

Kernan, Nathan, ed. *The Diary of James Schuyler*. Santa Rosa, CA: Black Sparrow Press, 1997.

La Moy, William T., and Joseph P. McCaffrey, eds. *The Journals of Grace Hartigan, 1951–55*. Syracuse, NY: Syracuse University Press, 2009.

Leigh, Ted, ed. *Material Witness: The Selected Letters of Fairfield Porter*. Ann Arbor: University of Michigan Press, 2005.

Levy, Julian. *Surrealism*. New York: Marstan Press, 1986.

Loughery, John. *The Other Side of Silence: Men's Lives and Gay Identities: A Twentieth-Century History*. New York: Henry Holt and Co., 1998.

Machiz, Herbert, ed. *Artists' Theatre: Four Plays*. New York: Grove Press, 1960.

McPhee, John. *The Headmaster: Frank L. Boyden of Deerfield*. New York: Farrar, Straus and Giroux, 1966.

Mee, Arthur, and Holland Thompson, eds. *The Book of Knowledge: The Children's Encyclopedia.* New York: Grolier Society, 1911.

Myers, John. *Tracking the Marvelous: A Life in the New York Art World.* New York: Random House, 1981.

O'Hara, Frank. Donald Allen, ed. *Early Writing.* Bolinas: Grey Fox Press, 1977.

———. *Poems Retrieved.* Bolinas: Grey Fox Press, 1977.

Padgett, Ron, and David Shapiro, eds. *An Anthology of New York Poets.* New York: Random House, 1970.

Parisi, Joseph, and Stephen Young, eds. *Dear Editor: A History of Poetry in Letters—The First Fifty Years 1912–62.* New York: W. W. Norton, 2002.

Perl, Jed. *New Art City: Manhattan at Mid-Century.* New York: Vintage, 2005.

Poggioli, Renato. *The Theory of the Avant-Garde.* Cambridge, MA: Harvard University Press, 1968.

Rhymer, Mary Frances, ed. *Vic and Sade: The Best Radio Plays of Paul Rhymer.* New York: Seabury Press, 1976.

Rivers, Larry, and Arnold Weinstein. *What Did I Do? The Unauthorized Autobiography.* New York: Aaron Asher Books, 1992.

Ruoff, Henry W., ed. *The Century Book of Facts: A Handbook of Ready Reference.* Springfield, MA: King-Richardson Co., 1910.

Sawin, Martica. *Nell Blaine: Her Art and Life.* New York: Hudson Hills Press, 1998.

Schuyler, James. *Collected Poems.* New York: Farrar, Straus and Giroux, 1993.

———. *Other Flowers: Uncollected Poems.* James Meetze and Simon Pettet, eds. New York: Farrar, Straus and Giroux, 2010.

Stevens, Wallace. *Transport to Summer.* New York: Alfred A. Knopf, 1947.

Tindall, William York. *Forces in Modern British Literature, 1885–1946.* New York: Alfred A. Knopf, 1947.

Tippins, Sherill. *February House.* Boston: Houghton Mifflin, 2005.

Truman, Harry. "Statement by the President of the United States," August 6, 1945.

Tytell, John. *The Living Theatre: Art, Exile, and Outrage.* New York: Grove Press, 1995.

Untermeyer, Louis. *Modern American Poetry; Modern British Poetry: A Critical Anthology.* New York: Harcourt, Brace, 1942.

Wells, Carolyn, ed. *A Parody Anthology.* New York: Charles Scribner's Sons, 1904.

Literary Critical Works About John Ashbery

Altieri, Charles. *Self and Sensibility in Contemporary American Poetry.* Cambridge, UK: Cambridge University Press, 1984.

Blasing, Mutlu Konuk. *American Poetry: The Rhetoric of Its Forms.* New Haven, CT: Yale University Press, 1987.

Bloom, Harold, ed. *John Ashbery.* New York: Chelsea House, 1985.

Bromwich, David. *Skeptical Music: Essays on Modern Poetry.* Chicago: University of Chicago Press, 2001.

Clune, Michael W. *Writing Against Time.* Palo Alto, CA: Stanford University Press, 2013.

Costello, Bonnie. *Shifting Ground: Reinventing Landscape in Modern American Poetry.* Cambridge, MA: Harvard University Press, 2003.

DuBois, Andrew. *Ashbery's Forms of Attention.* Tuscaloosa: Alabama University Press, 2006.

Epstein, Andrew. *Beautiful Enemies: Friendship and Postwar American Poetry.* Oxford, UK: Oxford University Press, 2006.

Fletcher, Angus. *New Theory for American Poetry: Democracy, the Environment, and the Future of Imagination*. Cambridge, MA: Harvard University Press, 2004.

Fredman, Stephen. *Poet's Prose: The Crisis in American Verse*. Cambridge, UK: Cambridge University Press, 1983.

Hammer, Langdon. Review of *Notes from the Air*. *New York Times Book Review*, April 20, 2008.

Heffernan, James A. W. *Museum of Words: The Poetics of Ekphrasis from Homer to Ashbery*. Chicago: Chicago University Press, 1993.

Herd, David. *John Ashbery and American Poetry*. Manchester, UK: Manchester University Press, 2000.

Hickman, Ben. *John Ashbery and English Poetry*. Edinburgh, UK: Edinburgh University Press, 2012.

Lehman, David, ed. *Beyond Amazement: New Essays on John Ashbery*. Ithaca, NY: Cornell University Press, 1980.

Levy, Ellen. *Criminal Ingenuity: Moore, Cornell, Ashbery, and the Struggle Between the Arts*. Oxford, UK: Oxford University Press, 2011.

MacArthur, Marit J. *American Landscape in the Poetry of Frost, Bishop, and Ashbery: The House Abandoned*. New York: Palgrave Macmillan, 2008.

MacFarquhar, Larissa. "Present Waking Life: Becoming John Ashbery." *The New Yorker*, November 7, 2005.

Moramarco, Fred, and William Sullivan. *Containing Multitudes: Poetry in the United States Since 1950*. New York: Twayne, 1998.

Perloff, Marjorie. *The Poetics of Indeterminacy: Rimbaud to Cage*. Princeton, NJ: Princeton University Press, 1981.

Reddy, Srikanth. *Changing Subjects: Digressions in Modern American Poetry*. New York: Oxford University Press, 2012.

Rosenthal, M. L. *The Poet's Art*. New York: W. W. Norton and Co., 1987.

Schultz, Susan M. *Tribe of John: Ashbery and Contemporary Poetry*. Tuscaloosa: Alabama University Press, 1995.

Shapiro, David. *John Ashbery: An Introduction to the Poetry*. New York: Columbia University Press, 1979.

Shetley, Vernon. *After the Death of Poetry: Poet and Audience in Contemporary America*. Durham, NC: Duke University Press, 1993.

Shoptaw, John. *On the Outside Looking Out: John Ashbery's Poetry*. Cambridge, MA: Harvard University Press, 1994.

Stitt, Peter. *Uncertainty and Plenitude: Five Contemporary Poets*. Iowa City: Iowa University Press, 1997.

Trotter, David. *The Making of the Reader: Language and Subjectivity in Modern American English and Irish Poetry*. London: Macmillan Press, 1984.

Vendler, Helen. *Invisible Listeners: Lyric Intimacy in Herbert, Whitman, and Ashbery*. Princeton, NJ: Princeton University Press, 2005.

———. "Understanding Ashbery." *The New Yorker*, March 16, 1981 (108–36).

Vincent, John Emil. *John Ashbery and You: His Later Books*. Athens: Georgia University Press, 2007.

Ward, Geoff. *Statues of Liberty: The New York School of Poets*. New York: Palgrave, 2001.

Williamson, Alan. *Introspection and Contemporary Poetry*. Cambridge, MA: Harvard University Press, 1984.

Acknowledgments

For interviews on Rochester, Sodus, Pultneyville, and Buffalo, I thank: Georgia Anson, Lawrence Anson, Annaliese and Jack Bopps, Sylvia and Phillip Bornath, Magdalena Bout, Kendra Burnap, Eleanor Clapp, Sally Smith Fay, Buddy Gaylord, Jinny Gilbert, Mary Ann Boller Henderson, Joan Williamson Hickey, Doc Malchoff, Abner McKee, Anne Healy McMahon, Joan Buckman Micha, Marie Wells Ostendorf, Elsie Parsons, Chester Peters, Mary Grosz Raymer, Nancy Meulendyke Schopf, Evelyn Sergeant, Jo Little Sibley, Norma Jean Snyder, Kate Hobbie Storms, Hazel Wahl, Margaret Jordan Wahl, Betty Lou Burden Warrington, and Caroline Williamson. For information on later years, I am particularly grateful to: Ellen Adler, Judy Amory, Bill Berkson, George Bradley, Les Brown, Pat Hoey Cooper, Anne Dunn, Freddy English, Helen Epstein, Jonathan Gregg, Nancy Sippel Gregg, Gillett Griffin, Maxine Groffsky, Karen Koch, Katherine Koch, Albert Kresch, Gerrit Lansing, Alfred Leslie, Alvin Novak, Maureen O'Hara, Larry Osgood, Debby Taft Perry, Tere Lo Prete, Robert Silvers, Harrison Starr, Larry Taft, Elaine Tennant, and Malcolm White.

I am indebted to: Christina Davis, curator of the Woodberry Poetry Room, who made possible the preservation of the lost film *Presenting Jane*, in coordination with Haden Guest at the Harvard Film Archive; Nancy Kuhl, curator of poetry in the Yale Collection of American

Literature (YCAL) at the Beinecke Rare Book and Manuscript Library; Anne Lozier, archivist at Deerfield Academy Library; Leslie Morris, curator of modern books and manuscripts at Houghton Library, Harvard University; and Karen Muchow, historian at the Alden Historical Society, for her detailed historical sleuthing. I have also appreciated the opportunity to study collections from: the Cooperstown State Historical Library; East High School in Rochester, New York; the Francis Parker School in Rochester, New York; Sodus Central School; the Sodus Free Library with the helpful assistance of Bette Bugni; the Rochester Historical Society; the Rochester Central Library; and the Wayne County Historical Society.

For thoughtful work preserving photographs from John Ashbery's private collection, thanks go to Timothy O'Connor. Emily Skillings, John Ashbery's current New York City assistant, has been consistently insightful. Eric Brown at Tibor de Nagy Gallery has been supportive and helpful at every step of this project, and I am also grateful to Andrew Arnot at Tibor de Nagy. Nathan Kernan, James Schuyler's biographer, is a model of scholarly generosity. Rosanne Wasserman and Eugene Richie have shared their vast knowledge with such good nature. Forrester Hammer provided remarkable assistance while an undergraduate at Harvard, including a memorable campus tour of John Ashbery's dorm rooms.

For illuminating conversations about Ashbery, poetry, and biography that moved forward my thinking, I thank especially: Misha Amory, Mark Bauer, Becca Boggs, Olivier Brossard, Antoine Cazé, Richard Deming, Marcella Durand, Edwin Duval, Tom Healy, Lena Hill, David Hobbs, Matthew Frye Jacobson, David Lehman, Ava Lehrer, Ellen Levy, Ron Padgett, Robert Polito, Jenni Quilter, Archie Rand, Marc Robinson, Susan Rosenbaum, Bernard Schwartz, Emily Setina, Josh Siegel, Mark Steinberg, Rachel Trousdale, Michael Wenthe, Catherine Whalen, Thomas Whitridge, Ruth Yeazell, and Stephen Yenser.

Grants and fellowships for research and writing during various stages of this project made continuation of work possible. I appreciate this support from: the American Council of Learned Societies; the

American Philosophical Society; the Howard Foundation of Brown University; the Harry Ransom Center at the University of Texas at Austin; the Houghton Library, Harvard University; the National Endowment of the Humanities Summer Stipend; and the University of Minnesota Rare Book and Manuscript Library. A sabbatical year at West Point would not have been possible without the help of Kristina Fox and the encouragement of scholar and then head of the department, Colonel Scott Krawczyk.

I could not have done this work without Carol Rupert Doty, who openly shared not only details about her (literally) lifelong friendship with John Ashbery, but also provided me with a place to stay in Rochester on multiple trips, and was terrific company. Her sudden death in August 2013 was a shock and is still a source of sorrow. My enormous gratitude goes to her daughter, Beth Doty, and son-in-law, Phil Matt, who meticulously restored family photographs included in this book. Jane Freilicher, with whom I spent some of my very favorite afternoons on her couch in her warm apartment reading and chatting, has been deeply missed since her death at the end of 2014 at the age of ninety. I am very grateful to her daughter, Elizabeth Hazan, and her family for their friendship. Mary Wellington Martin has shared her sharp memories of Pultneyville with humor and grace. Bob Hunter sat for multiple interviews, allowed me access to a treasure trove of college letters, and finally read and commented on the entire manuscript. He has been a calm, intelligent, and wry source of information and conversation.

Langdon Hammer has generously given incisive criticism about writing and provocatively challenged my thinking about poetry and biography for nearly twenty years. I have relished many discussions on poetry and writing with Elizabeth Samet and about the art of biography with Linda Leavell. I have felt more than lucky in having Jonathan Galassi as my editor. Our conversations about creativity and poetry have been a highlight of this project.

Enormous thanks to: my parents, Dorothy and Eric Roffman; my other parents, Katherine and Fu-Ming Chen; my siblings Kim and

Franz Field, Ian and Jennie Roffman, Sharon, Irwin, and Aya; my nieces and nephews, Sam, Eli, Zac, Margot, Audrey, Kai, and Kenya; and my oldest friends Beth Niestat and Elizabeth Bassett. My sister-in-law Jennie Roffman read the entire manuscript three times, and it would be impossible to express how much I have appreciated her help. My husband, Melvin, knows how grateful I am for his sense of humor, good nature, and insight, but it is very worth repeating. To my son, Milo, I apologize for the lack of soccer references in these pages, and I am so grateful for your questions, curiosity, and enthusiasm despite this unfortunate omission. John Ashbery's poetry has been a regular part of our dinner table conversation since Milo could talk—"At North Farm" was the first poem he memorized, and well before I finished this biography, he had already composed his own two books on the subject.

John Ashbery and David Kermani agreed to this undertaking six years ago and have remained energetic and good-humored about it. They have allowed me to be in their house for years, among their things. David Kermani's *John Ashbery: A Comprehensive Bibliography* (1976) remains an invaluable resource, and Kermani has also brought his talents to the creation of the Ashbery Resource Center, a tremendous archive. John Ashbery sat for more than one hundred hours of interviews, and shared his books, music, photographs, new poems, private papers, and capacious knowledge and interests. Yet they have also allowed me to discover on my own how to think about what I was learning and how to write about it, and their patience with and respect for the solitude in which books are written have been remarkable.

Index

Illustration Credits